PEOPLE OF THE STORM GOD

Lost and Found Series

Classic Travel
Writing

PEOPLE OF THE STORM GOD

Travels in Macedonia

WILL MYER

Interlink Books

An imprint of Interlink Publishing Group, Inc.
Northampton, Massachusetts

This edition first published in 2005 by

INTERLINK BOOKS
An imprint of Interlink Publishing Group, Inc.
46 Crosby Street, Northampton, Massachusetts 01060

ISBN 1-56656-578-2

Cover Design: Baseline Arts
Cover Image: Will Myer

Typeset in Adobe Garamond
Printed and bound in Canada by Webcom

To request our complete 40-page full-color catalog, please call us toll free at **1-800-238-LINK**, visit our website at **www.interlinkbooks.com**, or write to
Interlink Publishing
46 Crosby Street, Northampton, MA 01060
e-mail: info@interlinkbooks.com

CONTENTS

FOREWORD

Will Myer wrote *People of the Storm God* following two separate visits to Bulgaria in late 1994 and to the Former Yugoslav Republic of Macedonia in early 1995. He was just 26 years old when he finished it.

Will was an exceptional person. He had a passion for learning and knowledge which was matched by his joy in disseminating what he knew without being pompous or patronising. His approach was original. His ability to make connections between different disparate areas and bring them together into a coherent simple whole, without losing the subtleties of inherently complex situations was amazing. A spin doctor would say that he was adept at joined-up thinking and communicating.

And, he was *fun*.

Will seemed to have an uncanny knack of travelling to a place just before the fabric of its political systems unravelled. After a trip to Yugoslavia in March 1991 he predicted the imminent collapse of that country and the bloodiness of the wars in Croatia and Bosnia. Later that same year Will was in Moscow when Mikhail Gorbachev was ousted by the Red Army and Boris Yeltsin emerged as the Saviour of Russia.

When I first met Will I was intrigued as to why a stereotypical English, Anglican, public school alumnus should have such a profound interest in Islam and in the Balkans. In my ignorant indifference Islam was another world religion and the Balkans were a troublesome area in school history books and conflict was always the fault of the Sanjak of Novi Pazar.

Will told me that he first started travelling in the Balkans when he was 15, in the summer of 1984. His father introduced him to the area and Will's fascination with religion, politics, psychology, sociology, geography, history and what makes people tick was first teased during the two-month long trip. They were in a restaurant in Romania where everything on the extensive menu was available but only an omelette could be served, when an obviously affluent, urbane and well-fed man came in, sat down, ordered a drink and lit a fat Cuban cigar. He was immaculately dressed in an expensive suit and wore a red fez.

Will asked his father how a Romanian could be so rich and sophisticated when Romania itself was so poor. My father-in-law, who is terribly erudite and speaks enough of many different Balkan languages to understand when someone else was a foreigner in the region, told Will that the man was probably a Turkish businessman. He then went on to explain a little of the turbulent history of the region in a way that captured Will's imagination and to describe the wonders of Islam: its theology, science, architecture and art, and how interaction between the Ottoman Empire and Occidental Powers had shaped the destiny of Europe. Will was hooked. He went on to learn as much as he could from books, experts, periodicals and news media and to make many more trips to the area.

The first foreign trip Will and I went on together was to Turkey and Bulgaria. I was amazed at the depth and breadth of Will's knowledge, his ability to interest me in subjects that I knew nothing about and to attract the attention of others through his words. When we were at Rozhen Monastery, just outside Melnik, Will was explaining the iconography of the murals to me and their historic and political significance whilst a tour guide was taking round a party of other foreigners. Gradually the more fluent English speakers amongst them abandoned their group leader to hear Will's account and to ask him questions. He simply made the chaotic comprehensible.

Will had arranged to start studying for a PhD in October 1995 at the School of Oriental and African Studies in London but he had a free year in which I encouraged him to write a book. *People of the Storm God* is the result of the research that he carried out in the autumn of 1994 and the spring of 1995. I hated him being away. The only brightness in those days before the information superhighway, cyber cafés and instant e-mail was the weekly letters of his exploits from which I would glean warmth.

After Will's death I searched high and low for those letters and for others that he had sent me from his other travels but with no success. I also was unable to find a copy either physical or electronic of the manuscript that I knew he had completed. I spoke of the fruitlessness of my search and my sadness with our friends. One of them, Jean Mortimer, said that she believed that she had the original manuscript in her loft.

In April 2002 Jean sent me the copy that she had. It was the only one in existence.

I finished reading Will's manuscript "Untitled: Travels in Macedonia" for the first time in May 2002, nearly seven years after its completion. Reading an old forgotten manuscript written from life is a strange experience. Suddenly, like a slinky falling down stairs under the force of gravity, you are pulled into the past and can touch it again.

I was transported back in time to a younger Will. Reading the manuscript jogged memories that had faded and refreshed emotions. I was able to connect with him and engage with his spirit. Will's words had the power to create new images too. It felt as if I were travelling with him, sharing his knowledge and experiences. I could hear him talking to me from across the years. This was a journey that he wanted to describe and he evoked it well. Too well for it to stay just with me; and so I decided to get it published; just as I had always promised Will I would, when I had the time. Of course with the blindness of inexperience I had thought he would be alive to see this happen.

As with Will's other posthumously published book *Islam and Colonialism: Western Perspectives on Soviet Asia*, there are some incomplete references, for which I apologise. Despite best efforts, there may also be transliteration errors. I would ask for forbearance, and hope that Will's understanding, knowledge and love for his subject can be shared and appreciated through this book.

✳ ✳ ✳

Will's aim in writing the book was to discover what creates identity in one of Europe's melting-pots and to share his knowledge and experiences of the Balkans. As such, it covers more than the process of travelling, sights seen, people met and the inner world of the traveller. It also includes some of the history of Macedonia, politics, religion, ethnicity and nationalism.

Obviously the political situation in the Balkans and Eastern Europe has changed significantly since Will's travels nearly a decade ago. The bloody bitter war between Serbs, Croats and Bosnians has been settled by the Dayton Peace Agreement; there have been conflicts in Kosovo with NATO and UN forces intervening to make peace; the former Serbian leader Slobodan Milosevic is being tried in the Hague as a war criminal; the former Yugoslav republic of Slovenia joined the newly enlarged European Union in May 2004; Croatia, Romania,

Bulgaria and Turkey are candidate countries that hope to join the EU in 2007. All the citizens of member states will in theory have the right to live, work and play wherever they wish within the EU federation. But *plus ça change, plus c'est la même chose.* Will and I grew up during the Cold War where the bogeyman followed a different political and economic paradigm to us. After the collapse of the Soviet Union in August 1991, Will felt that the clash of cultures, the defining of oneself in opposition to the "other", had reverted to a medieval battle between different gods. The "Axis of Evil" rhetoric of George W. Bush following the awful tragedy of the terrorist attacks on September 11, 2001 echoed Ronald Reagan's "Evil Empire" view of the Soviet Union only 15 years earlier. We in the West are involved in a costly war in Afghanistan; a similar operation had bankrupted the Soviet Union by the end of the 1980s. There has been another war between Iraq and a coalition of powers led by the US and Britain. Relaxing affluent holidaymakers are welcomed abroad for their contribution of tourist dollars to the local economy. At the same time, poor migrants hungry to work for a materially richer life are at best grudgingly accepted in their host nations despite their unquestionable contribution, both economically and socially.

Even though almost a decade has passed since Will's writing of this book, his analysis of Macedonian and Macedonians still holds, his experiences are still valid and his ability to convey the motivations of others still rings true. From Orthodox weddings and Easter parades, widows and witches, dervishes and mystics, through to political rallies and drunken evenings with shady characters, Will paints a beautifully vivid picture of this richly complex land and its peoples.

Shaoni Myer
London July 2004

THANKS

There are too many people without whom this book could not have been written to name them all, but some must be mentioned.

First of all thanks must be given to the peoples of Macedonia; Slav, Turkish, Albanian, Armenian, Greek, Vlah, Jewish and Gypsy. Each gave freely of their time to help me fit the pieces of the jigsaw together. Most especially I should mention Boris in Bansko and everyone at the Evangelical Church in that town, the mufti of Plovdiv, the mayor and imam of Gorni Kraište, Linda in Ohrid and the sheikhs of the Rifa'i *tekke* in Skopje and the Helveti *tekke* in Ohrid.

Dr John McGuckin in Leeds taught me most of what I know about Byzantine religion and politics and Bill Weaver was the first of my many teachers of Islam. A mention must be made of Dr Shirin Akiner of London University, who wanted me to go to Tadjikistan, and also to Sasha Rimsky, who taught me Russian believing I was going there. Without his patience I would not have been able to communicate.

I must also thank my father. In 1984 I bullied him into taking me to Romania and to Bosnia. I have been in love with the Balkans ever since.

Finally I must thank my wife Shaoni for letting me return to Yugoslavia despite her better judgement.

TO SHAONI

WITH THANKS FOR UNDERSTANDING.

WILL MYER
OCTOBER 1995

"With luck a traveller in Macedonia may hear six distinct languages and four allied dialects spoken in the same market place."
—H. N. Brailsford, *Macedonia: Its Races and Their Future* (1906)

"Each nationality dresses, speaks, cheats and worships after a fashion of its own and quite different from that of its neighbours, and each of them cherishes a traditional antipathy to all the others."
— G. F. Abbott, *The Tale of a Tour in Macedonia* (1903)

"The Macedonian Peasants themselves ... can hardly be said to possess any National Soul, or, for that matter, any soul at all."
—*ibid.*

"Violence was, indeed, all I knew of the Balkans: all I knew of the South Slavs."
—Rebecca West, *Black Lamb And Grey Falcon* (1939)

"Little is worth mentioning about these people, nor are their names without difficulty."
—Pliny the Elder (c.78)

PROLOGUE: "The Macedonian Question"

"I'm going to Tadjikistan," I announced in the summer of 1994, "for three months." This elicited two responses from assorted friends and family: "Where the hell is Tadjikistan?" or "Why?"

"I don't want you to go," said Shaoni, my wife, "you'll get killed."

"I doubt it," said my Uncle James, "he'll probably be kidnapped though." Shaoni shot him a withering look.

"Be sure you don't," she said to me. "My grandfather's expecting us in Calcutta in January."

I telephoned the Indian High Commission in London: "Do you have an embassy in Tadjikistan?" I asked.

"Where the hell is Tadjikistan?"

"It's near Afghanistan."

"Well then go to our embassy in Kabul."

"But I'm not going to Kabul. I'm going to Tadjikistan, and I'll need to get an Indian visa while I'm there."

"Look, I don't believe in this Tadjikistan. How do you expect me to help you if you can't say the name of the place you're going to correctly?"

Only the director of London University's Central Asia Research Forum thought it was a good idea. "We need to know about the Isma'ili community there," she told me. "Besides, if you do research on them you might get some money out of the Aga Khan." She introduced me to an Isma'ili from that remote corner of the former Soviet Union. "No problem," he said. "I will get you a letter of introduction. You will teach in my university in Khorog. We will pay you, but it will be in local currency. I will make all the arrangements." Tadjikistan was at the time the only country in the world still using the Soviet rouble, the kind with a portrait of Lenin on it. The Russians had refused to give them any new banknotes, regarding Tadjikistan as even more of an economic disaster zone than their own country.

A couple of months later my letters of introduction were ready, signed and stamped by the Tadjik minister for foreigners, as he styled himself. I presented them to the Russian Embassy to procure a visa. "You're mad," I was told, but I got the documents. I rang my contact to make the final arrangements. His mobile was switched off. I rang a number in Moscow he had given me. I rang Khorog. I posted a string of letters. I had lost contact with my contact. "Shit!" I said. Then civil war broke out again. Thousands of Tadjiks fled to the peace and security of Afghanistan. "Shit!" I said again.

"Why not go to the Balkans?" suggested Shaoni. "At least you like it there. But don't get yourself killed."

"They're not killing each other in Macedonia," I replied. "They should be, but they're not. I might see if I can find out why." And so I found myself flying to Istanbul in search of Macedonianness.

✻ ✻ ✻

Macedonia is a problem. It is such a problem that the French named fruit salad after it: *macédoine de fruits*. Four wars have been fought over it in the last eighty years, each bloodier than the previous one. They were fought to determine not only where exactly Macedonia is, but who lives there and what in state they should live. Depending on who you talk to, Macedonia is south Serbia, south-west Bulgaria or northern Greece. Some people take the view, utterly unreasonably in the eyes of the other protagonists, that it is none of these, but simply Macedonia. The problem has been made worse by the region's history. It has been part of numerous empires but the heart of just one. The Illyrians and Thracians who once formed the bulk of the population have long since vanished. They were followed by the Greeks, who temporarily lost control to Rome before that empire split up; the Eastern half of the empire, whilst continuing to call itself the Roman Empire, became more and more Hellenized.

The greatest of the Byzantine Emperors Justinian the Great, the last Roman emperor to use Latin as an official court language, is said to have been born in Ohrid, a city closely connected to the history of Macedonia and of its later inhabitants. Subsequently the area was swamped by Slavs and invaded by a Central Asian tribe, the Bulgars, who themselves became absorbed by the Slavs. It was then partially re-Hellenized and repeatedly taken and lost again as Bulgaria and Byzantium battled for supremacy in the Balkans. The Greeks finally lost the region following the depredations of the Crusades and an improbable itinerant army known as the Catalan Grand Company which—for reasons best known to itself—invaded from the east. It was not long before Latin control became as shaky as Byzantine had been, allowing the Serbs to move into the vacuum, only to fall out among themselves and allow another Central Asian tribe, the Ottomans, to sweep in. It was during the Ottoman period that the jumble of Slavs and Greeks was further confused by the advent of Spanish-speaking Jews and a gradual seepage of Albanians from the west and Gypsies from the east.

Greece, Serbia and Bulgaria are agreed: there is no such thing as a Macedonian. Greece might, just might, grudgingly admit that there could be such a thing as a "Slavophone Greek" whilst asserting that Macedonia is Greece and Greece only. Anywhere that is not Greece is *ipso facto* not Macedonia and has no right to use the name. Hence, when in 1992 a part of the former Yugoslavia declared independence under the name of Macedonia, Greece immediately imposed an economic blockade and vetoed any moves by the European Community to recognize the fledgling state, despite this recognition being extended to Slovenia, Croatia and, most bizarrely of all, Bosnia. In February 1991, London's *The Independent* observed that Greece had described as "preposterous, senseless and utterly unacceptable" a report to the US State Department that noted the existence of a Slavic population in Greece which it referred to as "Macedonian". To admit the existence of a separate Macedonian people would be tantamount to recognising the possibility of a separate Macedonian state.

Serbia is no less intransigent. The Slavs of the region are merely south Serbs. After all, the great Emperor Stefan Dušan made his capital in Skopje, which is now the capital of the independent state. Greece is welcome to the southern part of the territory, Aegean Macedonia, but the north is rightfully Serbia's. Edith Durham, a remarkable Englishwoman who became something of a Balkan heroine in the early years of this century, recorded a Serbian teacher in Tsetinje in Montenegro talking during the Balkan Wars when Serbia, Greece and Bulgaria were squabbling like starved hyenas over the moribund remains of the Ottoman Empire. The man was praising his country's victories, revelling in the annexation of more "Holy Serbian land". But, it was objected, Serbia cannot possibly make a claim to Macedonia, it is inhabited by Bulgarians: "Bulgarians put the definite article after the noun, as do the Slavs of Macedonia." "No matter," came the reply,

"Once our army has been there for two years there will be no articles after the noun."

Articles after the noun were an essential part of Bulgaria's claim. It argued that the majority of the inhabitants of Macedonia were Slavs and that these Slavs were, without exception, Bulgarians, much to the amusement of Serbia and Greece, who agreed that in the event of there being *any* Slavs, which Greece denied, then they were Serbs. Bulgaria, like Serbia, had an empire centred in Macedonia during the Middle Ages, indeed most of medieval Balkan history centres around the constant struggle between Byzantium and Bulgaria for regional hegemony. Macedonia was one of the three provinces of Bulgaria, together with Moesia and Thrace.

All of these claims to Macedonia were inspired by medieval history. As the historian Stavrianos pointed out in 1958:

> *The past—even the very distant past—and the present are side by side in the Balkans ... governments and peoples, particularly intellectuals, have based their actions on what happened, or what they believe to have happened, centuries ago. The reason is that during almost five hundred years of Turkish rule the Balkan peoples had no history. Time stood still for them. Consequently, when they won their independence in the nineteenth century, their point of reference was to the pre-Turkish period—to the medieval period or beyond ... peaceful inter-Balkan relations were scarcely likely in the face of simultaneous attempts to revive the medieval Greek, Bulgarian and Serbian empires.*

Things finally came to a head in 1912, during the First Balkan War. While Bulgaria was fighting the Turks in Thrace and coming within an inch of taking the city of Edirne, Greece and Serbia quietly carved up Macedonia between them. Inevitably Bulgaria, finding herself cheated of what she considered to be rightfully hers, rounded on her former allies in the Second Balkan War of 1913 and made further attempts at gaining the territory in 1915 and 1941, to no avail. Greece took the lion's share, about half the total area, known as Aegean Macedonia, and promptly expelled as many Slavs and Muslims as it could lay its hands on, replacing them with refugees from Asia Minor and Bulgaria. Serbia gained most of the rest—Vardar Macedonia, named for the river that flows through it—and began to enforce the use of Serbian, much to the annoyance of the natives, whilst Bulgaria had to make do with a tiny rump of the land it had originally conquered in 1878 and then lost again, and a massive complex concerning its *irredenta*, the Unredeemed Ones.

Not that the Macedonian Slavs necessarily saw themselves as unredeemed. In fact it is uncertain that they saw themselves as anything in particular. The Greek novelist Stratis Myravilis, who fought in Macedonia during the First World War, noted of the peasants (the urban population was composed largely of Greeks, Turks and Jews):

> *They hate the Serbs, who treat them like Bulgars, tyrannising them. They hate the Bulgarians because they have conscripted their children into the army. As for us Greeks, they accept us with a certain sympathetic curiosity, on account of one, and only one fact: our status as genuine spiritual vassals of "Patrik"—that is, the Ecumenical Patriarch ... this makes us privileged in their sight. Nevertheless, they want to be neither "Boulgar", "Srp" nor "Grts".*

Spyridion Trikoupis, writing in the nineteenth century, claimed "Blessed is the nation that professes one and the same faith. We (Greeks) possess this blessing—thanks be to God—and cursed by the nation is he who will conspire against the faith of the Greeks." What he meant by that is that anyone who is a member of the Greek Orthodox Church is, regardless of language, Greek and conversely anyone who is not, regardless of language, is not Greek. Over a century later another Greek writer, G. Arnalis, noted that

> *We have Turkish-speaking Greeks, who are loyal to Greece because they are Orthodox ... we meet Greek-speaking Turks from Crete, settled in Turkey ... even today* [1960], *with nearly four decades of peace between Greece and Turkey, the Muslim Cretan, who may still speak Greek as his vernacular, will never call himself a Greek, but, using the Greek language, he will refer to himself as a* Tourko-Kretikos, *a Turkish Cretan.*

Religion is just one of the factors complicating the Macedonian jigsaw. Although most of the Slavs in the area are Orthodox, and although most of the Albanians are Muslim, some aren't. Christian Albanians themselves divide between Orthodox and Catholic, but at least remain Albanians, but the Slav Muslims are variously known as Macedonian Muslims, Pomaks, Torbeshi or, confusingly, as Turks. The "Turks" are not of course to be confused with Turks from Anatolia, who continue to speak Turkish and who often claim that *all* the local Muslims are descended from the armies of Mehmed the Conqueror. Gypsies also often call themselves Turks, much to the disgust of those who can trace their ancestry to Mehmed's time. Sometimes all Muslims take the easy way out and refer to themselves simply as Muslims, which, whilst in keeping with the spirit of Islamic law, does not tell you in what language to address them.

In the nineteenth century the traditional manner of defining people by religion merged with the new-fangled European system dependent on language, and ethnographers began to draw maps based variously on religion and language aimed at proving that the inhabitants of Macedonia belonged to the particular ethnic group of the cartographer. They coloured in these maps using a different colour for each ethnic group. Looking at such a map of Macedonia is a sure way of contracting a migraine.

✳ ✳ ✳

So why bother with Macedonia? Why not simply write it off as impossibly Balkan, a word which seems to have supplanted Byzantine as meaning "impossible to understand and not really worth the effort"? Perhaps because this forgotten corner of Europe has affected world history to an almost unrivalled extent. The most famous Macedonian of them all, Alexander the Great, built one of the largest empires ever known. Cleopatra was descended from one of his generals, Ptolomy, while in Central Asia Alexander is still regarded as an ideal king and villagers in remote corners of Afghanistan, Pakistan and North-western India name their sons Sikander after him.

More than one Byzantine emperor was born in Macedonia and it was two local brothers known to history as Cyril and Methodios, born in Thessaloniki, who brought the Orthodox faith and a new system of writing to the Slavs, though the alphabet that bears the name of one of them, Cyrillic, was devised by their followers. It was in Macedonia that the neo-Manichaean heresy Bogomilism, which many believe to have influenced the Albigensians and other western heretics, took root. Later, another heterodox belief, this time Muslim, established itself. This was Bektashism, derived from the teachings of the Shi'i mystic Hajji Bektash; it was the favoured cult of the janissary corps, which was recruited from Macedonia as well as from Serbia and elsewhere in the Balkans. Although in theory the sultan's bodyguard and the guarantor of his power, the janissary corps had a strong influence on Ottoman policy until its dissolution in 1826.

The "Macedonian Question" was to cloud relations between the European powers in the run-up to the First World War, and it was in Macedonia that the Young Turk movement, which desperately wanted to modernize the Ottoman Empire along European lines in order to ensure its survival into the twentieth century, was founded. One of its leading lights was a young man called Mustafa Kemal, who left his birthplace in Thessaloniki to study at the military academy in Bitola, another Macedonian town, before defeating the Allies at Gallipoli, driving the invading Greeks from Anatolia and establishing the modern state of Turkey, where he is revered as Atatürk, the Father of Turks.

There is more to Macedonia than history, though. Indeed, a history that seemed to have ended with the partition of the territory has, with the collapse of Yugoslavia, come to life again. The press in Britain was agreed: after Bosnia, Macedonia. Ethnic and religious tensions would flare into an even bloodier war, one which could enmesh all the Balkan states—including the NATO allies Greece and Turkey—in a cataclysm that would pit all the myriad peoples of the region against one another. By the end of 1994 this had failed to come about: Macedonia was peaceful, but rumblings of war could be heard. I was determined to get there before it was too late.

Part One
LAND OF THE STORM GOD:
PIRIN MACEDONIA

SKULKING behind the main railway station in Pazardik on the Thracian Plain, was the toy train that was to take me to Bansko in Bulgarian Macedonia, a ramshackle affair of passenger carriages and goods wagons, looking like a string of mobile chicken coops, up to their knees in weeds. Expresses whizzed by on the main line, but I was not taking the main line. I was heading for the hills, for Macedonia. Narrow-gauge railways, because they are relatively cheap to build, tend to go to places where no railway was ever meant to be, either because of the extreme sparseness of the population or because of the difficulty of the terrain. That could be why I have always had a weakness for them; they represent a triumph of hope over reality. I do not believe that any has ever made money.

The cramped, smoky compartment rapidly filled with people: besuited elderly gentlemen, an army conscript, a young man with an attaché case and a seemingly never-ending swarm of old women carrying pots, pans and bags filled with God knows what, which very soon occupied the bulk of the space in the carriage. They shouted greetings to each other, comparing the prices of the goodies they had bought in the town. Eventually, in a cloud of stinking black diesel fumes, the train roared into life and lumbered off across the flat, fertile land, through tiny villages whose dirt streets thronged with chickens and dogs lazily luxuriating in sunny patches, slowly lifting their heads to observe our progress as we trundled along. A heady scent of ripe apples mixed with the exhaust pouring from the engine and the cloyingly heavy aroma of silage drifted through the open windows as we rattled through this dreamland. Gradually, conversations faltered and then died. One by one we drifted off into trance-like dozes, rocked gently to sleep by the rolling gait of the train, only to be reluctantly dragged back to reality as the screeching brakes announced our arrival in another tiny hamlet, where a handful of people would get off, a handful more get on, the dogs continued to lounge and the chickens scratched in the dry earth, before we resumed our leisurely amble through fields being worked by teams of horses.

Suddenly we were facing a wall of sheer rock which rose up, blocking our path, a grim boundary to the Thracian plain, a fortress which seemed to say "go no further, return to your farms and your orchards and your quiet contentment. Here be Dragons." We were leaving the peace of the plain and heading for altogether harsher, wilder territory. As the train began gently to ease itself up a narrow gorge from which the sun had fled, it clung precariously to a narrow shelf above a foaming river and the very land seemed to rebel as if trying to force us back. A rock, falling from somewhere far above, smashed through a window, narrowly missing one of the sleeping peasant women and sending broken glass spraying through the compartment. Animated discussion broke out as the shaken old lady was calmed and her pile of pots and pans redistributed away from the fatal window. Below, a small, tumble-down building became visible near the river, shrouded by trees. A sign on its roof announced "Jolly Guest House". I had nightmare visions of something out of the Brothers Grimm, imagining the unwary traveller waking up to find himself transformed into gingerbread, or enchanted by a combination of wild mushrooms and berries from the forest. Passengers on a descending train cheered and waved as we passed, as if glad to be leaving the very place we were inexorably making towards with their skins and minds intact.

At length we hauled ourselves out of the gorge, onto a rolling upland pasture, deserted except by small huts, *hizi*, surrounded by beehives like mother hens protecting their broods from some cosmic predator about to descend from the open sky. Where the slopes became too steep for pasture, the sun shining on the red and gold of the leaves of the forest made it look as though someone had spread a giant Afghan carpet over the hills. Here and there, never less than five miles distant, villages could occasionally be seen. The train continued to make stops at run-down stations with blue enamel signs over the doors of the various offices in French as well as Bulgarian: *Chef de Gare, Entrepôt, Billets.* How many people, I wondered, passed that way who could read those smart blue notices placed by the wild civilizing impulse of a far away bureaucrat. Had any Frenchman ever needed to speak to the *Chef de Gare* at any of these out of the way places, and if he had what were the chances of his finding that the station master spoke French? At every stop, a handful of people got off and disappeared into the expanding, desolate horizon, and their places were taken by a few more, the women dressed in "non-traditional Bulgarian clothes": the sorry remains of the Muslim costumes that had so enchanted Victorian travellers now reduced to a skirt printed in garish floral colours—onto which some of the younger girls had sewn sequins—worn over trousers, or in the case of one modish teenager blue jeans. On their heads they wore scarves as bright as their skirts. This was the land of the Pomaks, whose ancestors had kept their land and liberty by converting to Islam. It was also the scene of some of the worst atrocities of the struggle for independence and, a hundred years later, of the government's attempt to expunge all trace of Muslim life and culture from the country. Just out of sight to the East was the village of Batak, where in the 1880s Pomaks and the dreaded *bashibazouks*, irregular Muslim troops who were little more than rapacious bandits, slaughtered the Christians in their own church. The massacre came to the ears of the popular press in London and, perhaps for the first time, government policy changed as a result. Under Gladstone's leadership Britain swung from supporting the Turks against Russian imperial ambitions, executing a neat U-turn to oppose Ottoman policy in the Balkans.

Abruptly we left that wild upland, and after traversing a pine covered ridge from which the hills fell away steeply, teetered momentarily on the edge before plunging down through a series of tunnels to emerge into a lusciously green river valley whose steep sides hemmed us into a confined space where horses were roaming as if at will through the long grass. Flocks of sheep scattered in front of the train, pursued by the shouts of shepherds. Villages of solid stone houses with tiled roofs crowded up to the tracks as if glad to see us. Minarets, the tall pencil-like structures introduced by the Turks, which one associates with Western Turkey and the Balkans, thrust skywards indicating the source of this bounty. Peasants in carts drawn by horses, mules or oxen waved cheerily to the passing train. We had entered the valley of the Mesta, which rises here, giving life to an otherwise inhospitable terrain before flowing south to Greece to become the Nestos, the river that divides Thrace from Macedonia. It was into this river, now so benign in the bright sunlight, that the Thracian women had cast the head of the god-king Orpheus, still lamenting the loss of his beloved Euridyce. The Turks called the river Karasu, which means "Black Water". Ahead loomed the massive bulk of the Pirin mountains, their cloud-covered peaks bearing witness to their being home to the Thracian storm god Perun. I had at last arrived in what seemed an almost legendary country, Macedonia.

Huddled up close to its protecting mountains, Bansko lies on the very edge of an open basin through which the Mesta flows, the rich golden brown of its stone houses matching the fields. The old town was preserved by the Communists as a monument to the National Liberation in recognition of its colourful history in the late nineteenth century and remains a maze of narrow cobbled streets flanked by the high walls and stout gates of the traditional *kâštas*, the fortress-like homes developed to defend the people from marauding bands of bandits or Ottoman officials who were entitled to demand three days' free board and lodging. Behind these blank walls lives the family with all its provisions and livestock. Brightly coloured carpets drape over balconies, their basic brown enlivened with reds, ochres and yellows, in company with strings of burningly red peppers and the warm brown leaves of drying tobacco and the yellow of corn cobs, art imitating life in a harmony of rural hues. Barns overflow with provisions gathered in for the winter, hay for the animals, great mounds of pumpkins, potatoes and cabbage for the people. During the day and early evening old crones entirely swathed in black sit on benches outside their *kâŝtas*, chatting whilst shucking corn or spinning and carding wool, watching the world drift past in horse-drawn carts, motionless and timeless as the stones behind them. In the main street people sit in the clear mountain air under golden yellow chestnut trees soaking in the sun with their espressos and waiting for winter, when the town will transform itself into a resort for skiers of the more leisurely kind. The game of conkers has yet to be introduced, and children conduct their minor wars in a less ritualized manner, throwing the nuts at one another.

As I sat one evening taking coffee, I was approached by a burly man in his early thirties. "Do you speak German?", he asked. His name was Boris. I could have guessed as much. He looked like a Boris, with his shoulder-length hair, bushy black beard and flashing eyes. A great bear of a man, his bulk was accentuated by a padded leather jacket. He told me he was a disc jockey for the local radio station: "I spent three years in Bonn learning about the broadcast media. Originally a group of friends sponsored the station, but then the money ran out and we had to take advertising. What do you do? You're a teacher? You don't look like one. Where's your tie?"

"I try not to be bourgeois."

"Ha! Gimme five." We slapped hands, pretending for a moment to be African Americans. This proved to be Boris' favourite way of expressing approval. Evidently he had learnt about more than just broadcasting in Bonn.

"You're right, " he continued, "there's a lot of unemployment up here—people go to the cities but they still can't find work. All the same, I don't think there'll be any problems in the elections. That Zelyu Zelev (the president of the republic) has got his head screwed on all right. Thank God relations between Christians and Muslims are good now. We live in a democracy, you can be whatever you like. You can be Buddhist if you really want, what does it matter? Look, in a place like Macedonia you have to be tolerant, otherwise nobody would be able to live here. Look what happened in the past. I'm a native Macedonian, but that's not important. Who cares that I'm Macedonian and you're English? We're both people, and that's what counts. The name-changing idea was stupid, this idea that to be a Bulgarian citizen you have to be Bulgarian. I like the American idea. You talk about Irish Americans and Italian Americans. Just because you're Irish or Italian doesn't make you any less American. It's the same with your country, Great Britain. You're lucky that it's named after a place, not a people, so anyone who lives in that place can belong to it regardless of race or religion. That's like Macedonia."

"It hasn't always been true here, though, has it?" I interposed. "You yourself said that you were ethnically Macedonian, not Bulgarian."
Boris thought for a moment, wrinkling his forehead.

"Well, of course I *am* Bulgarian, but that's just my citizenship. I actually said I'm a Macedonian Slav. That doesn't mean Greeks and Turks aren't also Macedonians. Of course they are if they live here. I only wish the Greeks understood that."

"Mmm … The Greeks say that their population is entirely Greek and that Macedonia is solely within Greece."

"I know. Strange, isn't it? They make all this fuss about Macedonia, but Thrace is divided between Bulgaria, Greece and Turkey and they never say anything about that. It doesn't seem to bother them. I speak Greek …"

"You do? I didn't think anyone here spoke Greek."

"Yes. At school, Russian was compulsory, of course, and then we were given the choice of English, German or Greek. I thought that I could learn English or German at any time, so I chose Greek. After all, south Macedonia is in Greece, and I didn't think I'd get another chance. Everyone should speak four or five languages. You have an excuse, because English is an international language, through the medium of music, but the French and Italians should know better. We have MTV here, and I play English music on my show. It's the great leveller. By the way, do you want another beer?" We had moved on from coffees. I was drinking "Pirin" beer, the kind with *Makedoniya* emblazoned across its label, Boris had his country's national drink, *mastika*, an exceptionally noxious spirit similar to ouzo or raki. "Cheers!" he said.

"*Prost!*"

"*Nasdraviye!* Gimme five. English music is the best in the world."

"That and American."

"No, just English. What kind of music do you like?"

"All kinds. jazz," I mentioned some well-known jazz musicians, "Folk, rock ..."

"What kind of rock?"

"Well, it's a bit obscure. Have you heard of J. J. Cale or Richard Thompson?"

"Of course I have! Give me some credit, I'm a DJ. How about the Rolling Stones?"

"Everybody likes them. I like Bulgarian music too, Ivo Papasov and Trio Bulgarka. *Bezmusika, bezzizn*, I say." The drink was beginning to get to me.

"*Öhne musik, öhne leben*. No life without music. I agree. Trio Bulgarka are good, but Papasov is a genius. I once saw him playing the clarinet through his nose." I couldn't help but think that must be very uncomfortable. Ivo Papasov, a Gypsy, is the leading exponent of the style known as wedding music, an amplified version of the traditional idiom, which the Communists tried to ban in their efforts to turn all aspects of popular culture to the revolutionary cause. The immediate result of the ban was that the style became enormously fashionable. "Tell you what," continued Boris, "let's go to another bar and hear some Bulgarian music. There was a rumour that George Harrison likes it and it became very popular."

On the way through Bansko's all but deserted streets we met some people Boris knew. He knew many people: "They're musicians. This man has just bought some bagpipes. We will hear them later."

A low wooden door presented itself to the narrow, muddy lane. From within came the sound of laughter and a clinking of glasses. We ducked through the doorway into a small, smoky room whose stone walls were hung with the brightly coloured textiles of the region, vivid red against solemn black. Knots of people sat on benches at trestle tables talking to one another in raspy nicotine-impregnated voices, and eating grilled kebabs and chopped pickled cabbage. In a corner three men, with clarinet, accordion and a goblet-shaped drum, were playing and singing lustily, though, rather to my disappointment, the clarinettist never once offered the instrument to his nose. The complex rhythms and wild melodies of their music wound their way around us, while the men's stentorian voices spoke of a strong people preparing for war or simply revelled in their masculinity. The nineteenth century seemed to have come terribly close. I felt as though I had stumbled into a cameo in a film—"The Robber's Lair".

"We will drink wine," announced Boris. "Bulgarian wine is the best in the world." An earthenware jug was brought to us by a waitress who looked strangely out of place in her black and white uniform, like a refugee from a Budapest café lost in the badlands of the interior. Boris poured the wine into goblets, draining and refilling his almost before I had had a chance to taste mine. The wine was richly intense, the colour of blood, its spiciness clinging to the side of my throat.

"How did you get here?" asked Boris. "By train? Good God! That must have taken forever. Only Pomaks use the train, and Pomaks smell." Somehow the drink had affected his Macedonian tolerance, his internationalist urbanity.

"Tell me about relations between Pirinska Makedoniya [in Bulgaria] and Vardarska Makedoniya [formerly in Yugoslavia]," I urged.

"Ah! You've been lying to me! You told me you don't speak Macedonian, but you know the names of our country perfectly. Of course we get on well. Many people have friends or relatives over the border. We understand each other perfectly. By the way, do you like football? Manchester United are going to win the European Cup. We get two hours of English football a week on television. It's beautiful to watch, the best in the world. *Prost!*"

"*Nasdraviye!*" Suddenly the nineteenth century had vanished, taking its wild remoteness with it, and we were left in the new international world, bound together by the fortunes of a football club in the north-west of England.

"Come on," urged Boris, "We must hear some more music." He led me through a maze of backstreets to another doorway concealing another crowded, smoky room. This one was the same as the last, but with bagpipes. New arrivals asked to be seated away from the band. Bulgarian bagpipes are even more excruciating than the Scottish or Northumbrian varieties. The piper, a stocky young man with a swarthy face, curly black hair and no front teeth, kept jumping about in a most disconcerting manner. I was getting very drunk.

"I must go home," I said feebly.

"Just one more drink ... Wine! Bring us wine!" Boris shouted. "Tell me, what religion are you, Protestant or Catholic? Most Bulgarians are Orthodox, but we've got everything, Catholic, Protestant

... There's an English Protestant church here in Bansko. Many people here are Protestants." The idea of a rogue Anglican parish high in the Pirin was too much for me. I had to leave. Outside I gulped in the cold mountain air. Above my head were more stars than I had ever seen before. It was as though someone had taken a giant brush and flicked paint across the heavens, a cosmic Jackson Pollock. Close to the horizon, Orion strode between two peaks, his bow pointed at a monstrous Taurus as if to defend Macedonia from some horribly destructive force. Cautiously, I felt my way back through the deserted lanes to my lodgings.

The Muslims of Kraište and Gorni Kraište

Not far from Bansko is the village of Kraište. Apart from a small railway station, named not after that village but for another more distant, Christian one, there is little to distinguish it from any other in the region. On a hot Friday afternoon I walked down a main street whose only signs of life were a few chickens desultorily scratching in the dirt and a knot of young men playing football. The air was heavy with the scent of wildflowers and hay. Somewhere a donkey brayed. All around lay farmland where men and women were busy sowing next year's crop by hand. Slightly further off loomed the mountains, their rocky peaks showing white against the clear blue sky. Just up a slight hill stood the mosque, only its minaret giving it away, distinguishing it from all the other square, red-tiled buildings, each set in its own farmyard. A plaque over the door in both Western and Arabic script dated it to 1948. A porch was floored with new, locally made kilims, brown with red, white, green and yellow stripes, each loom-sized strip of cloth stitched to its neighbour. The building was locked, despite it being the time of the noon prayer that all Muslim men must make as a congregation on Fridays, but the door of a lean-to addition opened to reveal a *mekhteb*. Inside, a wood-burning stove took pride of place in the middle of the room. As well as more kilims, there were a few wooden benches. A blackboard hung on the wall in the company of a poster depicting the Kaaba, and a pile of brand new Qur'ans were stacked on the floor. The mosque was perfectly peaceful, and it was tempting just to sit on the porch listening to the humming of the bees and enjoying the view, but I had come because I wanted to talk to some of the region's Muslims.

As I left the village, making for its sister, Gorni Kraište, I was hailed by a shepherd who scrambled up a bank and leaned on his staff to talk to me. It was impossible to guess his age from his leathery, weather-beaten face.

"Where are you from?" he asked. "We don't get many foreigners here. Some Arabs came once, and left some Qur'ans, but I don't think I've ever seen an Englishman before." He looked around, sucking his teeth pensively as if half-expecting regiments of English to spring from the ground. "Would I call myself a Pomak? No. The Bulgarians like to call us that, but I just think of myself as Muslim. This whole region is inhabited by Muslims, except for a few places. About four kilometres from here there's a Christian village, Belitsa. Also in Banya there are Christians, but here everyone is Muslim. I don't really think about these things much. This is a democracy and you can be whatever you like. All that nonsense about name changing is over now, Allah be praised, but things are still bad for Muslims because there's no work in the villages where we live. It's a pity you couldn't have come tomorrow, because I've got a friend who's studying German in Blagoevgrad but he only comes at the weekend. You could talk to him. You could always try in the bar down there—you can't buy alcohol of course—and talk to the businessmen, but I think they will only want to talk about money. I must get back to work." His sheep had scattered over a wide area by this time, and he leapt down the bank to gather them in. I continued along the road, through pungent pine woods. Once a bus passed in the opposite direction leaving a cloud of black diesel fumes hanging in the still air. Birdsong drifted through the air, and the toot of a train, barely audible, drifted across the valley.

At length I arrived in Gorni Kraište, which announced itself with a jumble of wooden frames for drying tobacco. The plants themselves, now shorn of their leaves, still stood in the fields. Although noticeably poorer than its neighbour, the village sported a large new mosque, again on a hill just beyond the houses, its central dome sheltering the three smaller domes of the porch, in the Ottoman style. Prayers were just ending as I arrived. Groups of brightly dressed women hurried away in knots to their chores, but some of the men lingered.

"*Salaam Aleikum!*" I greeted one of them.

"*Aleikum salaam.* Where are you from?" I told him. "Do you speak Bulgarian? Russian? Come!" I was led into the presence of a large man, clearly the local big-wig, whose suit stretched too tightly over his ample stomach. He was engaged in urgent discussion with some builders who were reluctantly shovelling sand into a cement mixer. My nature was explained to him and we exchanged the necessary pleasantries by way of establishing our relative social standing.

"So you speak some Russian?" he asked, "Do you know Turkish?"

"No. Are you Turkish?"

"Of course. We all are. There is no such thing as a 'Bulgarian Muslim'—they were invented by the Communists. It's what I call neo-Byzantinism. Many years ago, where we are now was part of the Byzantine Empire, then we Turks came from Anatolia and added it to our Islamic Empire. The Communists wanted to deny that, and put Bulgaria back to what it was before, but now we can practise religion and use our own names."

He led me to the bare interior of the mosque. A turbaned imam was sitting under the dome, saying additional prayers to himself. He ignored us.

"How do you like our mosque? It's quite something, isn't it? Up here is the women's gallery, and here (opening a small door and fumbling for the light) is the minaret. On second thoughts, you'd better not go up there. I don't think its finished yet. We're raising money for it in the village, but building materials are very expensive, which is why it's taking so long to finish." Someone came running up from the village, shouting that my guide was wanted on the phone, so he left me outside. Before long I was joined by the imam, who came out, jamming a beret onto his head to replace the turban. He took my hand and pummelled it, searching my face with watery grey eyes. He was not old, perhaps 28, but his cheeks were sunken, and his mousy hair and hesitant moustache made him look older. His voice was very soft, gentle. I got the impression that he had seen more hardship than his years warranted.

"*Salaam Aleikum.* Are you a journalist?"

"No, I'm writing a book about Islam in Bulgaria. I like your new mosque. Is it true you raised all the money for it in the village?"

"Well, the villagers have given what they can, but it was founded with money from Turkey. I had to go to Sofia to study, but now we have a *mekhteb* under the mosque, so everyone can learn Islam properly. Do you have mosques in London?"

"Yes, many. Muslims from all over the world live in London. There is also a *madrasa*. In one of our cities, the head of the city soviet is a Muslim." The imam's eyes widened in disbelief as he tried to comprehend the idea of an Islamic Britain. We had been walking down the hill, and now arrived outside the town hall.

"Excuse me," he said, and greeted a small cluster of people, using the Turkish word *marhaba*. They responded in kind and began to talk animatedly in a mixture of Turkish and Bulgarian. I was led into the building, up crumbling stairs to the shabby office of the man I had spoken to previously. He was shouting in Bulgarian into a telephone, seated behind an immense wooden desk. A group of villagers was seated around the walls, under battered and dusty books, looking at him as if in supplication. This was less an office than a court, where people came to lay their grievances before the Big Man. I was motioned to a chair immediately before the desk. Slamming down the receiver, he rotated his considerable bulk towards me.

"Have a cigarette," he said. "What do you want to know? And clear off, all of you! Get some coffee." Crestfallen, his suitors departed. Moments later, coffee was brought.

"Well, I've heard that there is now a Turkish political party in Bulgaria ..."

"Don't say that! That is what our enemies say. It is called The Movement for Rights and Freedoms. Is there 'Turkish' in its name? No! It is open to anyone, and we work in alliance with other parties. We don't want nationalism here, there is no place for it. They have nationalism in Yugoslavia, and look what happened to them. Now Bulgaria is a democracy, and we must respect and work with all peoples."

"Is it possible to learn Turkish in school?"

"It's taught as a special subject. There's a single curriculum, which must be taught, but our children learn Turkish as well. As for name-changing, don't talk to me about that! If you were called Isma'il, you had to pretend to be Ivan. Why? What is your *narodnost* [literally, 'peoplehood']? English? But I've noticed you call your country Britain, not England. And why should a country have only one *narod*?"

We were joined by the imam, who sat rather nervously on the edge of one of the hard wooden chairs. "Can you tell me," he asked, "are there many problems for Muslims in Britain?"

"Some. It can be difficult to get *halal* food in school."

"That is a very big problem."

"Yes. Also Muslims cannot marry in the mosque, they must go to the town hall. But I think the biggest problem is lack of unity. There is no leader, no grand mufti. Pakistanis only go to Pakistani mosques, Turks to Turkish ones. Islam in Britain has become almost nationalist."

I thought for a while. "Also, *ezan* must only be in the mosque, you can't have it in public."

"And *ezan* is in Arabic? Do you know it in Arabic?"

I started out, mangling the holy language, but dried up after *Muhammedin Rasul Allah*. The imam finished the phrase for me.

"Do you have any Sufi groups here?" I asked. "I ask because there are many in Yugoslavia." At first the imam didn't understand: "You mean like in Iran, people who follow Jafar as-Sadiq [Shi'ites]?"

"Er, no, *dervishler*." I used the Turkish word.

"Oh no, we have none here!" He explained dervishism to the mayor, who seemed nonplussed. "Do you have them in England?"

"Yes, there's a Naqshibandi *tekke* near where I live." I could see British Islam plummeting in his estimation. We descended to the ground floor, where there was a café, an echoing barn of a place with a couple of pool tables and a plain concrete floor, simple tin tables and plastic chairs. The mayor brought espressos, sweetened to the Turkish taste.

"Are you married?" he asked.

"Yes."

"Children?"

"No."

"You should have. I have two, the imam has one. What does your wife do?"

"She works in a bank."

"Manager? Cashier?"

My Russian wasn't up to explaining the workings of an investment bank. I hardly understand them myself, so I said, "She buys hard currency." That met with approval. Buying and selling hard currency has only just become legal, and it carries great social cachet.

"Ah! Pounds! Dollars! How much does a teacher earn?" I told him. "Good God! And how much is a loaf of bread? Good God! Well, your prices are stupid, so your wages have to be as well. Here we have a big problem. Many people are unemployed, and even if you have work it's hard to earn enough to eat. What about John Major? Do you think the Workers' Party will win power from him?" In Russian, the same word, *rabota*, means both work and labour, but I don't think Mr Blair would be too happy with the idea of the Workers' Party. Too socialist by half.

A television in the corner of the room was broadcasting a news bulletin. The studio seemed to be suffering from an unseasonable blizzard. The reporter was doing a fair imitation of a frog, as her words were jumbled by static. "Is this Turkish television?" I asked.

"Yes. We get it by satellite." Turksat, Ankara's latest move to export Kemalism to the furthest reaches of the Turkic world. It is actually aimed at Central Asia, propaganda to bind the emerging states to Turkey, but here it served to bolster the villagers' sense of Turkishness. In the modern media age it is becoming harder and harder for any government to tell its people what to think, which is why the anti-Muslim drive was doomed almost from the start. Fences are no longer enough to keep the world at bay.

"How are you getting back to Bansko?" the mayor asked. "By train? Hey! Ahmet! Is there a train to Bansko this evening?" A seedy-looking man with a droopy moustache, dressed in a scruffy approximation of the state railway's uniform, who was doing nothing in particular replied. "At seven. Who is that guy?" The imam was looking at his watch.

"I think you have *namaz* at five," I hinted. He looked relieved.

"Yes, I must get back to the mosque or I will be late." He rose.

"Wait," I said, "I want to give you this for the mosque." I handed him 100 leva, about £1. He sat down again in confusion.

"I can't take this much money!"

"Think of it as *zakat.*"

"But you're not Muslim, are you? How can you pay *zakat?*"

"We all believe in one God. What's the difference. Besides, I want to give." He pondered this for a moment.

"Are there problems between Christians and Muslims in your country?"

"Not as such. There's racism, but that's not connected to religion."

"What about between sects? Are you Catholic?"

"No, Protestant. There's no real problem, except in Northern

Ireland, where Protestants and Catholics have been fighting for over 20 years." They were aghast at the prospect.

"That's like Bosnia! Allah preserve us from that!" I asked what they thought of Bosnia: "We try not to. It's none of our business. Relations between Christians and Muslims here are good, and *insh'allah*, God willing, they will stay like that. Why should we want to fight?"

As I walked back, the sun was setting, glinting pinkly off mountain tops freshly dusted with snow the previous night. People were beginning to return to their villages, the women and children driving cattle before them, the men riding in carts which ambled along the road. The smell of wood-smoke hung in the air as a hundred grills and ovens were prepared for the evening meal. A ten-year-old boy, riding bareback, raced his horse across the meadows. By the crossroads the same young men were still playing football. It was a long way from Bosnia.

I sat down at the station and began to write up my notes. A lanky station master with his cap pushed far back on his head wandered over to watch me. "It's very beautiful here," I commented.

"Yes," he replied, "very, but there is no work, so perhaps it is not so beautiful."

Night fell. Over the road I thought I could see fireworks. Then there was an almighty bang and all the lights in the valley went out.

The Christians of Bansko

A Christian island largely surrounded by Muslim villages, Bansko's church, Holy Trinity, was built to proportions far larger than those prescribed by the Turks, hidden from view as it is behind stout walls. A silver birch draped its leaves gracefully over the memorial to some local hero in the courtyard, while under the porch the inevitable group of black-clad women, aged anything between 40 and 80, gossiped about who was seeing whom. Outside the gate children returning from school refreshed themselves at a fountain that constantly flowed with pure mountain water. Within the gloomy interior, just visible through clouds of incense, a priest and a choir of two were engaged in worship. A handful of people drifted in and out, but the worship of the Orthodox Church goes on regardless of the presence of a congregation. The bass voices of the trio by the iconostasis combined to an effect that was mysterious and dark. Rather than soaring like angels, the words seemed to come from the deepest recesses of the men's souls, emerging in a low rumbling growl to spread themselves thickly like treacle across the floor. Here was no joyous worship but a deadly serious meditation.

✳ ✳ ✳

The Ottoman *millet* system classified people according to their religious affliation, and the area of authority of a church aligned to a particular group could become the basis of a new territorial state. In 1866 the Ottoman granting of autonomy away from the Greek patriachate in Istanbul to the Bulgarian Exarchate Church—where, if there was the support of two-thirds of the adult male parishioners, a parish could switch allegiance to the Exarchate Church—led to the establishment of the Bulgarian state in 1878. However, this new state was severely truncated from its original form in the San Stefano Treaty of 1878 at the end of the Russo-Turkish war of 1877–8 due to pressure from Britain and Austro-Hungary. This so-called Greater Bulgaria, based on the parishes who had opted for the Exarchate Church, had included most of Macedonia, which, in 1878, remained under Ottoman control. As the three rival Orthodox Balkan states—Greece, Bulgaria and Serbia—began to inch closer to Macedonia, each sought to assert the authority of its church over the people living there: membership of a particular church implying membership of the relevant nation and thus serving as a possible basis for an *irredenta*. It was here that the Macedonian Question raised its head. Who were the inhabitants of Macedonia, and to which state should they belong?

Each of the three states squabbling like hyenas over the decaying corpse of the Ottoman Empire was quite certain that Macedonia was an integral part of itself. Greece, fired by the concept of the Great Idea— that the Greeks were the descendants of the ancients and had a holy duty to re-establish the Byzantine Empire—looked to the heritage of Alexander the Great and Aristotle and claimed Macedonia as their own. That large numbers of its inhabitants spoke languages other than Greek was irrelevant. They were all members of the Greek Church, they went, if they went at all, to Greek schools (since the schools were run by the church they had little choice) and therefore they were Greek, even if they had temporarily forgotten their mother tongue. Serbia observed that its Emperor Stefan Dušan, who in 1346 proclaimed himself

Emperor of the Serbs, Greeks, Bulgars and Albanians, had had his capital in Skopje, the heart of Macedonia. Dušan died in 1355. Barely 30 years later almost the whole of the Balkans had fallen to the Turks with the great Serbian defeat at Kosovo Polje. The Serbs had been the last Christian rulers of Macedonia, and the land was rightfully theirs. Patriots in Belgrade began to proclaim that the Skopje dialect was the "purest" form of Serbian, and Bulgarian priests, whom they called "cassocked conquerors" were accused of "corrupting" the language.

Foremost among those priests was Father Paisii. His statue stands in the square outside Bansko's church, its pedestal always covered in fresh flowers which children protect from the depredations of passing goats. A native of Bansko, Paisii became a monk at the monastery of Hilander, the establishment founded on Mount Athos in 1198 by the Serbian Tsar Stefan Nemanja and his son, Rastko, who himself became a monk under the name of Sava, later becoming Serbia's patron saint. Here Paisii worked on what was to be the first history of the Bulgarian people. Completed in 1762, it was one of the first books to be written in modern Bulgarian. In it he asserted that "the Bulgarians were the most glorious of all the Slavic nations, they were the first to have tsars, they were the first to have a patriarch, they were the first to be Christianised, and they ruled over the greatest area." That area included Macedonia. Was not Ohrid the seat of the ancient Bulgarian patriarchate? Was it not in Macedonia that the great Tsar Samuel's army was defeated by the Byzantine Emperor Basil II, the "Bulgar-Slayer"?

A century later, Dimitâr Mladenov claimed that Stefan Dušan was in fact a Bulgar, and that the people of Macedonia spoke Bulgarian. Ironically, Mladenov, who was educated in a Greek school, wrote his early correspondence in Greek. The Serbs were not going to take such a claim lying down. In 1886 the Society of St Sava was founded in Belgrade to combat "Exarchist Bulgarianism", the claim that Bulgarians were a separate nation deserving of their own church and that Macedonians were among them. "The name Bulgarian", wrote the Serb propagandist C. Stoyanovich, "does not designate the Bulgarian nationality, but is simply derived from the Latin *vulgaris*, meaning slow-witted, peasant, farmer." The etymology could be doubted, but the point intended is correct—"Bulgarian" was often simply used as a term of abuse to designate a peasant, not that that ever put the Bulgarians themselves off.

Unfortunately for the propagandists, the actual inhabitants of Macedonia do not seem to have thought of themselves as anything much, beyond "Christian" or "Muslim" and showed a marked indifference concerning intellectual arguments as to which nation they belonged or to which church they should belong. More forceful means of persuasion had to be resorted to. As Stavrianos puts it in his *The Balkans Since 1453*:

> *The miserable peasants were torn this way and that, and retribution was sure to follow whichever decision they made. If they declared for the Exarchists they could expect a visit from Greek bands. If they remained under the Patriarchate, they were hounded by the Bulgars as traitors.*

Favourites among the pastimes of the persuaders included setting fire to the beards of recalcitrant priests, or even locking entire congregations into their church and setting fire to it *pour encourager les autres*. Not surprisingly, a person's ethnic and religious identity (the two being seen as essentially the same) tended to vary according to who was doing the asking:

> *It was not uncommon for a family to have a member in each camp, for an individual to pass through several phases of religio-national orientation, for a village to switch sides at random, and … for these changes to be coerced.*

So wrote Ivo Banach in 1984. To make matters worse, not only were the Orthodox busily slaughtering one another but the Bashibazouks were equally busy engaging in what became known to Victorian Britain as the Bulgarian Atrocities, as they attempted to bludgeon anti-Ottoman sentiment out of the local Christians. One way of avoiding this mayhem was conversion to Protestantism. By doing so, not only were you put beyond the range of the Patriarchist versus Exarchist controversy but you gained the protection of the Western powers against any marauding Bashibazouks who might be loitering in the vicinity.

✳ ✳ ✳

Away from the centre of Bansko, further up the hill, stood an unprepossessing concrete-rendered building, entered through an arch on the ground floor. Above was the legend "Evangelical Church, Founded 1868" Upstairs, in a pine-floored hall, I found a congregation of about a hundred listening to a choir that sang to an easy rock beat. The light, warm room was a stark contrast to the gloomily damp Holy Trinity. Facing the congregation, on a podium piled high with fruit and vegetables, stood the pastor, a solidly built, slightly portly middle-aged man with short steely hair and a neatly pressed suit. Above him signs read "Enter with humility into the House of the Lord" and "God is Love". With a majestic sweep of his arms he bade the worshippers rise, and they burst into song to a synthesizer accompaniment, almost shouting the words in their glee. Then, holding his arms apart above his bowed head, the pastor blessed them and the meeting broke up. People shook hands and murmured greetings bubbled to the ceiling. A few old women dressed in the regulation black dress, blue headscarf and embroidered apron were present, but the overwhelming majority of those in the room were clean-cut and fresh looking young men and women in their 20s and 30s. They spoke English with a ready felicity. The synthesizer player approached me, her instrument under her arm. She must have been around 25, with short brown hair, black trousers and a fake pearl necklace resting on her pink jersey.

"Hi, I'm Anna. Where are you from? London? I live in Sofia myself, but I've come back to Bansko today, because it's Thanksgiving."

"You mean Harvest Festival."

"Do I?" Her grey eyes slowly took in the room. "I think all the Evangelicals are here today. Perhaps we are ten short. Are you born again in Christ?"

"No, I was born in the Church of England, and once was enough." Evangelicals tend to bring out the worst in me.

"But I think we must repent our sins and let Jesus into our hearts, then it doesn't matter what Church we belong to anymore. There was a big revival of our Church about three years ago, but now the newspapers are running a campaign against us. They say our pastors brain-wash us and encourage us to take drugs and to give them all our money, but you can see it's not like that."

Ivan, a Cliff Richard look-alike who seemed to have teleported from a southern US Baptist university and who wore a small gold cross pinned to the lapel of his tweed jacket, concurred.

"They confuse us with people like the Hare Krishnas, all those cults that are active in Bulgaria now. Since the revival a few years ago, when I was born again, the Church has grown very slowly. There's a lot of prejudice, and this feeling that if you're Christian, you should be Orthodox. As far as my parents are concerned, I'm Orthodox, because of my baptism, but I've only been to an Orthodox service perhaps twice. I met Jesus here, and came to know Him. This is where I feel comfortable." I had a nasty feeling he was going to ask me to be one of Jesus' Little Sunbeams, but he didn't.

"You're from London? A friend of mine went to Bible College in London. He now has a church in the extreme south, near the Turkish border. This is the oldest Protestant church in Bulgaria, though. It was founded by American missionaries ... yes, they're back. There was one singing in the choir this morning. Methodists, Baptists and Congregationalists came and divided the country between them. The Methodists took the north, and the Congregationalists the south, with a few Baptists." Spiritual imperialism. It happened all over the Ottoman Empire. Protestant and Catholic missionaries, riding on the back of Western commercial and diplomatic supremacy, became active towards the end of the last century. Finding it virtually impossible to convert Muslims, they fell on the local Christians like beagles on a fox and began tearing up the ancient Churches of the East, wolfing down whole communities in gulps. Concessions forced out of the Sublime Porte put Protestants under the protection of Britain and the United States, while Catholics by and large came under a French wing. Naturally, in the Balkans, those who were left regarded the converts as turncoats, apostates and traitors, a fifth column being used by outside powers to control the destiny of the fledgling nations, to deprive them of their newly awakened sense of nationhood, of historical culture.

Ivan showed me a photograph hanging on the wall under a line of portraits of previous pastors, all with their dates. It showed a large group of people sitting outside the church building, around the turn of the century.

"First of all, they met in a coffee shop. I once saw a photograph of the outside of this church and the congregation was so big you could hardly see the building. During the Communist period, though, people were frightened. There must have been only ten people who came.

There's a lot of ignorance about Christianity here. I and some of my friends travel round the country preaching the Gospel. We're having a meeting here for young people tonight. You're welcome to come if you like, but it'll be in Bulgarian, not English."

Later that sunny Sunday afternoon as I walked through Bansko in search of a beer, I heard music flowing from a *mehana*. Inside, a group was sitting over the wreckage of a meal. Three wine bottles and a *mastika* bottle, all of them empty, stood on the table. The people sang heartily, while two danced the *hora*, the circle dance of the Balkans. "Another *hora!*" they cried as the music came to an end. Another was danced. And another. And another, whilst those who were too drunk to dance clapped their hands and sang. One woman, who must have been 50, moved with a rolling swagger of her hips, forcing an onlooker to join her in a Greek dance usually reserved for courting couples. Whether the music was Greek or Bulgarian was immaterial, they danced on. The dances of Macedonia remain the same, wherever they come from, and no distinction is made as to a tune's source or a song's language. Boris' voice came to me again, "Music is the great leveller."

"More wine! Another *hora!*", and they effortlessly slipped into a disco beat without once missing their step. The room was alive with dance, and it struck me how rare it is now in Europe that you see traditional dance or hear traditional songs performed spontaneously, with everyone knowing the steps and the words. These days folk music has become divorced from the "folk" whose music it ostensibly is, being performed by rather po-faced individuals who are being self-consciously folkloric. But dance is meant to come from the heart, it is not an art form to be put on before a critical audience. Seeing this thronged room reminded me of how far we have come from our own traditions.

* * *

That evening the Evangelical Church was less full than it had been for the morning service, but the congregation no less enthusiastic. Ivan led the service in the company of another young man equipped with the regulation short hair, square chin, jacket and tie. A wood-burning stove crackled and spat in the middle of the floor, as if faintly disgusted with the goings-on. Ivan preached an over-long sermon well, taking the Epistle to the Philippians as his text. Anna deserted her synthesizer to come and translate for me. Ivan was extolling the virtues of taking Jesus into your heart and explaining the doctrine of Justification by Faith, attacking the Orthodox for being obsessed with ritual. He warned the assembled company that they alone carried the Light of Christ within them and that they should not hide this light but let it shine forth. They should steel themselves, as the Apostles had done, against adversity. "Don't let them write you off as a sect!" he admonished, "Bulgarians have always wanted to be free, but some think that means freedom from the rule of the Lord! We must show them that true freedom lies in letting Him govern our hearts and minds." It was all a bit sinister— freedom as servitude, the certainty of the Elect. I was reminded of James Hogg's Justified Sinner, a man who could do anything in his certainty that he was already saved.

They launched into the final hymn. Somehow the singing sounded oddly turgid, slowly progressing in a mournful dirge, despite the attempts of a few to enliven the tune: "Alleluia, Al-eh-lu-lia-a-a-a-a [*clap*], the Lord's my Sa-a-vi-our-our-our-our ... Alleluia, Al-eh-lu-lia-a-a-a-a [*whoop*], the Lord's my Sa-a-vi-our-our-our-our ..."

As the congregation broke up I was accosted by another clone.

"Hi, I'm Gary!" he grasped my hand. "What are you doing here?"

"Do you mean in Bulgaria, in Bansko, or here specifically?"

"Well, I was going to lead by degrees to the last. What church do you go to?" I was tempted to say I was a Zoroastrian, but I don't think he would have understood.

"I don't go to any," I replied. "I'm nominally Anglican, whatever that means."

"I think I know where you're coming from" he pounced. "I was brought up as an Episcopalian"—Gary was from California—"but, although I respected the tradition, I had all these questions they couldn't answer. I found the answers in the Bible. You know, there are many commentaries on the Bible, well someone once told me that the Bible makes an interesting commentary on the commentaries."

"That's a very Protestant point of view. Personally I find most of the Bible impossible to understand."

"That's unbelievable! If you let it speak direct to your heart ..."
Fortunately I was saved the explanation of what would happen then by
the approach of the pastor, whose name, incredibly, was Boris Karloff.
He would never have made it in Hollywood. A man less like
Frankenstein's monster would be hard to imagine. I had been
harbouring a theory: would anyone have converted to Protestantism if
there had already been a Bulgarian Church, using Bulgarian in its
worship rather than Greek?

"No, it's not that at all. There was a spiritual void which the
Orthodox could not fill. The time was ripe for Protestantism, and the
missionaries saved us, just as the time was ripe in England when Wesley
was alive. Remember, it was Evangelicals who first translated the Bible
into Bulgarian. The Orthodox used Old Church Slavonic, which
nobody could understand any longer. We saved Bulgarian Christianity.
If there's anything else you want to know, just ask and I'll show you the
church archives." Before I had a chance to do so he was dragged away
by his wife.

"How come you're here?" I asked Gary before he had a chance to
ask me to make room in my heart for Jesus.

"I work in the Bible College in Sofia," he answered. "Those were
two of my pupils leading the service tonight." Moral support or quality
control? Anna joined us.

"You see, the Americans look after us," she said, "but we don't get
any money from them any more like we did after 1989." Gary grinned
foolishly. "Many young people came into the Church then, but about
half have drifted away now, because of the Orthodox prejudice against
us. Most of the people here were brought up as Orthodox, but that
Church couldn't understand their questions. The Orthodox are very
weak at the moment—they're split because some people think the
patriarch gave in too much to the Communists—but now there's a
seminary in Sofia, and I think they will have many missionaries soon
and then they will be strong. We're all worried about the future. I'm at
Bible College in Sofia, but I want to study something else as well.

"Bansko's very strange, very conservative. They don't like new
things here. In Turkish times Muslims were frightened to come into the
town, because they would be killed, so there aren't any here, only in the
villages. They call themselves Turks, but you know they're not really. All
the Turks left when we were liberated. They're Bulgarians who

converted and they shouldn't call themselves Turks. Do I think of myself as Macedonian? Well, I was born here, but I'm Bulgarian. We all are, but if the people in Skopje want to call themselves Macedonian and not Bulgarian, that's fine by me. It's up to them. Perhaps tomorrow we can meet up and go to the library. My mother works for the Cultural Institute, and she might be able to help you."

"I'd like that, thank you. By the way, where did you learn such good English?"

"Just around. Actually, I find you quite hard to understand sometimes. I'm more used to speaking to Americans, but I much prefer the English accent."

✳ ✳ ✳

But Protestantism never really caught on in the Balkans. National identity was too powerfully caught up in the Orthodox Church, so the mayhem continued: are you Greek, Bulgarian or Serbian? In 1893 in Thessaloniki the most notorious of the Balkan secret societies, the VMRO, or Internal Macedonian Revolutionary Organization was founded. From the start VMRO was ambivalent as to whether Macedonia should be a part of Bulgaria or, as one of its leaders—a young school teacher named Gotse Delchev—at times proclaimed, "Macedonia for the Macedonians". Just three years later, a rival group was formed in Sofia, the Macedonian External Organization, known as the Supremacists, which had the explicit avowed aim of Bulgarian annexation of Macedonia. The story of Delchev, who was born in what is now Greek Macedonia and who is claimed by both Macedonians and Bulgarians as a "national" hero, and the VMRO was to haunt me throughout the rest of my time in Macedonia.

Anna's Mother

That Monday I met Anna beside the statue of the revolutionary poet Ivan Vaptsarov in Bansko's main square, near a poster which had "1893–1993—100 years of struggle—VMRO" written on it. We tracked her mother down in a café, where she was sitting taking coffee with her cronies. She was a large, motherly woman with sparkling eyes, who effusively welcomed me to her town. "*Ochen priyatno*," I replied, "it's a privilege."

"*Ochen priyatno! Ochen priyatno*, he says! What a nice young man! And such good Russian! But Anna told me you're a teacher. You don't look like one. You're meant to have a big beard and wild eyes!" She collapsed into a fit of giggles. When she recovered she said, "I'll see what I can do for you. I may be able to fix it for you to see the local leader of the VMRO, but I think he's gone off to make a revolution somewhere."

She led me to the Palace of Culture, a concrete and glass monstrosity which was by far the largest building in Bansko. Her office, behind the library, was furnished with an uncomfortable three-piece suite, a desk, empty bookshelves and two accordions which lay on the floor. "Everyone here likes to play traditional music and to dance," she explained. "Now, your books."

She came back with *A History of the Revolutionary Struggle in Bansko and a Record of People's Songs* and a pile of back numbers of *Macedonian Review*. "Read the Journal and Discover the Truth on the Macedonian Question and the Revolutionary Struggle of the Bulgarians in Macedonia" they suggested. I decided to defer that pleasure until later. Anna picked up the history and began to translate.

"This is very old fashioned Bulgarian," she complained, "it's hard to read." The book was published in 1954. "Oh look! There's a bit here about our Church. It says that the American missionaries were not like the Orthodox priests, who 'wore dirty clothes and had a low intellectual level and rushed through services so they could go and drink wine'." I thought they sounded rather a congenial bunch. Anna continued: "The Protestants were careful not to offend the Orthodox, except one time when the missionary went to Holy Trinity Church and preached against the icons. He had to leave town."

"I'm not surprised." Anna looked at me with eyes that at once understood and pitied the idolaters. She may have been thinking of her own experience.

"It says here that he could only come back under Turkish protection, when Protestants had their own church, schools and government [under the *millet* system]. This passage is typical! It calls Protestants 'twisted' and 'disconnected from national traditions' because they thought that much of folk custom had pagan roots. There is a story about a Protestant girl who, how do you say? Did something with her eyes?"

"She averted them?"

"Yes, she averted them when she saw some people dancing the *hora*, because she thought it was pagan." That would have been a particular crime to the book's Communist author, since ideologically speaking anything that is Of The People is good, even if pagan. Besides, Protestantism was a foreign import, and Alienated the Masses from their Great National-Historical Awakening and the March Towards Socialism.

"I never knew this!" exclaimed Anna. "It says that there used to be a large Turkish population in Bansko, but one day the Christians killed them all and told the authorities they had died of cholera."

As I was pondering the concept of a religion-specific disease an old lady came in with a bag of books which she laid on the table. They were obviously of Christian content. Anna eyed them suspiciously.

"Do you know Elena Vait?"

"No."

"She leads the Church of Seven Apostles, I think it is called in English."

"Helen White? The Seventh Day Adventists?"

"Something like that. They're in Bulgaria now, along with Jehovah's Witnesses and Mormons. I don't understand it. Usually it's hard to get a visa for more than one month, but the Mormons get them for two years in America. They deceive many people, because they look good and clean, but they tell lies. They add to the Bible, and you can't do that." She was building herself up for a tirade, but her mother stopped her. "Would you like to eat lunch with us. Only my mother says we must go now, because when men get hungry they complain. You can come back at three."

We wandered back towards the church through the sun-drenched lanes. Anna's family lived, four generations under one roof, in a newish building hiding, as tradition demands, behind a high stone wall. I was introduced to Granny, a tiny walnut of a woman who fluttered her hands and smiled often to reveal a total absence of teeth, Anna's sister, who looked like her but with a perm and a grave expression, the sister's husband and their six-year-old daughter, a lively child who insisted on showing me the catalogue of Barbie's new wardrobe. While Granny heated up the food we sat on sofas in their cluttered front room among a jumble of bric-a-brac.

"You say you have no religion," accused Anna, "so how can you teach it?"

"Do you need to be a writer to teach literature?"

"No, you don't, but without religion how can life have meaning? Christ gives meaning to my life."

"Turks say the same about Islam."

"But only one religion can be true. A friend of mine was interested in Buddhism, but after he had read a bit, he saw that the texts were written hundreds of years after Buddha died, so how do we know they're true? Islam came after Christianity, and is based on it, but they twisted it."

"A Muslim would say that both Christianity and Islam came from God, so of course they say the same thing, but Islam is more recent, and it hasn't been corrupted."

"Muslims claim that an angel spoke to Muhammed, but how can we know that? You can't see an angel. But we know the Bible is true— even Josephus says that everything about Jesus is true."

Then why did he remain a Jew? At least Muhammed took the trouble to dictate the Qur'an as soon as it was revealed. Simple faith is always the hardest to engage in debate with. Besides, I had not come for a theological discussion. I was saved by the announcement that lunch was ready. We sat around a table in a sparsely decorated room lit by the sun filtering through apple trees in the garden. Granny brought us soup, bread, stuffed cabbage, pickled vegetables and baked apples which she laid on the table all at once before retiring to her bed in the kitchen to play with her great-granddaughter. We ate slowly, savouring every mouthful.

"Do you have food like this in England?" Mother demanded.

"Only the apples. I think Bulgarian food is very like Greek food."

"Yes, it is. We have friends in Greece, Slavs like us, and we have been there many times. Also I have been to Ohrid, which is very beautiful." A complete circuit of Macedonia.

✳ ✳ ✳

That afternoon I turned my attention to the *Macedonian Review*. Originally founded in 1924, it ran to thirteen volumes before being closed in 1943, to be revived in 1991. The editorial to the first part of volume fourteen proclaimed "[We] will defend the truth about the Bulgarians of Macedonia, will prove their national identity and the character of their epic struggles for cultural and political independence, will uphold the Bulgarians' national spirit in this historically Bulgarian land which has suffered so much". There followed a series of articles virulently slandering Greece and Serbia, page after page devoted to the heroes of Macedonia who fought for a Free Bulgaria, to discussions of Macedonian folklore and language which allegedly proved not only that Macedonians are Bulgarians but that they are the *true* Bulgarians, surpassing all others in their Bulgarianness. I packed it in after a couple of hours. Too much nationalism all at once gives me a headache.

Living for the *Hora*

I returned to the Petrevich, the *mehana* Boris had taken me to the previous evening to hear the bagpipes. My next door neighbour, who sat huddled in the corner nursing a bottle of Coke, was called Mihail.

"I should say that I'm about half Macedonian and half Bulgaria," he said. "I feel both equally. I support the Union of Democratic Forces but with the Bulgarians split about evenly between them and the Socialists, the Muslims hold the balance of power. Fortunately there's no tension with them at the moment. All I'm really interested in, though, is listening to this music. It's very important to us. We like to sing and to dance. It's our national tradition and we're proud of it. I was born here, and I've never been anywhere else. Never wanted to." We were joined by his friend Petko, also in his 20s and sporting a checked lumberjack shirt and a teddy-boy quiff.

"I'm wholly Macedonian, not Bulgarian," he asserted. "Never mind what that idiot says. VMRO is very popular here. All the young people support them." The ambivalence over whether the original VMRO was pro-Bulgarian or for a Macedonia separate from Bulgaria lives on, with different organizations in both Macedonia and Bulgaria pushing the different agendas and both utilizing the VMRO name and heritage. Petko continued: "We are rediscovering our heritage after the Communists suppressed it. The only thing we have in common with Bulgarians is that our language is similar. Do you like our music? Is it like English music? You see, this is why we don't fight with the Muslims—our real religion is music. We live for the *hora*."

As if to prove his point there was a skirl on the pipes and the audience leapt to its feet to dance.

"Come, now we will dance *hora*," said Petko.

"But I don't know how."

"It doesn't matter."

And it didn't, as clasping our neighbours' hands above our heads we danced the sideways conga of the Balkans, the leader keeping his right hand clenched behind his back as a gesture of defiance to the Turks, the dancers urging each other on with whoops and cries.

"That feels better! My heart is glad now," said Petko, as we sat down panting. Mihail had not moved an inch. Petko went on, "I'm from Bansko, but I've been all over. I'm a lorry driver for a private firm, doing the Istanbul to Belgrade run to break the sanctions. Not that I like the Serbs, it just brings in good money. All Macedonians are pleased that Vardar Macedonia is free of the Serbs now. One day we may be able to unite, and then we'll only have to worry about Aegean Macedonia. Things are very bad in Vardar Macedonia at the moment because of the Greek blockade. I don't know what's wrong with the Greeks. Sometimes I think that they're a bit mad. Europe should have recognized Macedonia when it recognised Croatia. Because they weren't recognized the Macedonians can't trade and they have nothing. We must help them. Ah! They've stopped playing that Bulgarian rubbish. Now we'll hear some real Macedonian music. There is a *hora*. You will dance."

The whole room had erupted at the change in the music. The *hora* parted to admit us and then closed up again, looping around itself to make the most of the limited space. Round and round we circled while the music leapt and swirled around us, an intricate, wild pulsating tapestry of sound. Syncopated rhythms clashed against each other as band and dancers slipped effortlessly from one tune to another, the clarinettist extracting a range of wails, shrieks and yelps from his instrument to set against the writhing fingerwork of the accordionist, whilst above it all the pipes sang in their eerily mournful voice, a hand drum underpinning the whole. I could see why the American missionaries had feared paganism and witchcraft. Gradually the pace quickened. Faster and faster we circled to this mad cacophony till nothing seemed to exist outside the dance. And on and on it went …

Eventually we returned, exhausted, to our table, to be joined by a young woman. Mihail perked up considerably.

"This is Irena, the Bulgarian," announced Petko. "She speaks English. Hey, Irena! Say something to the foreigner!"

"Do I have to speak Russian?" she asked anxiously, twitching her nose like a frightened mouse and putting a cigarette to her lips. She did not inhale.

"You can speak English if you like," I encouraged her.

"Do you speak English? Oh, you *are* English! And you learnt Russian because you *wanted* to? We were forced to. Now everybody wants to learn English, but it's difficult without the materials. I learnt at home in Smolyan. We have a teacher from England called Jane. Have you been to Smolyan? I was born there, but my mother's from Bansko. I'm here to visit my cousin and to rediscover where I'm from. Of course I like the VMRO. Everyone does. Do you think," she asked eagerly, "that now that Vardar Macedonia is free, all three parts can be united in an independent state?"

"No. The Greeks won't have it. I can imagine Vardar and Pirin Macedonia being joined, but not as an independent state. Sofia would never allow it."

She was dispirited. "Ah yes, Sofia. They dictate everything, but what do they know? Just a load of *nomenklatura* and criminals who take, take, take and never give, when in the villages there is no work and people have to leave their homes. I would like so much to go to London, to travel, but I have never left Bulgaria. Where would the money come from?"

At that juncture a group of young men burst through the door, covered from head to toe in cowbells, and started to dance the *hora*. CLOP-clop, CLOP-clop, CLOP-clop-clop, CLOP-clop their bells went in unison, like a coven of deranged cart horses. Then they vanished as suddenly as they had appeared.

"What the hell was that?"

"Oh, that's just to let us know that it's only two months to New Year. It is the tradition." I dread to think what the actual New Year's celebrations involve. As I walked home I could hear the sound of bells all over the town, CLOP-clop-clop, CLOP-clop.

VMRO and Ilinden

The following day Anna took me to the town museum to see the curator, who she said was an expert on the VMRO. He inhabited a smoke-filled room stuffed with battered leather furniture and piles of dusty books. A portrait of a monk, whom I took to be Father Paisii, hung behind his desk. Shafts of bright sunlight fell on a disordered heap of papers, magazines and letters strewn liberally around him. A clock ticked quietly to itself as we sipped on glasses of tea.

"Macedonians," he said, taking a cigarette in his long, delicate fingers, "are Bulgarians really." He blew a cloud of smoke towards the ceiling. A dead fly fell to the floor. He began to ruffle through a sheaf of papers, eventually pulling one out. "Look, here's a copy of a letter sent in 1890. Do you see what's on the letterhead? 'Bulgarian Church in Solun [Thessaloniki]'. At that time the majority of people, just, who lived in Macedonia were Bulgarians. Let me give you some figures from 1905. They were published in Paris, so they must be true. Bulgarian Christians: 1,172,136; Bulgarian Muslims: 144,608; Greek Christians: 190,047; Greek Muslims: 9,640; Others: negligible. So you see history tells us that Macedonia is Bulgarian really." Somehow nearly 60,000 Jews had vanished, taking with them all the Turks, Albanians and Gypsies. This was a dispute between Bulgarians and Greeks: to whom does Macedonia belong, the inheritors of Aristotle or the inheritors of the Thessalonian brothers Cyril and Methodios? The census figures, if that is what they were, were being used for political ends. Ottoman censuses are notoriously unreliable anyway. Figures for 1906, based on the *millet* system, give a total of 1,145,849 Muslims including Turks and Albanians; 623,197 Greek Orthodox and 626,715 Bulgarian Orthodox, but the "Greek Orthodox" included a number of Slavs loyal to the patriarchate, whilst the "Bulgarian Orthodox" attracted many Serbs in the region. So there was a Bulgarian church in Thessaloniki. That showed that there were Christians who did not want to be members of the Greek Church, but it did not prove that they were Bulgarians, or that they thought of themselves as such.

"You speak of Bulgarian Christians and Bulgarian Muslims. Apart from their religion, how do these communities differ from one another? Is their music different, for instance, or their dances?"

"Totally different. It is only language and architecture that they have in common. It is hard to see Turkish influence in Muslim buildings; Turkish buildings, rather, are copies of Bulgarian ones. As far as language goes, you will find many Turkish words in the Bansko dialect. For instance, they say *pencere* for 'window', not *okno*, which is proper Bulgarian. But there are no Turks here. Some of the people in the villages call themselves Turks, I don't know why. Whatever they call themselves, their lifestyle is the same as that of Bulgarians." Was he saying that Muslims are at once exactly like and exactly unlike Christians? In any case, and regardless of nationalist theory, surely if someone believes himself to be a Turk, then to all intents and purposes that is what he is. The curator lit another cigarette and went on.

"The Greeks tried to say that anywhere there were a few Greeks, in Plovdiv or Melnik for example, was Greece, so they established schools in those towns. Greece was much richer than Bulgaria, because it was independent, and it could afford to do this. What happened? The Bulgarians, like Neofit Rilski who went to these schools did not lose their national identity, but they founded Bulgarian schools after the model of the Greek ones. Gotse Delchev taught here, all the local schools came under his control, so he could form links to Bulgaria via the education system to supply guns. Bansko was a major centre for the VMRO. Six *chetas* were formed, each with its own *voivoda*, and there was heavy fighting in Razlog—at that time the word referred to this whole district, not just to the town down the road. There were never very many Turks here. The land was too poor to support their soldiers, or even for a decent *vakif*, a religious endowment, so this became a natural refuge for the *chetas*." The term *voivoda* essentially means warlord. These figures became great folk heroes and the subjects of epic verse. Each had his own little gang, or *cheta*, with which to wreak havoc. A member of a *cheta* is called a *chetnik*. The tradition was revived in Yugoslavia during the Second World War, when Serbian nationalists joined the *chetniks* and devoted themselves to slaughtering both the occupying Germans and, with equal aplomb, Tito's Communist Partizans. The *chetnik* tradition is just one of the factors making the war in Bosnia such a nightmare. After all, you can't be a warlord and become a folk hero without a war, and no true warlord accepts any authority save his own.

"Were the *chetniks* all Bulgarians?" I asked.

"Good question. Under its original charter, only Bulgarians were allowed into the VMRO, but later when they were calling for Macedonian autonomy, they opened it to anyone who was opposed to the Ottoman tyranny."

"And did any non-Bulgarians actually join?"

"Very few. Some Serbs, some Greeks. The Muslims mostly thought of themselves as Turks, but those who thought they were Bulgarian joined. In general, when Muslims and Christians shared a village they got on, but in the 1850s there were two bands of Bashibazouks who terrorized all of Macedonia. Eventually they were all killed by the Christians. This proves that our revolutionary tradition is older than that in the rest of Bulgaria. All the *voivodas* were Bulgarian, except for one, whose mother was a Vlah."

"What's a Vlah?" asked Anna.

"You have to go far, far back into history to answer that one," the curator replied, leaning back in his chair and examining his nails. "Some people say they're the descendants of the Roman legions, but their ancestors could have been the original Thracians. Or maybe the Illyrians. Their language is a Latin one, quite like Romanian. They used to be nomads, like the Saracatsans, who spoke Greek. The Romanians tried to stir up trouble with the Vlahs, they said they were Romanians because of the language, and because their name sounds like Wallach (Vlach), after the Romanian province of Wallachia. I don't know if there are any left now. I think they were all absorbed by the Bulgarians.

"Anyway, before Ilinden, VMRO's biggest action was here, when they kidnapped an English woman, Miss Helen Stone, and held her to ransom. She said very good things about them. That was in 1902. Then there was Ilinden, which was a disaster. After Ilinden, many Christians tried to flee to free Bulgaria, over the mountains near Belitsa. There was a *cheta* of just 25 people to protect them from thousands of Turkish troops, which they did for three hours. They all died. We call this our Thermopylae."

I had to explain the Spartans' defence of Thermopylae to Anna. She was staring at me fixedly.

"I'm sorry," she said, "but I'm fascinated by the way you write. I've never seen anybody use their left hand before. It was forbidden under the Communists."

"After the Balkan Wars," went on the curator automatically, "VMRO was active in all three of the countries Macedonia had been divided into. It even made its own small state in Pirin Macedonia until the Sofia authorities suppressed it in 1934, which was very ungrateful of them. VMRO saved our country. After we lost the First World War the treaty of Neuilly forbade us from having an army. The Greeks took advantage of that and invaded up the Struma valley, but VMRO raised an army of 60,000 and stopped them. I can't tell you anything about VMRO today. I'm a historian, not a politician."

Ilinden, St Elijah's Day 1903, marked what was to have been the Macedonian revolution. The VMRO—which in the space of just ten years had not only established a standing army of nearly 10,000 but operated a parallel state administration including a system of taxation and a postal service, under the noses of the Ottoman authorities— mounted a rebellion, hoping that ultimately a Balkan federation comprising Bulgaria, Serbia and Macedonia would be established. Unfortunately, the rising had been poorly planned. Gotse Delchev himself, who was probably the most able administrator in the movement, had had an unlucky run-in with the Turks, and was killed earlier in the year. After three months, the rebellion had been crushed, and VMRO split into a number of competing factions.

The daring assault on Miss Stone had been part of the preparation for Ilinden. Short of funds for the purchase of arms, the *cheta* commanded by Yane Sandanski decided that kidnapping a prominent foreigner would not only be financially lucrative but would bring world attention to their struggle, almost certainly the first time that a kidnapping had been arranged for the benefit of the *Illustrated London News* and its ilk. They settled on Dr House, the head of the American Protestant mission in Thessaloniki, but he rather unobligingly cancelled a trip he had planned to the interior. There was, however, his deputy Miss Stone. Sandanski's friend Cernopeev later recalled:

> We heard that Miss Stone was in Bansko and would be travelling south in a few days. Down we rushed to Bansko. I did not mind Miss Stone so much. She often preached against us, telling the poor peasants that God would right their troubles, not "the brigands". All harmless stuff—nobody took it seriously.

The hapless evangelist was carried off on the 3 September, along with her companion, Katerina Tsilka, who was pregnant at the time. Katerina had given birth to a baby girl by the time they were released. Sandanski demanded a ransom of 25,000 gold Turkish pounds, but eventually settled for 14,000, which he spent on guns. On her release, Miss Stone, who seems to have been a doughty woman, remarked, "in our hearts there awoke the hope that these people, who provided us not only with bread but even with flowers, would decide not to kill us." Perhaps it was the flowers. Sandanski himself was later to die during the Second Balkan War, in 1913.

Gotse Delchev

Gotse Delchev had a town named after him by the Communists. The road there from Bansko runs through the mountains following the course of the Mesta downstream as it winds its way through a narrow gully. Once it had left the open basin around Bansko, the bus passed only one village, named after the river, throughout its 30-mile journey. The valley floor was intensely cultivated, with tiny scraps of vividly green land separated from one another by rows of slender poplars. Small conical haystacks squatted in the fields like outsized fungi. On either side rose walls of brownish-pink rock, home only to the goats which scrambled out of reach of solitary goat-herds. Every so often the bus would stop, and people would get off in ones and twos, making for narrow paths into the hills. Behind these fortress-like barriers, high up, lie Pomak villages where the name-changing campaign was met with violence.

Soon the valley opened out into another basin, dustily brown. Women in *salvar*, Turkish-style trousers, walked by the side of the road carrying armfuls of straw, ignored by the men trotting past in their carts. Before long we were bumping through the cobbled streets of Gotse Delchev itself, to come to a shuddering halt in the town's chaotic bus station.

Previously, Gotse Delchev had been known as Nevrokop, but this was insufficiently revolutionary, especially in view of the fact that as Nevrokop it was the seat of a bishop. Today, priests appear in public wearing ecclesiastical garb once again, and they seemed to swarm through the town. Everywhere you looked there was a stove-pipe hat, in the cafés, in the bakeries, in the street. It was a strange feeling seeing them there, after the invisibility of the clergy under the Communists.

In the main square Delchev himself sat in effigy, his bronze moustache proudly erect, a bandoleer casually slung over his shoulder. No-one had left flowers. Behind him a small church hunkered down among some trees as if trying to conceal itself from the imperious gaze of the starkly brutal Hotel Nevrokop opposite. Inside, a slightly simple-

looking man with tightly curled hair and a gap-toothed grin was splashing red paint onto the pulpit.

"Hello!", he shouted down to me. "Do you like our lovely new icons? That one's …"

"John of Rila."

"So you know our Bulgarian saints! What religion are you, Catholic?"

"Church of England." He looked a bit baffled, so I added "Protestant."

"Oh, I have never heard of your English Church. You should have come on Sunday, then the church would have been full. This year is the hundredth anniversary of the Bulgarian eparchy [diocese] of Nevrokop, so I am painting the church to celebrate. Before, there was a Greek bishop, but the people didn't like him, and so they went to Tsarigrad and asked the Sultan, 'Can we have a Bulgarian, please?' and he said 'Yes', so they were happy. From that day on we have had a Bulgarian bishop and we have been friends with the Muslims." His words all tumbled out in a rush. Then, as abruptly as he had started, he dried up and stood watching me, fidgeting, unsure of what to say or do next. Some of the older icons still bore Greek inscriptions.

"Have you been to our lovely monastery?" the painter resumed. "It is very beautiful. You can go most of the way by bus, you'll only have to walk about eight kilometres, and they'll let you stay the night." By this time we were quite close to the door. "Here, take this," he said, handing me a small booklet which he took from the counter where religious paraphernalia was sold. "It is a history of our church since 1894. See, here is a photograph of our monastery, and of the cathedral, Saints Cyril and Methodios, over the road. Nowhere else in Bulgaria are two churches so close together. This church is very old and very small, and when the Turks left it was decided to build a big new one, but they left this. Have this as well."

He handed me a book. *The Life of Christ.*

"But I can't read this. It's in Bulgarian."

"I know. Now you must learn our language properly. Take this as well." It was a plastic medallion of the Virgin. A paper sticker on the back read "Price: leva 1.50." That was 1½ p or less than 5 cents.

"I can't take all of this!" I protested.

"Why not? Is it because you're Protestant? We are all the same in the eyes of God, Protestant, Orthodox or Muslim. People always try to make *granitsi*, borders, between each other. There should be no *granitsi*. They are bad."

* * *

Later, I spotted another small church shrinking modestly into the side of a hill. In its musty interior, heavy with the dust of lifetimes, an old lady sat knitting whilst flies buzzed angrily against the glass of a lantern-like dome above her head. The woman appeared to have been sitting there for ever, like one of the Fates knitting her country's fortunes—a simple thread would have been insufficient for Macedonia. She looked up and beckoned me towards her.

"Have a seat where I can see you." She peered at me with sparkling blue eyes. "Where have you come from?" I was unsure as to whether this was simple curiosity or a metaphysical question. She seemed imbued with the wisdom of centuries. "You come from London! Oh, I am so pleased to see you. I have never seen an Englishman before. You should have come on Sunday, because then the church is full. Now there is only me. We have three churches here, praise God, and a

monastery in the hills, where the Muslims live. They come to town but they don't live here. They mind their business and we mind ours and everything is just fine. Look at our beautiful iconostasis." Apart from a couple of new images of John of Rila and Saints Cyril and Methodios, essential to mark the church as a Bulgarian one, all had had their original, presumably Greek, inscriptions, painted out and replaced with Bulgarian texts.

"Do you have such a beautiful iconostasis in your church?" she asked. She used the dialect word *hram*, the word used in Serbian, rather than the official *tsârkva*.

"We have no iconostasis in my church," I replied, rather shamefacedly. She drew in her breath sharply, sucking her teeth and swaying in anguish.

"But where do your saints live? Magdalena," she called to another woman, a thinner version of herself, who had appeared in the door "this Englishman says he has no saints in his church! Can you imagine!"

"I have heard of such people," Magdalena replied. "He must be a Protestant. They say that Protestants have no saints, only the cross, poor things!" She turned to me. "That's right, isn't it? As you see, we Bulgarians have many saints. They look after our church." The first lady concurred that this was indeed the true function of a saint.

"You know," she said, "you remind me so much of one of my sons. I have four sons, and Magdalena has three daughters, so we are almost perfect friends! Do you have a wife? Where is she? In *London*? Oh, we women suffer so much!"

✳ ✳ ✳

I wandered back towards the market through almost deserted streets lined with frames for drying tobacco. Gotse Delchev lives, if that is the word, off tobacco production, an industry largely dependent on the Muslims in the villages. The town was hard hit when they packed their bags and left rather than become good socialist Bulgarians. Now, though, Muslim men and women thronged the marketplace with their bags of vegetables, the men wearing beards and berets and the women gaudy *salvars*, embroidered waistcoats and aprons and a blue or black raincoat, the whole topped off by a scarf or a wimple from which their hair hung in long black tresses. Nobody seemed to be buying anything. A tattered fly-bill demanded "Macedonia for the Macedonians" above a map showing the area surrounded by three wolves. Beneath was a potted history of Macedonia since the turn of the century, written not in Bulgarian Cyrillic but in the Macedonian Cyrillic used in Vardar Macedonia. "Macedonia has been denied its historic destiny!" it screamed, "Support the United Macedonian Organization, Ilinden."

Ilinden was formed in November 1989 under the name Independent Macedonian Organization to assert the existence of a separate Macedonian nation within Bulgaria. It had obviously now become more radical, demanding the enlargement of the Republic of Macedonia to include the Pirin and Aegean regions. *Macedonian Review* was scathing: "[its] inadequate, unrealistic political conclusions, ideas and actions, as well as the language of nationalistic and ideological labelling are the fruit of an alien national ideology adopted and inspired from abroad", the magazine ranted in 1992, using the paranoid language of the Communist era. "Macedonism" refers to the heretical belief that Macedonian Slavs are distinct to Bulgarians, whilst "alien national ideology" meant "idea of which we do not approve". Communists did not have feelings, they had ideologies which, if they were Communist ones, were in tune with the deepest yearnings of the Working People. Competing ideologies had to be subversive and always came from overseas, probably as a part of the Great Capitalist–Zionist Plot to weaken the Brotherly Feelings and Internationalism of the Working Masses. VMRO was treated by the same magazine rather differently: "amidst the contradictions and intricacies of today, the VMRO, taking up the banner of struggle, is committed to overcoming the disastrous injuries caused by Macedonism to the unity of the Bulgarian Nation." That was a point made abundantly clear by VMRO itself in September 1991 when it proclaimed that

> *Many efforts have been made by the Serbian chauvinists to sever the people of the Vardar valley (former Yugoslavia) from their Bulgarian roots ... the Internal Macedonian Revolutionary Organization–Union of Macedonian Societies greets you dear brothers of Vardar Macedonia ... let us work together for our future spiritual union and for the peaceful demolition of the frontiers between us.*

VMRO (Bulgaria) is the spiritual heir of the Supremacist, or pro-Bulgarian, movement which captured one of the splinter groups of the original VMRO that developed after 1903, fighting for a Greater Bulgaria. So just what was the attraction? Why support a political party whose time had already been and gone by 1903 and which was suppressed by the Bulgarian government in 1934?

* * *

A battered white Lada, its boot overflowing with anonymous sacks, lurched through the market. It bore Greek number-plates, a reminder not only of the proximity of the Greek border but also of the fact that there remains in Greece a Slavic community, the so-called "Slavophone Greeks", the descendants of those who could not or would not join in the exchange of population in 1923. Despite being bound by the Treaty of Sevres to guarantee educational rights and the use of Slavic for official purposes, it was not long before Slav-language schools were being closed and icons being repainted with Greek texts. In 1926 the use of Slavic place-names was prohibited.

During the war, Aegean Macedonia was—with the exception of the key port of Thessaloniki which went to the Germans—occupied by the Bulgarians, who immediately set about Bulgarizing the territory in a regime of remarkable brutality. Greece claims that 200,000 Greeks were expelled from the area, though the Bulgarians put this figure at just 70,000. Many chose to live under German or Italian occupation rather than under the Bulgarians. Not surprisingly, after the war, and a civil war in which many Slavs fought on the side of the Communists who at that time were advocating VMRO's old goal of a Balkan Federation, Greece felt it had had enough of Slavs altogether. In a curious parallel to the Bulgarian treatment of Turks and other Muslims, the use of Slavic personal names was proscribed, as was the public use of the Slavic language. The vast majority of Greek Slavs emigrated to Yugoslavia and to Australia, particularly to Melbourne, where they continue to engage in a war of words with the local Greek community. Those who remained did so either because they were too poor to emigrate, even to Yugoslavia, or because they were content to become Greeks. Nationalism had reached its logical conclusion: if loyalty to a state is dependent on membership of a people, which is the basic premise of the nationalist argument, then foreigners cannot be loyal to the state and must be expelled. You simply can't trust them.

At least the Greeks, Turks, Slavs and Albanians who found themselves uprooted from their homes and forced to move to the new nation-states had a place to go to, and were often helped to get there. One Balkan people was not so lucky. That building the Lada was rattling past, it couldn't be … but it was—a synagogue. A rusty Star of David surmounted its domed roof, stubbornly resisting what seemed to have been attempts by an unseen giant hand to wrench it off, and defying the secular message of the lines of washing hung from its windows. In Tomar, the Portuguese town which the Knights Templar made their own, an elderly man whose care-worn body gave the impression of being just an empty shell, had shown me around the local synagogue. "This building is useless now," he told me. "You need to have ten sane adult males to worship, and there aren't that many of us left."

The Jews of Spain and Portugal fled *en masse* in 1492 when offered the choice of Christianity or death by those great and enlightened monarchs Ferdinand and Isabella. They went east, to where another ruler, recognizing the benefits of having a group of people from the same culture as Maimonides (1135-1204), offered them sanctuary under the protection of Islam. The Sephardim, who continued—and, where they survive, still continue—to speak their own mixture of Hebrew and Spanish, Ladino, settled throughout the western Ottoman Empire, but most especially in Macedonia and Thrace. The city of Thessaloniki at one time had a majority Jewish population. Of all the Macedonians, they were not concerned with the question of what state they should live under, and so they survived the Balkan Wars and the first wave of "ethnic cleansing" in the 1920s, only to suffer the more horribly in the subsequent cataclysm. Their Balkan refuge of the last 400 years was no longer safe. Most were to perish in Treblinka. Fewer than one-tenth of the Jews of Greece survived the war. Vardar Macedonia could count a mere 55 survivors.

In Bulgaria matters were slightly different. The government was too busy persecuting Greeks to bother much with Jews, and, besides, when deportation orders were announced, pro-Jewish riots broke out in Sofia with the backing of the king and senior church figures, a phenomenon which must be unique in history and not at all what might be expected of the modern Balkans. Nevertheless, as a sop to Germany, Jews were required to wear a yellow Star of David, and Bulgaria was powerless to stop the long strings of cattle trucks making their way north through its territory towards Poland. Although the majority of Bulgaria's Jews survived the war, Europe was clearly no longer safe for Jews, and most fled to Israel in the early years of the Communist regime.

✳ ✳ ✳

Gotse Delchev was too full of ghosts, too full of suffering and tensions not fully resolved. Despite its art deco high street and the elegant Turkish *konak* occupied by the Union of Democratic Forces, VMRO's concrete bunker seemed closer to the reality of the town. Nobody walked with the swagger I had come to expect in Bulgaria, and conversations were conducted in hushed voices, as if that some force, visible or invisible, might hear and take offence. Even the market was subdued. Regardless of the assurances that there was peace and that everyone was friends now, there was another peace which had not yet been made, that with the dead. I fled back to Bansko.

Laments and Bagpipes
Bansko was at peace with itself. A cow stood contemplatively, or perhaps just vacantly, in the middle of the road, blocking the path of an approaching cart, which was drawn, rather lopsidedly, by an enormous bullock and a tiny donkey. An old women swept up cowpats on a patch of waste ground, carefully depositing them in a small cart she pulled behind her while the reddening sun gradually drifted behind the mountains and the air became blue and crisp. I have no idea what she wanted them for, fuel possibly, but I had visions of incantations to be made over an open fire, spells cast with the aid of dried toads or larks' tongues. Hidden in its fold in the mountains, hemmed in by high peaks, this is a land of mystery, a place where time, the time we know, which is measured by clocks and diaries, has no especial meaning. Gradually the wizened old ladies in their uniform black, long plaits of hair hanging from under their scarves in memory of an all but forgotten youthful beauty, emerge from behind the great stone walls of their *kâšta*s, those enigmatic fortresses where for centuries their families have

taken refuge at night, and take up their posts in the lanes and alleyways of the town. The songs of the women are eerily haunting. Sung in a minor key, their melodies are a drawn out, wavering lament, each phrase ending in a kind of half-swallowed sob. The songs are called *dertliška*, from the Persian word *dertli* meaning "worry" or "grief", and they tell of life, of love, of sadness and of pain, a never-ending lament for the hardness of the lives of women whose menfolk leave them to hide in the hills, making war on the Turk.

Those days are over now, but still the women sit, endlessly spinning, spinning, completely motionless save for their fingers. What do they think of in these few twilight hours they have earned for themselves? Of the cruel history of their people? Of which spells to employ to ensure a suitable match for grandchildren and great-grandchildren? Or are they simply calculating how long it will take to finish the task in hand? Some may have been alive when Bansko was still a part of the Ottoman Empire, just 80 years ago. They seem ageless, timeless, yet their time is coming to an end. Their shrunken bodies and wrinkled faces suggest endless toil and untold suffering, which their progeny cannot begin to comprehend. "For me this is fascinating," Anna said to me in the museum, "I never knew any of this before. Sometimes I think you know Bulgarian history better than I do."

"Do you mind if I join you?" Ratko, "Richard in English", was the personification of Zorba the Greek, a tall, lanky man with long wiry grey hair, a droopy moustache which trailed in his beer and a tanned, weather-beaten face. Either Zorba or the Knight of the Sad Countenance. "If you're interested in Macedonia," he continued, "you should speak to my friend Ivan just over there. He understands English, but he can't speak it. He knows all about VMRO." Ivan was everything Ratko was not, a stocky man with neatly trimmed black hair and moustache and a wry smile. He let Ratko dominate the conversation.

"The first thing you should know is that there is no such thing as a Macedonian," proclaimed Ratko. "We are all Bulgarians, and have been for centuries. When Macedonia was divided, the Serbs tried to turn the people of Vardar Macedonia into Serbs, but they failed, so instead they said 'You are Macedonians' to make them forget who they really were so that they would become dependent on Belgrade. The Greeks expelled most of the Bulgarians from Aegean Macedonia and replaced them with refugees from Asia. There is only a very small Bulgarian community there now, and the young ones are forgetting who they really are and becoming assimilated. When I was in Canada, a good friend of mine there, a Bulgarian from Aegean Macedonia, asked his son what he thought he was, and his son replied 'a Greek'. But although people from many different nations, Greeks, Serbs, Jews, Albanians, have lived here, the people of Macedonia have always been Bulgarian." His eyes were ablaze as he took a long slurp of his beer, wiping the froth from his moustache.

"When did you go to Canada?"

"In 1967. It was forbidden to leave the country, but I escaped across the border to Greece. I had my routes, my methods, but I was a very young man then, just 21, and foolish. I didn't speak a word of any language but Bulgarian. At that time there were very few Bulgarians in Canada, but some people in Halifax, Nova Scotia, helped me get a job in a construction firm. It went bust so I had to get a job in another company, but that went bust too. When it looked like Communism was going to end, I came back here and looked for work in construction, but now, like many Bulgarians, I'm unemployed." Ratko was obviously a curse to the labour market. He carried on.

"I'm worried that there'll be a big swing to the Socialists at the next election. People are scared—Bulgarians aren't used to unemployment or business failure, and they don't understand inflation. Of course I learnt about all that in Canada. It could turn out like in Poland, with the Communists back in office. I expect most people around here will vote for VMRO though. You've heard of these people 'Ilinden'? I think they've got just 25 supporters in Bansko. They've swallowed the Serb propaganda about there being a Macedonian nation, which of course there isn't."

At the mention of VMRO, Ivan brightened considerably. He began to talk animatedly in Bulgarian. Ratko translated: "He says that VMRO are true patriots. Bansko was a centre of their activity in the old days, and we're very proud of the fact that there were never any Turks here. Have you heard the story of Miss Stone? You see, back then the leaders of VMRO were very good politicians, Gotse Delchev and the rest of them. They knew the Great Powers, especially Britain, did not want Macedonia to join Bulgaria, so they called only for autonomy, but that was just a stepping-stone. The ultimate goal was unity with Bulgaria. VMRO today wants the same thing. There's a party of the same name in Vardar Macedonia too, but I don't know what they want. You'll have to ask them in Skopje.

"I have drunk enough beer here now. Shall we go to Petrevich? We can hear *gaida* played. What do you call *gaida* in English?"

"Bagpipe."

"Like in Scotland," put in Ivan with a grin, downing a glass of whisky. "Let us go to Petrevich and hear bad pipe!"

As usual, Petrevich was heaving and a *hora* was being danced. Three people had established their own private *hora* on one of the tables. Ratko eyed them critically. "They're not from round here," was all he would say. We sat down at a table which had been wrapped around a tree which no-one had had the heart to remove when the *mehana* was built, and were brought beer, and whisky for Ivan, kebabs, salad and loaves of bread. Ratko began to eat, stuffing the food into his mouth as if afraid that it wasn't real and might vanish at any moment. Ivan had another whisky.

"The man with the *gaida*," said Ratko through his food, "is a Gypsy. That is why he plays so well. That means he's probably Muslim, but who's to tell? You know, a lot of Bulgarians supported the name-changing campaign, but I never did. I saw the effect it was having. I worked with Muslims on building sites here, and old men would come up to me in tears and say 'You're a Bulgarian. Tell me, I have been Mehmed all my life. Why must I now be Mihail?' It doesn't matter if I call myself Ratko or Ramazan so long as it is what I choose, but the government has no business telling me who I am. Only a Fascist could come up with an idea like that."

The band began to sing a lustily upbeat number. I asked what the song was about.

"It's about a Bulgarian boy who falls in love ... all the usual bullshit," said Ratko. A beatific smile had spread across Ivan's face by now. "Where are you going tomorrow? To Yakoruda? This man," indicating a complete stranger, " is going there tomorrow. He will give you a lift in his car, but it is only a Moskvich, not a good car. How will you talk to people in Yakoruda?"

"In Russian. It worked in Kraište."

"If they understood you in Kraište, they will understand you anywhere," opined Ivan.

Yakoruda

Yakoruda is a town of 13,000 people near the head of the Mesta valley, some two hours from Bansko by the snail-like train that only Pomaks use. Or rather, it is two towns. A small pocket of *Mitteleurope* huddles around the white, barn-like hulk of the Church of Saints Cyril and Methodios, on Cyril and Methodios Street facing the blank-walled barrack of the Cyril and Methodios Lycée. You get the feeling someone is trying to make a point: "this town is both Bulgarian and Christian". Erected during the 1920s and 1930s, this part of the town could be almost anywhere, save that someone has taken the trouble to put up some posters extolling the virtues of VMRO, and seems strangely incongruous in juxtaposition to the rest of the town, which sprawls around it sending exploratory tentacles up side-valleys encrusted with pines. Here, where the asphalt runs out and is replaced with dirt, is the true Yakoruda, the Muslim quarter. It resembles nothing so much as a giant farmyard. Chickens scratch in straw-lined streets where dogs lounge, ignoring the desultory traffic of horse carts slowly plodding uphill. Beehive-shaped haystacks are everywhere, punctuating the rows of traditional houses with their stone barns on the ground floor and projecting upper storeys. Here and there rather grander, more elegant Turkish *konaks* built from lath and plaster collapse gracefully with the languor of the fainting heroines of Victorian melodrama. Strings of red paprika and onions hang from the eaves in the company of sheepskins only recently parted from their late owners while the balconies are brightened by colourful rugs draped from their railings. Goats bleat plaintively behind heavy wooden doors. There are no shops since each *kâšta* is a virtually self-sufficient fortress. What little buying and selling that needs to be done takes place in the market square by the river. Chainsaws buzz as the townsfolk prepare wood for the coming winter whilst the haunting melodies of Turkish and Bulgarian folk song float from open windows to mingle with the sweet smell of peppers being fried over open fires in the streets and the heavy richness emanating from bubbling cauldrons of *gyuvetch*, meat and potato stew enriched with onions, tomatoes and peppers. It seems hard to imagine anything more peaceful, yet Yakoruda too has a bloody, and not distant, past.

In 1990 there were protests in the town against the local authority's reluctance to re-register Muslims under Muslim names. The situation was exacerbated by the fact that a Muslim girl, Aiše Mriškova, had died after being assaulted by a Christian classmate at that barracks-like school. The local mosque had been bombed. All was not well in this rural elysium.

Just where the tarmac ran out stood the bombed mosque, shrouded in wooden scaffolding. Fake marble columns were being added to the walls. Men were making their ablutions as the *ezan* faintly gurgled from loudspeakers fixed to the minaret: "*Allah-hu Akbar! Ash-hadu ala-illaha illallah! Ash-hadu anna Muhammed ar-Rasul Allah!*", the triumphant cry first uttered by Bilal when the Muslims took Mecca from its pagan overlords and which unites Muslims the world over. I sat in the garden amongst scraggy rose bushes and awaited the end of prayers.

A rotund old woman with a kindly smile and dancing blue eyes sat next to me, prayers being optional for women. She took my hand and looked intently into my face. "Where are you from?" she asked. "From London! That's a terribly long way for you to come on your own!" Conversation was difficult, since she spoke no Russian and I no Bulgarian. "There are many Muslims in this town, but we live at peace with the Christians," she said in response to my request. "The only problem is the lack of work for the young people. They leave the mountains and come here, or go to Turkey. I went to Turkey once, but I didn't like it. I speak Turkish, but my home is here in Bulgaria, so I'm a Bulgarian."

A shifty looking middle-aged man sidled up to us. "This journalist has come from London!" said the old lady. I had said nothing about being a journalist, but how else could the presence of a foreigner who asked questions be explained?

"Does he speak Bulgarian?" the man said in a tired voice. "Only Russian? Well, they're much the same thing." He joined us. "We're mostly Turks here. We outnumber Christians by more than three to one, but all the same they control the council and take all the best jobs. It shouldn't be like that in a democracy. We can't speak Turkish or write Turkish, and we've got no work. All we have is our names back, and that's not enough."

Worshippers, roughly a hundred in number, were coming out of the mosque by now. Mostly elderly men—there were no women among them—they wore berets on their heads, although here and there the bobble cap favoured in Turkey could be seen, and one man wore a white lace skull-cap like those worn by Muslims in Britain. Almost without exception they had the watery blue eyes of Slavs. They used the customary Turkish greeting, *marhaba*, and conversed in the curious mix of Turkish and Bulgarian I had heard in Kraište. At length the imam appeared, a dignified old man with more gold than teeth in his mouth, standing erect in his embroidered fez and black cloak. I was introduced as "the journalist".

"Do you speak Turkish?" he asked me in that language as he led me into the building, a simple hall painted light green, "We are all Turks here, no 'Bulgarian Muslims'. There was bad oppression under the Zhivkov regime." He ground his hands together in a crushing gesture. "Things were very bad then, but now we have our own names back, we have a *mekhteb*, and we are restoring the mosque ... Do we get money from Turkey? No, we raised it all ourselves. The totalitarians forced the mosque to be *kapali*, closed, but now we have it back and things are good. Now, if you will excuse me, I have much work to do and I must lock the mosque."

Later, as I sheltered from the drizzle that had begun to fall in a café where a bored waitress doled out espressos, I was joined by a bowed old man in a brown suit, clutching a homburg, whom I had seen at the mosque. He asked me whether I spoke Turkish. "German-language? English-language? You *are* English! Welcome Englishman—boy! What is your name? My name Mehmed. No more Bulgarian name. Bulgaria-land good?" His English though fragmented was quite comprehensible. "When I young man, I speak English very good, but now I old man and I forget. Only person in Yakoruda speak English. They, only Bulgarian, Turkish. When I young man, I go Capital-Atina [Athens]. Army. *Voina* [war]. I learn Greek, English. I speak very good Turkish, very good Greek, but English I forgetting. In English land *dzamiya*?" I'm not sure that he believed my claim that there are many mosques in England. "I go now. Goodbye Englishman!", and the Turk who conquered Athens on behalf of Bulgaria and learnt to speak Greek departed as suddenly as he had come, shuffling through the rain into the gathering dusk, another enigmatic piece of the Balkan jigsaw.

* * *

The train lurched its meandering course through the night back to Bansko.

"Where are you from?" asked the ticket inspector, a jovial man with a round ruddy face framed by tight black curls. Despite the slovenly way in which he wore his faded blue uniform, he seemed to have taken some trouble over polishing the red star which adorned his cap badge. "From London! I have been to London. A very beautiful place. I remember the museum. Also Victoria Station. Victoria Station is very beautiful—the best. You know Victoria Station? I stayed near there. Every day I went to Victoria Station. Do you think I could get a job in London?" I told him I thought it highly unlikely. There is scant demand for Bulgarian-speaking ticket collectors, even at Victoria. He caught sight of my wedding ring.

"What have you done with your wife? Left her in London, eh? Good idea. Perhaps when we get to Bansko we can eat together in the station restaurant." I told him I had already arranged to meet a friend for a beer, an entirely gratuitous lie.

"Never mind," he said, "Some other time. You must be used to meeting lots of people in London. The whole world is there, Americans, Bulgarians. There are even black people. I have seen them in Victoria Station.

"I must go now to check the rest of the train, but next time be sure you're on the 10.40 from Bansko or the 3 o'clock from Septemvri. I'm on those trains and you won't need a ticket." He wandered off, muttering "Victoria Station" to himself and chuckling. The builders of the London, Brighton and South Coast Railway could hardly have imagined that more than 100 years later Bulgarian railwaymen would dream of their London terminus. It seemed a curious legacy.

* * *

Maria Pamplova was 100 years old when she died in 1962. I came across her grave in the cemetery of Dobriniše, a Christian village tucked into the hills just at the point where the Mesta enters its gorge below Bansko. Her photograph on the headstone shows a wizened, thin-lipped woman with her scarf wrapped tightly around her head, betraying a toughness born of the vicissitudes of her century. When she was born there was no Bulgarian state, or even a Bulgarian Church. She was already 50 and quite conceivably a grandmother when the Turks finally left Macedonia. Perhaps her son had fought, even died, with the *cheta* in the struggle to bring about that event, or in the Second Balkan War or the First World War, disputing with the Greeks and the Serbs who should govern the newly liberated territory. Her grandson must have re-fought the same battles in the Second World War, occupied Thessaloniki or even Athens with the old Turk from Yakoruda. Then, in 1944, just 32 years after the departure of the Turkish overlords Maria found herself living under another vast empire whose masters controlled their subjects far more tightly than the Turks had ever done, an empire with its capital not at Constantinople, the "Second Rome", but in the city to which the Orthodox had looked during the Ottoman centuries as the "Third Rome"—Moscow. In a single lifetime Bulgaria had gained and lost its freedom, and its church had come into existence, flourished and then been brutally strangled.

Maria must have known Iliya Stapev, who lies nearby. Though some seventeen years her junior he outlived her by only a year. Despite his bushy moustache and the jaunty angle at which he wore his cap, he could not conceal a great sorrow lurking behind his eyes. Did he take part in the Ilinden uprising or run guns to the *chetniks*, or was he just the hapless victim of the Turkish reprisals? And what of the men of his generation buried here who died young in 1925? Could they have been members of the VMRO force which turned back that Greek army which came storming up the river Struma to wrest this land from Bulgaria? No matter. These people's troubles were now over, and they lay at rest on the hill overlooking their village where another generation of women, widows themselves as old as the century, came to tend the graves.

Pirin Macedonia has gained a brief respite from its history, and the citizens of Dobriniŝte were taking advantage of the fact to sit in the sun in the village square, drink their coffees or beers—*Pirin Makedoniya* brand—and talk politics while stray horses wander unmolested through the streets. Those with a bit of money are investing it in rebuilding their houses, a sure sign of faith in the future. At regular intervals the clang of a church bell broke the almost soporific calm. In the garden around the church a young woman was sitting reading a psalter, occasionally giving a rope a desultory tug to make the bell ring another time. "It's the tradition," she said.

I took a last walk through the old town of peaceful Bansko, along the narrow alleys thronged at this evening hour with goats returning from the hills to the sanctuary of the *kâšta*, their pendulous udders swaying and their bells setting up a flowing tinkling, dancing like a stream, as they fanned out to dispose of any stray scraps of vegetation while their minders stopped to pass the time of day, and the snow-capped peaks of the Pirin range that dominate the town gradually turned from pink to blue to grey as the sun set. In times past a family's fortune depended on that of its goats. As well as eating their flesh and making cheese of their milk, the mountaineers used goats' hair to make the carpets with which they decorated their homes and Muslims floored their mosques. Their bones could be turned into flutes, while their skins held wine or water or formed the essential component of the *gaida*, the air reservoir. During the Ottoman period, when Christians were forbidden to carry arms lest they turn them against their masters, goats' horns served as daggers. Useful animals, goats. Useful, but smelly.

I had just finished a meal of the local spicy sausage served with a cabbage salad and washed down with heavy red wine, and was beginning to write up my notes when I was joined by a threesome, Dimitâr, Todor and Maya, who crowded onto my table, which was the only one free.

"Where are you from," asked Dimitâr, "And what do you want to drink, beer or raki?" Todor and Maya shook their heads in encouragement. "What do you do? A book about Macedonia! You must be very clever. I'm a wood-carver, a Macedonian Bulgarian. Macedonians are a kind of Bulgarian, but a special kind. have you danced the *hora*? When you dance the *hora* you know what it is to be a Macedonian. Vardar Macedonia is a very beautiful place, but they've got no money because of the Greeks. At least they're free from the Serbs now. Serbs are very strange people—in fact I think they're mad. As for VMRO, I don't know how popular they are but they're friends with the Turks so they're quite powerful. All they're really interested in is guns.

I've no idea what they want to do with them. But it's all politics. They have politics in Yugoslavia and look what good it's done them. I'm a worker. I do my job and I'm not interested in politics." A waitress wearing a clinging black skirt placed drinks on the table. "Look at the arse on that!" exclaimed Dimitâr appreciatively.

"I'm married."

"Married? Pah! Throw away that ring! You're in Bulgaria now!" Maya grimaced.

"I don't think so. Maya knows why I say that. Here's a photograph of my wife." I took the picture out of my wallet and passed it over.

"She's very beautiful, but she doesn't look English."

"She's Indian. She grew up in England." The information took some time to sink in.

Todor wanted to know whether I liked football. I would have liked almost anything to avoid discussing my virility with Dimitâr. We compared the relative merits of Tottenham Hotspur and Manchester United. It's amazing how doors around the world open on the utterance of the sacred words "Kevin Keegan" or "Kenny Dalgliesh", though a younger generation only responds to "Ryan Giggs" and "Ian Wright". Maya was getting bored.

"What do you think of Bulgarian food?" Maya asked.

"I think it's very tasty, especially *kyufta cheta* and *gyuvetch*."

"But have you not tried any of our local specialities?"

"I've had *Banska sutdzukia*," I offered, indicating the remains of sausage on my plate. Not good enough.

"We also have another kind of sausage, and our *gyuvetch* is famous. You must eat it, then you will know that our food like our music is the best in the world."

Blagoevgrad

The administrative centre of Pirin Macedonia is Blagoevgrad, formerly known as Gorna Dzumaya but now named for yet another revolutionary hero, Dimitâr Blagoev. The town, nestled in the valley of the Bistritsa just at the point where it flows into the Struma, could hardly differ more markedly from the villages of the Pirin mountains. The Communists tore down much of the old town and replaced it with tree-lined avenues of modern buildings, which, though not unpleasant in this new age of cafés and bright lights, must have been grim under the old regime. Smart bars with outside tables take the place of *mehanas* and there is an urban bustle to the place which puts you more in mind of Sofia or Plovdiv than of Gotse Delchev.

The effigy of Delchev strikes a suitably heroic pose in the main square, yet this is one of the least "Macedonian" towns I know, with its sleek sophisticated air and noticeable ethnic homogeneity. Before 1912 the population was predominantly Turkish and when they left they were replaced by refugees from Greece and Serbia seeking sanctuary in the newly established Bulgarian state and fervent in their love for that country. The only surviving mosque, a typically unpretentious Balkan house-with-a-minaret, is now a café. That is all that survives of 500 years of the town's history. Istanbul seems as far away from here as it does from almost anywhere in Europe, yet the Turks were here for longer than almost anywhere else in the continent. So do great empires vanish without trace, first Byzantium and then Ottoman Turkey. The legacy of the Russian overlords will be harder to erase.

What became of Gorna Dzumaya? Nothing is left of the old town save a clutch of *konaks* around a church which dates from 1844. The Turks forbade the use of domes in Christian architecture and ordained that no church should be larger than a mosque, so that, though large, this is a low basilica decorated on the outside with murals depicting among other things a somewhat tame Last Judgement where a skinny looking serpent—rather than the usual flame-red monster—is being force-fed sinners, many of whom seem only too happy to go. Elsewhere figures clamber up and tumble off a Wheel of Fortune. A smiling Virgin sits in the wheel's hub surrounded by the signs of the Zodiac and allegorical depictions of the seasons. Summer is represented by an effete young man playing a lute. Gone is the harsh severity of the saints who inhabit the surviving medieval churches, replaced by a luxuriant paganism where Summer can be represented by Orpheus and where a person's fate is as much the work of the stars as of the Virgin. It is a naïve art for a naïve faith far removed from what was introduced here, which was a barely understood world made concrete, not in the stylized serenity of the best icons, but in a peasant language. Two Turks look on aghast as St Michael the Archangel brandishes his sword over a recumbent figure from whose mouth a devil escapes. The symbolism is hardly subtle. Protecting the church on either side of the door Saints Cyril and Methodios look out with doleful eyes as if shocked and depressed by what has become of their creation.

On Sunday morning the church was packed. A new priest was being ordained and the bishop, an old man with a flowing white beard and a frail voice, was in attendance. A gaggle of priests swarmed around him as he liberally splashed holy water about, his head wobbling precariously under an enormous gold crown. He delivered a short address on the Nature of Women, a subject about which he can have known almost nothing, since Orthodox bishops are also monks. A female member of the congregation heckled him loudly until a priest swept her into a stall at the back, using his sumptuously embroidered chasuble or cloak as a broom.

As the liturgy ended and the bishop's minder, a sly young monk, packed him into his car, a sort of anarchy broke out as the remaining five priests began to conduct different services simultaneously. A stream of young women appeared bearing babies tightly wrapped in blankets. The infants were liberally doused in holy water and each presented to the icons in turn whilst the priests who held them in their arms mumbled incomprehensible magical incantations. Old ladies were asking other priests to intercede for them in front of the icons and wandering around distributing funerary bread to anyone who would take it. In the centre of the nave a further two priests waited on a young couple who were getting married. The whole life of the community was here in this *mélange*, simultaneously celebrated under the watchful gaze of the saints. After a while I became confused as to exactly what I was eating—was this baptismal, marital, or funerary bread? It was good bread too: not the horrible little wafers, which stick to the roof of your mouth, that Catholics and Anglicans use.

I caught one of the priests having a quite cigarette outside the church during a pause in the proceedings.

"Oh yes," he said, "there's been a massive upsurge of interest in Orthodoxy. Of course there are more people here today because it's Sunday but all the same …"

"When I was in Bansko there were only old people in the Orthodox church but many young people in the Protestant one," I observed.

"I think the Protestants were more prepared for the end of Communism then we were. Also they had help from outside, but as you

see now even very young children are being brought to the Orthodox Church. We have nothing against the Protestants though. Why should we? We had a funny relationship with the Communists. They closed down all the village churches but they paid to maintain the ones in the cities. Even Communists would come to church on special occasions and of course they were buried as Christians, but will you excuse me?— there is another wedding. Enjoy your stay in Gorna Dzumaya."

Gorna Dzumaya. To the Orthodox Church Blagoevgrad never was. Indeed, in the area around the church, where in intervals between their religious duties priests chopped wood to feed the building's stove, the brash new town may as well not exist. Orthodoxy, with its heart in monasticism, has always been particularly adept at ignoring reality when it suits its purpose to do so. Things do not in their essence change for the Orthodox, no matter what the substance may be, a neo-Platonic viewpoint that ensured that the Greek and Bulgarian revolutionaries could rely for support on monks for whom the Byzantine and Bulgarian Empires had never ceased to exist in essence, even though in substance they existed only in the Church.

Back inside, the priests were continuing with a seemingly never-ending succession of marriages that I watched with mixed emotions. At once I was happy for the shy, nervous young couples who stepped forward, as well as sad, lonely and nostalgic. Sooner or later all solitary travellers feel that way, far from their own communities and divorced even from their own language. I wanted my wife with me. My feelings were heightened as each couple circled the makeshift altar before which they were married as Shaoni and I had circled the fire symbolizing the god Agni on our own wedding day.

Like everything else in the Orthodox Church, the wedding ceremony contains more ritual and more symbolism than its Western counterpart. Bride and groom stand before the altar holding candles that are tied together by a ribbon, with the best man behind the bride and the bridesmaid behind the groom, each also holding candles. Whilst the priest places crowns on the candidates' heads, it is the best man who solemnizes the ritual by swapping them around, an action confirmed by the bridesmaid offering the couple a glass of wine to share, its rim encrusted with sugar. Prior to this bride and groom have each eaten bread torn from the same loaf and dipped in the wine, which is finished by bridesmaid and best man before all four process around the altar. Thus not only are bride and groom publicly committed to each other but their sponsors are likewise jointly committed to supporting the marriage. All four would circle together again as they danced the *hora* with their guests after the wedding breakfast. There were many *horas* danced in Blagoevgrad that night.

In the evening I returned to the now deserted church. A solitary priest left off chopping wood to answer the request of a couple in their 20s for the baptism of their son Aleksandâr. They were very unsure as to what exactly was demanded of them but they were determined that their son should be baptized. The priest, whose ferocious beard was betrayed by a twinkle in his eye, put them right and marked infant and parents with the sign of the cross before embarking on another liturgy, this time accompanied by a single elderly man as chorister. The worship of the Orthodox Church goes on regardless of what anybody else is doing. I cannot conceive of a Protestant or a Catholic conducting a service in the absence of a congregation, but the Orthodox will. Perhaps that is the secret of the Church's survival.

Priests had been flitting in and out of the Royalist Club of Gorna Dzumaya all day. Like the Orthodox, royalists do not recognize revolutionary heroes such as Blagoev. I went into an almost deserted room where nobody spoke any language other than Bulgarian, not even Russian. There were portraits of the last king, Boris, and his son Simeon, who fled the country in 1946. Simeon seemed a kindly enough man and he undoubtedly had a regal bearing. The family name is Battenburg, which in Britain became Mountbatten. Virtually all the royal families of Europe are related to one another, and most, like Britain's, are German. During the nineteenth century Germany had a superabundance of princes. The surplus was exported: Greece, Bulgaria and Romania all received German monarchs, though Serbia managed to provide one of its own. Almost without exception they ruled badly until forced to flee to Estoril in Portugal, Europe's dumping ground for unwanted royalty, although Michael Hohenzollen of Romania has made repeated attempts to return.

The Royalist Club in Blagoevgrad comprises two rooms, one named Stara Zagora after an ancient Bulgarian capital, the other called Ohrid. No need to ask where the club's members stand on the Macedonian Question, but the cause of the royalists is not popular; I was the only person dining that evening, and when I received the bill I saw why. Simple though it was the meal cost three weeks' average wage. It must be hard to run a club for aristocrats in a country where there are none.

❋ ❋ ❋

Like all hotels run by Balkanturist mine was overpriced. Its restaurant preserved the best of Communist hospitality. All its tables were "reserved"—and empty. An excessively large staff lurked in the gloom around the bar. At length one of them bestirred himself.

"Can I have a glass of red wine," I asked, "and what have you to eat?"

"Everything."

"But what specifically? Do you have shish kebab or gyuvech?"

"No."

"Do you have chops?"

"No. There is tongue."

The tongue seemed to have been taken from someone's shoe. I was brought white wine. The following morning I checked out.

The Hotel Alen Mak in the town centre was far too smart, but in Macedonia Square, overlooking the statue of Gotse Delchev, was an unprepossessing building with the single word "hotel" written on its side in Cyrillic characters. The lobby was dingy. A painting of soldiers emerging from a trench hung over the faded green baize of a billiard table and a cabinet labelled "new books" contained biographies of military heroes and *voivodas*. It didn't seem very much like a hotel. A door was wrenched open from the inside to reveal a poky office in which three high-ranking army officers sat in a cloud of smoke, arguing. An old lady emerged. "What do you want?" she asked, squinting at me.

"Is this a hotel?"

"Why not? I will arrange a room." The soldiers were scrutinizing me closely as if to determine my potential as a fighting man. Then one of them spoke.

"Who are you, where are you from, what is your work and why are you in Blagoevgrad?" he demanded in an aggressive voice. I told him.

"Ah," he said. "Manchester United."

I had in fact stumbled across the Warriors' Club of Blagoevgrad. Beyond a penchant for wearing uniforms none of its occupants seemed very warrior-like. They were without exception very fat or very thin. My room was obviously designated as being suitable for Other Ranks, a Spartan lodging under the eaves with washing facilities down a corridor, on the wall of which hung another painting of the heroic victories of the Bulgarian Army. The army is rather short of such events, having fought few wars and lost all of them save one, unless you count Bulgaria's involvement on the Soviet side in the Prague Spring. Somewhere downstairs a woman was singing one of those eerily haunting folk songs, a *dertlika* telling "of life and love, sadness and pain".

✳ ✳ ✳

Markets are always fascinating places, where people from miles around gather to exchange goods and gossip. In Blagoevgrad the market is alongside a fetid trench optimistically known as the river Bistritsa. Traders from Vardar Macedonia were mobbing an exchange booth by the entrance. I have never seen such a bizarre range of currencies quoted—not just the currencies of neighbouring countries but the Hungarian forint, the Estonian kroon, even the Ukrainian coupon. Who on earth could want to buy coupons? They were worthless even in Ukraine. Most of the currency changing hands was Macedonian denars and German marks. What did the Macedonians spend their newly acquired leva on? Not on jars of honey or dried apricots nor on the heaps of fruit and vegetables piled on stalls and in the road, pumpkins for five pence a kilo, baby carrots for eight. Nobody showed any interest in the pornographic videos which shared shelf space with Disney, nor yet were there any takers for the giant copper still that a middle-aged woman sat beside all day before dismantling it and taking it home. They had come to buy consumer goods imported from Greece, circumventing the Greek blockade on their own country. I bought a strip of hand-embroidered cloth from an old woman. "Are you Russian?" she asked.

"No, English."

"Ah! My son lives in Chicago. He's been there ..." she thought for a moment "a year and four months. What is his work? Everything! Also he speaks good German. He lived in Germany for two years and six months." Once again Macedonia is exporting cheap labour.

"What are you doing hogging the foreigner?" demanded the woman at the neighbouring stall. "If he wants to buy something for his wife he should buy my lovely flowers! Where's he from anyway? Hey! Englishman! Buy my flowers!" she shouted after me as I walked away.

✳ ✳ ✳

That night I ate in a *mehana* where a truly execrable musician was doodling on a synthesizer. It was conveyed to him that I was English and during a break he came over and introduced himself as Grigorii.

"I hear that you're from London," he said. "I've always wanted to go there. I'm from a small village near Pazardzik. You're right that most people in Blagoevgrad don't come from round here, but that's one of the beauties of Macedonia. It's a truly diverse area, it doesn't matter where you're from. Our good neighbours come from the other side, and we share a language and a history so of course we're glad to have them. Everyone here will tell you they're Bulgarian. They don't try to separate themselves as Macedonian.

"I've always tried to play jazz, although I'm no good at it. Western music was forbidden by the Zhivkov regime but I felt in my heart that I should play Italian and English songs. I really feel that Bulgaria should be a part of the West but it'll take a long time to get there. We've never had true freedom before in Bulgaria, and most people are reacting to it in two ways. Either they think that freedom means anarchy and they become criminals, or they're afraid of the responsibility of having to think for themselves. When the Communists locked the churches they locked peoples' minds as well. God gave us minds so we could open them and become more like Him. That's another good thing about Macedonia. Because it's a meeting place of East and West, people tend to have open minds as God intended. I'm Orthodox of course, but not the way the Serbs are. They say they're defending Orthodoxy, but all religions say you must make peace, not war. Everyone in the Balkans confuses religion with nationalism, but that's an abuse of religion. Look at us, a bridge between East and West. We should be able to show the way to the world."

"VMRO," he went on, "used to run this country. They were great men in those days, Todor Aleksandrov and Gotse Delchev. The party now is just a shadow. In the old days they were like the Scots or the Irish, fierce mountain people who didn't want to be governed by anyone but themselves. Fighters. They're in opposition in Vardar Macedonia now but they could never pull off a stunt like when they shot the king of Yugoslavia. They're nothing now. I won't vote in the December elections, and if you ask people in the street most will say the same. I voted for the SDS last time, but that was a mistake. We had such hope, but it turns out that politicians are all just the same. The only rich people in Bulgaria today are politicians and *Mafiosi*. It's all black money of course. I'm just very disappointed with what's happened here. I think the only hope lies in military dictatorship for a bit, just to clean up the country and get things sorted out so that we can start again, but the army doesn't want to know. They've got problems of their own. Their wages are terrible."

An overt military dictatorship in Bulgaria would be the one thing to send the few Western investors packing, and in terms of international diplomacy it would be a public relations disaster, but would it really be such a bad thing? More than one EU member has endured a phase of military dictatorship and emerged unscathed as a democracy, most recently Portugal. The military can at least ensure the rule of law, a commodity in short supply in Eastern Europe since the old laws became redundant overnight and the old legislators could not even conceive of the laws needed in a capitalist state.

After Grigorii had returned to his instrument, Metodii and Maria, thin and haggard young people, emerged from the kitchen and sat on my table.

"What are you writing?" asked Metodii.

"A book about Macedonia."

"Do you want to know about Filip Makedonski, Alexander's father?"

"More recent than that. Were you born here?"

"Yes, I'm from Macedonia. I'm a Bulgarian. You should know that all of Macedonia, right down to Solun [Thessaloniki] is Bulgarian."

"Well I've read many books and they say many things ..."

"You should not believe in books," put in Maria. "You should go to Atun." So far as I knew *atun* was the Spanish word for tuna.

"You mean the Holy Mountain? Athos?"

"Yes, *Sveta Gora*. I can't go there of course, women aren't allowed, but you can go and you will see that they have many books there, pure Christian books, not propaganda, that show that Macedonia is Bulgaria. We speak the same language as the people who come across the border, of course we're the same people. Macedonia has always been Bulgaria really but we're tolerant of anyone who wants to live here. Macedonia is a place not a people. Who cares who lives here or what they want to call themselves? That chilli's very hot by the way. Don't put it on your potatoes."

"Do you like football?" enquired Metodii. "Manchester United is the best team in the world. You know old players—Gary Lineker, Kevin Keegan?"

"Bobby Charlton."

"The best! Have a beer."

"Grigorii's playing Macedonian music now," observed Maria. Half the customers were on their feet dancing enthusiastically. "Actually it's a tune from Yugoslavia. Serbs don't know how to dance. Neither do the Greeks, but Macedonians dance so well! We all speak Greek—we have to because they're our neighbours in South Macedonia—but they're not as good as us whatever they say. Many Greeks come here and they just can't dance! True they've got half of our country, but we don't hold it against them." As if to prove the point Grigorii launched into a Greek tune.

"VMRO are big people," said Metodii, "but all politicians are criminals. They've ruined the country to make themselves fat. I think the Socialists stand a good chance of winning the elections. People want to go back to the time when there was order and food was cheap. It was so cheap! I don't think I'm going to vote though. It's all crap."

Grigorii joined us again. "Can you teach me the words of some Beatles songs? I keep getting requests for them but I only know the tunes. You know, what I *really* want is a Hammond organ. If I could have one of them I would be happy."

* * *

"So you're the English writer I've been told about? The one with the book about Macedonia?" The speaker was a large 40-year-old man with close-cropped hair, who was crammed into a tight suit and who sprawled luxuriously in a corner of the *mehana*. "My name is Ognan. It must be very hard to write about Macedonia. We Macedonians never know whether we're Serbs or Bulgarians. Come, you will drink red wine with me. Bulgarian wine is better than French. We've been making it for longer. I was in Solun yesterday and I saw a great amphora in the Archaeological Museum with a picture of Dionysios on it. My heart felt warm and I understood these ancient people. Good wine and a good woman—that is what you need to make you happy. I have been in Greece, Yugoslavia, Romania, even in Switzerland and I can tell you that Bulgarian women are the most beautiful in the world. Greek women have fat hips. You like Bulgarian women?"

I said I was married and showed him Shaoni's photograph.

"She is as beautiful as a Bulgarian woman. You say she's Indian? The Bulgarians originally came from the Himalayas so that might explain it. But to get back to Macedonia. You must know that the Macedonians are Bulgarians. In fact Macedonia is the heart of Bulgaria. Out Saints Cyril and Methodios were Bulgarians and they gave an alphabet to the whole Slavic world. They didn't come from Solun, but from near there. The big cities were never Slavic, which is how we lost Aegean Macedonia to the Greeks."

It is often the case in Eastern Europe that an urban population is of a different ethnic group to the rural population. Until the Second World War the cities of the Baltic—Tallinn, Vilnius, Gdansk—were German islands in a non-German sea. Timisoara, the cradle of the 1989 Romanian revolution was, and to a large extent still is, the Hungarian city of Temezsvár. Bratislava, the capital of Slovakia, was once Pressburg. Bulgaria's Black Sea towns were for centuries Greek. It didn't matter—Slavs were peasants, Germans, Hungarians, Jews and Greeks were the bourgeoisie, and Eastern Europe's aristocracy was mostly German or Turkish. It was only after the First World War, when Eastern Europe was carved into ethnic states that problems arose. To whom did the state belong, the peasants or the middle classes? Was Transylvania Hungarian or Romanian?

"The Turks came and went but we stayed the same," the man said, ordering another bottle of wine. "We're Europeans, no different to the French or you English. We could be useful to the European Community. We're good workers—not like the Greeks, who only joined so they could live off your money. Between Solun and Kulata, on the border, there is not a single factory, but we have three here in Blagoevgrad alone, and they're good ones. We just need the investment. I used to be a policeman but now I'm manager of the Co-operative Bank—the best—and I know. Why won't Europe have us? America ignores us too and gives money to just anyone. But Americans are stupid. They have no history or culture. I have seen what they call 'culture' in the films. They shoot each other. I must ask, is that culture? Rambo? No! Many young people want to be like America, but that has to be wrong. We must join with Europe.

"That means we must build a proper democracy, but it will take a long time to come. At the moment no-one trusts the politicians. They're making themselves rich, but what is money if you have no heart? See, I am writing a song about this problem. It is a philosophical song. How can anybody live if they feel nothing? This is the ancient question. Come, I will take you to where you can hear the best musician in Blagoevgrad play. And for God's sake put your wallet away!"

We walked through the gloomy, almost deserted streets of the town towards the Hotel Alen Mak. In the basement waiters dressed in what was supposed to be "folk costume" were serving their well-heeled customers in half darkness.

"We will drink red wine," declared Ognan, placing himself behind a table where a swarm of waiters crowded around him. "The best red wine, from Melnik. Let us remember the god Dionysios! Also we must have roast potatoes with *kaškaval.*" *Kaškaval* is a cheese not unlike feta. Bulgarian roast potatoes are surprisingly good. A thin, seedy-looking character came over and address a few words to my companion. "This is the greatest musician in Blagoevgrad! Now he will play for us."

The man moved to a low stage and, plucking up a bouzouki, began to play. At once a group of immaculately dressed and coiffed young women leapt to their feet to dance the *hora*. They may have been regulars at the Lady Di Beauty Parlour near the Town Hall, but their hearts were in the Balkans. Who were these young people with so much money, I wondered. The same thought had occurred to me earlier in the Student's Union of the American University, where earnest young people were listening to a local jazz band which was under the direction of a German synthesizer player. The children of the former *nomenklatura*? Of whoever it was who smuggled opium, guns and stolen cars across the border? Revolutions are seldom so revolutionary as they seem at first sight. The new elite is often the old one in a new guise.

"Where are you staying?" Ognan asked. I told him but either it didn't sink in or he simply didn't believe me because he repeated the question several times. "On Friday I have a free day. We will go into the mountains with a friend of mine and we will go hunting." He mimed a rifle, and handed me his card. "Remember, who is Ognan? *I* am Ognan!" He leant back and beamed at me. I resolved not to be in Blagoevgrad on Friday.

"We will go now," he said abruptly, paying the bill ("you pay when I come to London"). We left, and he steered me towards what I thought was going to be another bar. It turned out to be a bingo hall. Serious men and women sat around tables hoping to win a small Citroën while a young woman, who looked monumentally bored, called out the numbers. Every so often someone would cry out "Bingo!" and red-coated officials scurried over to check the veracity of the claim. Playing bingo must be one of the best ways of learning the numbers in a foreign language, but Ognan was having no luck. He fell to cursing the gods, Dionysios especially. I made my excuses and left.

"We will go now," he said abruptly, paying the bill ("you pay when I come to London"). We left, and he steered me towards what I thought was going to be another bar. It turned out to be a bingo hall. Serious men and women sat around tables hoping to win a small Citroën while a young woman who looked monumentally bored called out the numbers. Every so often someone would cry out "Bingo!" and red-coated officials scurried over to check the veracity of the claim. Playing bingo must be one of the best ways of learning the numbers in a foreign language, but Ognan was having no luck. He fell to cursing the gods, Dionysios especially. I made my excuses and left.

Rila Monastery

The valley of the Struma was shrouded in thick fog as the bus left Blagoevgrad and began to lumber ponderously through a series of villages each poorer than the last where the mud-brick houses gradually collapsed under the weight of strings of peppers and maize hanging from the eaves. In the roads people were chopping wood to add to the great stockpiles they were building outside their homes against the coming winter.

The fog was lifting as we entered the small town of Rila, a collection of similarly crumbling mud structures flung across a narrow valley around a strangely incongruous modern main square. High on a hill, the lesser of the town's two churches was plastered with the death-notices common throughout the Balkans which the Bulgarians call by a word of Greek origin—*nekroloz*, "words about death". Though the church itself was locked two small icons had been hung on an outside wall which was blackened by the smoke of generations of candles, the latest of which lay bound to the wall by their own molten wax. The lighting of candles in sacred places must be a very ancient practice. As far away as Samarkand tombs are honoured by placing candles at them.

Further down the hill the Parish Church was decorated with a large mural showing the vision of Elijah the Tishbite, "a chariot of fire and horses of fire". The story is in II Kings 2 and relates to the prophet's ascension into heaven, but it is usually depicted as a cart containing a divine being crossing the heavens. There are few Balkan churches which do not contain this imagery, and many people, including Edith Durham, have seen in the veneration of Elijah the remains of the cult of a sun god, the Legions' Mithras (a temple of Mithras survives, or

survived until recently, in Jajce in Bosnia) or Sol Invictus, the
Unconquered Sun some believe was the true object of Constantine the
Great's devotion.

The fog had now lifted entirely to reveal high snowy mountains up
which crawled a patchwork quilt of trees, rust-coloured beeches against
dark green pines, with here and there smudges of yellow from some
other tree I didn't recognize, eventually giving out against wall of sheer
rock. A couple of small villages huddled in a valley floor that was half
in shadow even at midday. The bus stopped in the middle of nowhere
and the driver descended to pick fresh herbs from a meadow. Eventually
we rounded a corner and there before us loomed the massive bulk of
Rila Monastery.

If monasticism is the heart of Orthodoxy, then Rila is the heart of
Bulgarian Orthodoxy. St John of Rila, who was born in the
Macedonian village of Skrino near Kyustendil, lived in a cave in an
almost inaccessible part of the mountains for at least seven and perhaps
as many as twenty years up to his death in 946, refusing to emerge even
for the benefit of Tsar Peter. Even during his own lifetime he was known
as "the Miracle-Maker" and his cult is followed throughout Bulgaria. By
the eighteenth century the monastery his followers had founded near
the cave had fallen into disrepair, partly as a result of having been sacked
more than once, but a campaign for its restoration was begun in the
nineteenth century under the guidance of one Neofit of Rila, a native
of Bansko. Many in Bulgaria regarded the rebuilding as a sacred duty,
and the finest masons, woodcarvers and painters gave their services free
of charge. The structure they created is one of the most remarkable in
Europe.

I asked a monk who was selling icons and little wooden crucifixes
by the main gate whether it would be possible to stay the night. "Try
reception," he answered laconically. I did. It was tightly shut. An old
lady, bent double, was laboriously sweeping the vast stone-flagged
courtyard with a besom.

"You must see Father Valaam, cell seventy-four," she told me. I
climbed wooden staircases and prowled galleries through the
labyrinthine complex until I found the right cell and knocked on its
solid oak door. After what seemed like an age there was a scuffling
behind the door and Father Valaam, a young monk with piercing dark
eyes, a bushy beard and long tousled hair, emerged. He did not look

pleased to see me. I got the impression that I had interrupted his meditations. Nevertheless, he allowed me access to a Spartan but clean room in the guest wing with a shower that didn't work and a window which opened over the small river that came rushing down the mountain and washed against the monastery's stout walls.

Rila can only be described as an architectural masterpiece. Row upon row of arcaded galleries are stacked one on top of the other around the central courtyard, their curving lines flowing effortlessly together. Cartoon-like figures can been seen playfully painted in odd corners. Here and there strange fragile wooden balconies jut out with no visible means of support where monk or pilgrim can sit in peace and survey the near perfect stage-set in which squats the massive though comfortably rounded bulk of the church. As if in echo of the compound, high mountains rise jaggedly all around. Despite the crowds of day-trippers who throng the courtyard, the whole has an air of perfect tranquillity, the serenity which led John of Rila to seek out this remote spot in the first place.

The church itself is highly decorated, or rather over-decorated, with frescoes of an almost garish brightness, a confusing procession of apocalypses, saints and admonitions to sinners. A giant representation of the Garden of Paradise from which flowed the four Heavenly Rivers of Tigris, Euphrates, Nile and Psion (variously associated with either the Danube or, more probably, the Indus), harbours Abraham, Isaac and Jacob whilst St Peter unlocks the gates to admit the Saved. A sun possessed of a smiling face and with hands and feet which explode in sheets of flame is commanding an angel against a backdrop of sinking ships and collapsing cities. Less obscurely, a devil sits at a rich man's banquet while feeding the victim's soul into the gaping maw of a fire-breathing serpent. Angels pull a rope to activate a Wheel of Fortune while further devils with scythes rake despairing figures off the declining side. The wheel is quartered to represent the seasons, with spring at the beginning of the cycle and winter at the end. In the squinch of one of the porch's domes a group of peasants dances a *hora* to the sound of pipes and drums. The whole creation is an expression of a wildly exuberant peasant imagination. These rustic jollities and surreal mystical images are far removed from the traditional stern, long-faced and droopy-moustached saints of medieval churches. The Ottoman period took the Church out of the hands of intellectuals and aristocrats and gave it to peasants, who instead of abstract reasoning created a joyous world where Turks are pitchforked into hell while honest Christian folk sing and dance.

Even here, the intellectual centre of the Bulgarian Church, pagan sun and moon motifs are to be seen on the church's door, on a fountain, even under the eaves by the monks' cells. Ancient beliefs survive best among peoples who have little need for education. Education is the great destroyer of traditional beliefs, whether in Bulgaria, Britain or the Muslim world. Ironically, it was that great guardian of tradition, the Orthodox Church, which led the way in establishing Bulgarian-language education, ultimately bringing to an end an order which had lasted for four hundred years.

The beginning of the end can be glimpsed in the church's interior. On the doors of the immense gilt walnut iconostasis, the finest product of the Samokov woodcarvers, are European-style coats-of-arms. I recognized only two, but icon-like they had explanatory inscriptions. Bulgaria, Macedonia, Wallachia and Moldavia, Serbia, Montenegro and Herzegovina, Bosnia and finally Russia and Muscovy. The "arms" of the Balkan areas then under Ottoman rule and those of the state they looked to for salvation. Bulgaria's ambivalent relationship to Macedonia was neatly encapsulated in those arms. Bulgaria was symbolized by a gold rampant lion on a red ground. Macedonia's shield was similar but with the colours reversed. In one of the transepts lay a polished marble slab adorned with funerary wreathes and fresh flowers. It was the tomb of Boris III, Bulgaria's last Tsar, the German king who led his country into a disastrous alliance with Germany and Italy in the hope of recovering Macedonia.

"Actually," I heard someone say, "only his heart's here. No-one knows what happened to the body. It was stolen."

Resting under an embroidered cloth in front of the iconostasis is the body of John of Rila. A monk stands guard and on request lifts the lid of the coffin for the benefit of pilgrims, revealing a tiny body entirely swathed in a shroud save for one hand. Most contented themselves with a simple kiss, but one woman prostrated herself thrice before the saint under the approving gaze of the monk. An open drawer under another icon revealed fragments of bone claimed to have been the property of a wide range of saints, including Mary Magdalene. The Orthodox set great store by relics. As the sanctity of a holy person can be transferred to that person's icon, so it continues to inhere in his or her bodily remains after death, and it can be invoked for succour. There is a parallel in Central Asia, where devout Muslims will run their hands over saints' tombs in the hope of gaining some of that person's *baraka*, or divine blessing. Protestants and "orthodox" Muslims alike hold that this bestowal of power on inanimate objects is pure idolatry, but it seems no less credible than many other claims of religion. After all, holiness is holiness. How can it be bounded by space or time?

The doors of the monks' cells presented a blank face to the world. All except one, which was adorned with an ornate brass knocker and a plate likewise of brass. "Archimandrite Vitalii", it read. The Archimandrite, middle-aged with a grey beard and a noticeable paunch, was a man of few words. In fact I never managed to get more than five consecutive words from any of the monks. Perhaps they were saving themselves for the weekend, when scores of trippers and genuine pilgrims would descend on them. As it was, I never heard the Archimandrite speak except when reciting vespers in a powerful voice to an almost empty church. There can be no more than ten monks at Rila and I don't believe that all of them were present. Father Valaam was called upon to repeat umpteen "Hallelujahs" while a choir comprising another monk, two novices and an old layman sang "Lord Have Mercy!" over and over. The solemnity of the occasion was rather spoilt by the yapping of a small white terrier which followed one of the monks wherever he went and by the fact that while Father Valaam breathlessly continued his endless "*Gospodins*" and "Hallelujahs" the choristers kept up a hubbub of chatter amongst themselves.

Slightly further up the valley from the monastery a new hotel had been built for the benefit of pilgrims, where I dined off delicious fresh fish and the monks' excellent wine. Returning to the monastery, I found the heavy oak gates piercing its blank walls locked shut. On my ringing the bell a voice on the other side called out "Who's there?" "It's me, the Englishman. I'm staying here."

"You're staying *here*?" asked the voice incredulously before a tiny postern was swung open to let me in.

In the dark, with the trippers fled, an absolute still reigns over Rila. The only sounds are of water splashing in the courtyard's fountains and footsteps echoing around the endless galleries as black-robed monks flit by like bats. Yellow light spills from a room near the gate where a police detail is stationed. Bored young men are drinking beer and playing cards with plates of cold fried eggs at their elbows. A cat is sitting motionless on the threshold of one of the cells and a calm nacre moon is gazing down, flooding the range of buildings with a cold silvery light. There is perfect peace, the peace which John of Rila sought when he came here to meditate on the mysteries of the soul. From my window I could hear the rushing of the river and the outlines of the mountains stood out blackly against the night sky.

I was awoken at six the next morning by the bell ringing for Matins. Thick fog shrouded the monastery and a heavy rain was falling. I wrapped myself tighter into my blankets and muttered dark imprecations against St Basil, who ordained that the monastic day should start at so ungodly an hour.

Melnik

"We're going to Melnik," said Pat, an Australian former school teacher who was "doing" Eastern Europe with a couple of her friends. "We've heard they have good wine there."

"The best in the Balkans. I'm headed that way myself."

We travelled together south along the rain-sodden valley of the Struma towards the town of Sandanski, the supposed birthplace of Spartacus, whose statue overlooks the main highway. From ancient times it has been a spa, and was at one time known as Sveti Vrach, which means holy doctor. Now it carries the name of the Voivoda Yane Sandanski, as if there was some kind of direct link between him and the revolutionary slave. The previous month, in October 1994, the illegal nationalist group United Macedonian Organization–Ilinden, whose posters I had seen in Gotse Delchev, had distributed leaflets at the Pirin Folklore Festival in Sandanski demanding the annexation of Pirin by Vardar Macedonia and calling the Bulgarian Army one of occupation. The group was founded by a man called Solunski—"the Thessalonian". From time to time the organization attempts to hold rallies at Sandanski's grave, where they are almost invariably assaulted (or so they claim) by the police.

We had to change buses. I went to see whether it was possible to pre-book rooms in Melnik; Pat and the others went to the post office in the hope of sending their vast hoard of ceramic ashtrays and cups, bought for next to nothing at Rila, back to Australia. That was difficult,

---

the more so since none spoke any language other than English and the postmistress spoke only Bulgarian and Russian. I was roped in to translate. Each carefully packaged parcel had to be opened, inspected, repackaged, and customs forms filled in in triplicate and French, an endlessly complicated procedure. Pat had a card for the telephone with some spare credit on it. She wanted to phone Australia.

"You can't," said the postmistress, "there's no line. Nobody in Sandanski knows any Australians."

We boarded a crowded bus heading back into the hills. The heavens opened again, turning the side roads into seas of mud. Some Bulgarians were sharing a bottle of vodka on the back seat and attempting to pick up the Australians, burbling incomprehensibly in what they thought was English. "Macedonia for the Macedonians!" read the roadside graffiti. Eventually we were dumped in the pouring rain at Melnik's bus-stop, just outside the village and opposite a small ramshackle cottage.

"Well, what do we do now?" asked Pat.

"Look for a room." The shutters of the cottage were flung open and a sunken-cheeked old lady leaned out.

"Are you wanting a room?"

Inside, we sat steaming beside a wood-burning stove while our landlady brought us a bottle of young red wine which fizzed slightly on the tongue.

"From my own grapes," she explained.

✳ ✳ ✳

If there is one place in Macedonia where you might expect to meet the old gods, prophetesses or witches, it is Melnik. A narrow valley holds the town, or rather the village, bounded by the sheer cliffs of yellow mud which give it its name. Over time the cliffs have been eroded into fabulous, unearthly shapes made more surreal by the clouds that drifted across and through the landscape, depositing their burden on the hills. It is a fitting setting for a town of ghosts.

As late as 1880 Melnik was a city of 20,000 with a weekly market that rivalled any in Macedonia. Its mainly Greek population grew rich on the trade between Thessaloniki, Constantinople and Europe. Now, barely 600 people live here, surviving on wine, tobacco and tourism.

Melnik fell victim to war and changing patterns of trade—the Sofia to Thessaloniki railway follows the Struma, away at the foot of the hills which shelter Melnik, not only bypassing the town but obviating any need to stop there.

When G. F. Abbott, the ethnographer-cum-anthropologist from London University and sometime correspondent for the *Manchester Guardian*, visited Melnik at the turn of the century, he found it "an oasis of Hellenic language, culture and tradition in the midst of a district occupied by a Slav peasantry: honest, industrious and sober but withall dull." Melnik was just one of several such "oases". Kastoria, now in Greece, was another island in a Slavic sea. To Abbott's surprise, many of the citizens' family names were those of the Byzantine emperors. The names Paeleologos, Comnena and Lascaris were, he declared, "as common as our Tom, Dick and Harry", and a curious caste system survived. Members of the "aristocracy" never married into families considered to be lower class (the distinction had nothing to do with personal wealth). Melnik was dying even then though, due not only to changing patterns of trade but also to the alleged presence of no fewer than 50 *voivodas*, each of whom would be only too willing to relieve travellers of their burdens. "No Melnikiote worth robbing ventures five minutes' walk beyond the boundaries of the town," observed Abbott, who himself travelled with a heavily armed caravan: the weapons, being forbidden, had to be concealed.

Melnik's remaining houses either huddle together along a usually dry river-bed which divides the village's only true street, or sit in isolation scattered up the hillsides. Solid stone ground floor storerooms support elegant and airy upper living quarters that project over the unpaved alleys on wooden struts, town houses without a town. Narrow cobbled roads lead up the valley walls past ruins and yet more ruins. Everywhere lie the shattered remains of once-great houses and churches as overgrown and desolate as any Salamis or Troy. Donkeys, stray dogs and tortoises are the only animals that inhabit a city reduced to rubble less than a century ago, irretrievably gone in the fury of the Balkan Wars. Today's villagers have no hesitation in blaming the town's demise on the Turks, but the destruction could equally have been wrought by Bulgarians, Greeks or Serbs.

There is a solitary old man among the ruins, a last survivor with his feet wrapped in rags, a torn leather jacket on his back and an old-

fashioned flying helmet on his head, who squats before a fire he has built for himself under the shelter of a stunted hawthorn. As a cold penetrating rain fell it was easy to imagine the ghosts, singly or in small groups peering out of the undergrowth at the casual visitor wandering this graveyard of a civilization. They are sad withered figures with large beseeching eyes and they ask a single question: "Why?"

※ ※ ※

It is still possible to catch a brief glimpse of the wealth and sophistication that was Melnik in a surviving house which has been restored as a museum. Such houses were described in detail by Abbott, who as a rare foreigner, and an Englishman at that, could be presumed to be sympathetic to Greeks, was led unwillingly around many of them and obliged to consume *rakija* with their occupants. The ground floor comprised a massive storeroom extending into caves carved out of the rock behind. To one side was the *divan*. The word, which is Persian, means an assembly or the place of assembly (and by extension the seat on which those assembled gather). It was here that the wealthy merchant whose home this had been transacted his business. A flight of stairs led up to living quarters richly decorated in the Ottoman style. Large windows with stained-glass details looked out over the village and on the floor were kilims of the highest quality. The panelled walls were decorated with delicate paintings of cypress trees, flowers and birds; only a small cross carved discretely above a fireplace evinced that this was not the Istanbul home of some Ottoman grandee. Even the panelling of the ceilings was done in the geometric patterns I had last seen in the great mosques of Aleppo and Damascus. The Church may have preserved the ethnic identity of the peoples of the Balkans, but the wealthy still aspired to the prestigious Perso-Byzantine style of the metropolis.

It says much about the nature of the Ottoman Empire that one of the *rayah*, or the herd, as non-Muslim subjects were called, could rise to such wealth. It was wealthy merchants such as this who in Macedonia, Greece, Bulgaria and Lebanon sponsored the new European-style schools that were so crucial in propagating the idea of the National Revival. This single house utterly belies all the rhetoric of the "Turkish Yoke" so beloved in the Balkans. Christians were not kept in poverty by the Turks: many of the Turkish peasants of Anatolia were poorer by far than anyone in the Balkans, was imperial Russia any more "advanced" than the Ottoman Empire? There is no guarantee that Balkan society would have been substantially different even in the absence of the Turks, but it always feels good to be able to blame a foreigner for your troubles. It is even doubtful whether many people even appreciated their new post-Ottoman freedom. A Bulgarian novelist by the name of Maksimov wrote in his book *Tselina* of 1892 that

> *The peasant has but the vaguest idea of our transition from servitude to independent life: for him it matters little whether he pays tax to Ahmet or Ivan. In fact Ivan is often more distasteful to him than Ahmet, for Ahmet could more easily be fooled or bribed ... the meaning of state, rights and duties for the peasant add up to tax-payment and sending his son off as a soldier.*

The Church of St Nicholas in Melnik squats half-way up a cliff overlooking the village. Its light and airy interior revealed a few old men and women huddled around a stove whilst the priest filled the nave with his sonorous voice, answered by a wavering "choir" of a single old woman. She sang in the plaintive, constricted wail of the *dertliška*, the stern tones of masculine authority answered by the haunting melodies of the hill women.

Most of the icons were missing from the iconostasis and the remainder without exception bore Greek inscriptions. One of them was dated 1823, and someone had provided Bulgarian subtitles on pieces of card stuck beneath them. Cyril and Methodios were absent from the main programme, but their image had been added underneath St Catherine. Pride of place belonged to the Greek St Spyridion, a shepherd who continued to tend his literal flock even after elevation to the rank of bishop provided him with a metaphorical one. On the lowest level were charmingly naïve panels depicting the Fall interspersed with landscapes and still lives of flowers in vases. I asked the priest about the icons.

"Well," he replied gently stroking his beard, "first they were Bulgarian, then they were Greek. You see here," he waved his hand towards the icon of St Nicholas, "it says *hagios*. We say *sveti*. Now we use Bulgarian again but nobody bothered to change the icons, I think because everyone's so confused as to who we are. It doesn't matter. An icon is an icon regardless of what language it's written in.

"As for the Vardar Macedonians and their so-called 'Macedonian Orthodox Church', the patriarch hates it, but they can do what they want so far as I'm concerned. Everyone else does around here. If you live in an imaginary country you can imagine whatever you like."

❋ ❋ ❋

Rozhen is one of the foci of that imagining. Every so often UMO–Ilinden gathers at the monastery to demonstrate the separateness of the Macedonian people. VMRO and members of the Bulgarian government likewise go there, usually on the anniversary of the Ilinden revolt to demonstrate the unity of the Macedonian and Bulgarian peoples. It is not so much the monastery itself which excites these pilgrims as the village church, outside which the body of Yane Sandanski lies under an enormous marble slab on which is written "Patriot, Struggler for a Free Bulgaria." Or perhaps for a free Macedonia—whatever that means.

The rain held off as the three Australians and I climbed the hill from the tiny and run-down village of Rozhen towards the monastery, allowing a bright sunlight to suffuse the valley. Beyond the sandy cliffs that dominated the foreground rose hills green as I had never before seen Macedonia, a deep, luscious green. Further off high snowy mountains marked the horizon.

"Will you buy my wine?" asked a shawl-wrapped old woman at the monastery gate. "No? How about a photograph, or I have mountain herbs. Perhaps an icon or a calendar?" The latter featured a mildly pornographic photograph. I was looking beyond the woman, though, at the distant mountains. "It's wonderful isn't it," remarked the old woman. "Beyond the mountain over there is the town of Gotse Delchev. He was a very brave man, a very good man. On the other side of *that* mountain is Greece. When the Greeks came here in 1924 all the village had to take refuge in the monastery."

Once again the Bulgarian Church was proving the salvation of its people in a more than purely theological sense, yet behind those stern walls lies a little piece of heaven, a miniature Rila whose delicate wooden galleries encircle a small basilica which is tied down by a spider's web of grapevines. The church is covered with frescos inside and out. Executed some three or four hundred years before those at Rila they have none of the peasant naïvety of the latter but rather the solemn grace of the frescos at Ohrid and in other medieval churches of the erstwhile Yugoslavia. Again, all the inscriptions were in Greek and the Slav favourites, Cyril, Methodios and Elijah were absent, replaced by John Chrysostomos, the Golden-Mouthed Greek theologian, and Wisdom, personified as Sofia.

It was a Sunday and a steady stream of visitors was depositing flowers and candles before the icons in this Greek church that had sheltered their ancestors from the Greeks. A single monk was singing hymns in honour of the Virgin in the company of a group of youthful pilgrims. In the village the locals were doing a roaring trade in wine and honey. We entered the only *mehana* and played cards for what seemed like an eternity until the returning bus to Sandanski ground to a wheezing halt in the square outside before crawling back along the narrow mountain road to deposit us beside Sandanski's statue in Melnik.

✳ ✳ ✳

That night a large party was drinking jug after jug of the heavy red wine of Melnik, singing, laughing and of course dancing the *hora*. Two of my Australian companions, citizens of Melbourne, joined in, to much applause and cries of "Bravo". They were of Italian descent and had learnt the steps from Greek friends, but it didn't matter. As the *hora* ended, a sprightly middle-aged woman and a young man engaged in a dance the meaning of whose writhings could not have been more explicit. Dionysios had crept into the room to be with his votaries. Gods are immortal, and though they may fall from fashion they continue to live on the hilltops or in the caves where the people store their wine, only to steal forth when good Christian and Muslim folk lower their guard.

Vanga the Witch
The following day I was alone again. My companions were racing for Istanbul. My landlady, who spent all day padding around the house and brought me breakfast in bed, declared "you must sleep with sugar under your pillow. Vanga will use the sugar to read the past, the present and the future. She is never wrong in her predictions if your question is genuine and your heart is pure. Also, be sure to be in for dinner. There will be beans tonight."

"Vanga is not just a phenomenon, she is a super-phenomenon," I was told in the coffee shop over the road where the owner, the postman and the bus driver would spend all day playing cards together. "Her predictions always come true. You must go and see her. She speaks to foreigners all the time."

"She talks to people on other planets," I had been assured in Blagoevgrad, "but now she is very old and the planets don't speak to her so much any more. But she is a very powerful woman. Everyone listens to her." I was fascinated. "The idea for building the church was launched by the famous clairvoyant Vanga. It was constructed in Rupite, near Petrich. According to Vanga, thousands of years ago there was a town in that place which was destroyed. She says that her power comes from that town."

Vanga was born Vangelia Gušterova in 1911, in the town of Strumitsa in Vardar Macedonia, not far from where Basil II had had the eyes of Tsar Samuel's army put out in 1014. At the age of twelve she lost her sight, but in a vision of a "stranger on a white horse" who held a spear she was granted the gift of clairvoyance. St Petka, who habitually carries her own eyes in a small dish, commanded her to go to Rupite, and Vanga makes daily offerings to the saint, but her crowning glory came in 1994, when President Kirsan Ilyamdzinov of Kalmukistan made her an honorary citizen of his republic. Kalmukistan comprises an area near the Lower Volga in Russia and its unlikely inhabitants, a Mongolian tribe, follow the Tibetan version of Buddhism, recognizing the Dalai Lama as their spiritual leader. I became determined to visit Rupite.

Climbing through dripping pine trees above Melnik I emerged on a small plateau a good hundred feet above the town. Deep gullies surrounded me on all sides, and sandstone pinnacles ended abruptly in flat grassy summits. Further off were the mountains, great whale-backed massifs covered with snow. It was a fairy-tale landscape and it was here that the medieval city of Melnik was established on a crag, which ensured it only needed a single defensive wall. On this natural acropolis lived a man named Alexei Slav, a *voivoda* who, like others, carved himself a fiefdom out of the decaying remains of Byzantium. It was he who had invited the Greeks to Melnik from their homes in Plovdiv to create the centre of arts, trade, religion and learning which lasted until the Balkan Wars.

Scattered among the undergrowth lay the ruins of this medieval city, the remains of the single defensive wall, a cistern and the apses of a huge church which still contained the battered traces of a fresco of Christ the King. The only sign of life was a wren hopping over the fallen columns. Someone had tied brightly coloured rags to the branches of a tree near the old church in a votive custom which links Melnik through Turkey and Armenia to far away Bokhara. Suddenly the ruins took on mystical significance. I wondered what had prompted this supplication of the gods who still lived on the hills among the wreckage of human activity.

✳ ✳ ✳

"Come, come!" said my landlady, "You must come in here where it is warm. Winter has come and you must sit in here by the fire and drink some wine and have *kaškaval* and chillies before the soup and beans." She ushered me into a back room which served as kitchen as well as living room and bedroom for her partially paralysed husband who had lost the use of the right-hand side of his body. He was a sad-looking man with a deeply lined face and large grey eyes who wore a cardigan over his pyjamas and spent his days watching television and smoking Arda brand cigarettes, the cheapest. They stared at me writing with my left hand. "You see," she said, "it *can* be done." He looked unconvinced, and called for raki to be poured.

"What we miss most about the Communists," he said to me in a wheezing voice punctuated with coughs, "is the prices. Everything was so cheap, but now there is no work, even if you *can* work, so there is much unhappiness. How much does kebab cost in a restaurant?" They gasped with astonishment when I told them—fifteen pence each. "Meat is so expensive! We own very few animals now so we can't get it. Everything is expensive now. Tomatoes used to be five leva a kilo, but now they cost five times as much. At least we have a garden. How much are beans in a restaurant? You've never seen them on a menu? Then we shall eat beans tomorrow." He lapsed into silence again but his wife continued, handing me an enormous bowl of cabbage soup.

"Do you have parents? How about your wife? Yes? And her grandparents live in India! I thought she looked very dark in her photograph but I didn't know. I've never seen an Indian before. Of course Macedonians are Bulgarians. Anyone who tells you otherwise is a liar. Cyril and Methodios were just Slavs, but they founded our Bulgarian Church in Macedonia, in Ohrid. There are Greek icons in the church here because there used to be many Greeks here, in the days when there were 3,000 houses and 75 churches. That was before the war. There are no Greeks now. I can only name five churches here, and only two of them are used. We've lived here all our lives. The only other place we've ever been is Sofia. Our children, two sons and a daughter, live there because there are factories and jobs, so we're all alone, but they visit in the summer and then the house is full.

"You know Yane Sandanski? With the statue in the park? He was the great freedom-fighter from Melnik. His house is now the town museum. He fought for VMRO and died in the First World War saving us from the Greeks, but then VMRO was suppressed in 1934. All of that, the *voivodas*, is history now. It is good that you are writing about

Macedonia. East Europeans don't know West European history and you don't know ours—we're only just rediscovering it ourselves—but we're all Europeans and we must understand one another.

"Let me tell you about Vanga. When she was very little, a great storm came and she was picked up—whoosh!—into the sky, and when she came down she could not see with her eyes, but only with her heart. She came here once when someone was sick in the head. She found a church which nobody knew of before, and told this man to sleep there, and he was cured! She is a phenomenon. She talks to Marko, but St Petka likes her best. She has had a new church built for St Petka. It is so new we haven't seen it yet ourselves. She is something unique to the Bulgarians of Macedonia, special for us. There won't be another like her. Now she is ill. I do not think you will see her." She paused for a moment, wobbling her head from side to side in that peculiarly Bulgarian gesture.

"We're all Orthodox here of course", she added. "If you go to Gotse Delchev you'll see Bulgarian Muslims, but the Turks live in the Rhodopes and in Thrace." I remarked that the Muslims of Pirin called themselves Turks but seemed to use only one word in five of Turkish in their speech.

"Naturally. What would you expect? They were taught to think like Turks but not to speak like them."

✳ ✳ ✳

"Am I a Bulgarian or a Macedonian? Don't be stupid, I'm a Jew of course! Do you speak Spanish? I was brought up to speak Ladino. That's our own language, Spanish written in Hebrew characters." Once Elias mentioned it I suppose it was obvious, though I would have guessed that he was Armenian. I met him and two French people, Jean-Claude and Maria, in a *mehana* one evening. Tired of speaking Russian, I was attracted by the sound of French and introduced myself. We shared a jug of wine, and Jean-Claude laboriously explained to me that the French are not racist, they're simply frightened by the proximity of the Maghreb: "We tried to make Algeria part of France and failed. We don't want France to become part of Algeria."

"Have you seen the synagogue in Gotse Delchev," asked Elias, "by the bus station? There used to be thousands of us in the Balkans but everyone was killed, except the Jews of Bulgaria. Most have gone to Israel now, I can't imagine why. There are only 3,000 of us left. I'm from Plovdiv, the greatest city in Bulgaria. It should be the capital—it's just an accident that Sofia is instead, because you British gave Plovdiv back to the Turks. If everybody left everybody else alone the world would be a much happier place."

I met the three of them the following day by chance. Elias was looking for somewhere good to eat, so I steered them to my favourite *mehana* where we ate *stomna kebab*, a spicy stew named for the earthenware vessel it is baked in, and drank more wine. The French couple were agreed: the presentation was superb and the wine better than the previous night's.

"We're going to Rupite this afternoon," said Elias, "do you want to come? I have a car." We exchanged pleasantries, and then had to stop and translate everything into French.

"My father came from Bulgaria," explained Jean-Claude, but I don't speak the language. He went to Paris to study and never went home. Elias is a kind of cousin."

We climbed into Elias's battered Lada, myself in the front so that Elias could talk to me in Russian, and crawled off through the hills.

"*Ah, comme c'est joli!*" exclaimed Maria from the back. The cloud had lifted to reveal a gently rolling landscape framed by the majestic mountains.

"*Oui, c'est très joli,*" agreed Elias resting both hands on the dashboard and craning around to look at the view behind.

"*Attention au chemin!*" We had come close to falling over a cliff.

We crossed the Struma, dodging enormous lorries registered in Vardar Macedonia which were racing for the border and took the turning for Rupite down a poplar-lined road signposted "Granny Vanga's Church".

"What are these cars with the red sticker on the number-plate?" asked Maria.

"They come from Yugoslav Macedonia—free Macedonia," I said.

"And so you mean people here in Bulgarian Macedonia are *not* free?" demanded Elias, annoyed.

"That's just what they say in Yugoslavia."

In the middle of what looked like a building site squatted a concrete edifice which followed the classical cross-in-square plan and bore a pink copper dome. "Chapel of St Petka, built in 1994 by Vanga", a sign over the door proclaimed. It was the first new Bulgarian church in 50 years, and had taken two years and the labour of fifteen men to build using the money donated by some 2,500 people. The architects had given their labour for nothing, as had the painter Svetlin Russev who worked on the external murals and the icons in the wooden screen, sub-El Greco works in garish reds and yellows. The iconostasis was the work of fourteen months, donated by the sculptor Gregor Paunov. Vanga herself appears on the outside wall in a grotesque parody of the Virgin, her blind eyes rolled heavenwards in prophetic mode.

Although the church had cost 10 million leva, Elias assured me that Vanga reserved her prayers for those who had been able to donate just five leva each. When the church was dedicated, it is said that "thousands of admirers from Bulgaria, Greece, Macedonia and Romania" had come to pay their respects. The event was broadcast live on nationwide television.

"What do you think of it?" Jean-Claude asked Elias.

"You must ask the Professor of Religion."

"There seems to be something much older than Christianity going on here," I said to cue. "I told you last night about how Vanga is said to speak to Prince Marko, and about his supposed connexion to the Thracian Rider, the god Medaurus. In this I can see the coming cult of a saint. I expect that many Catholic saints started off like Vanga. The people here are not honouring Petka, they are honouring Vanga."

Vanga, or St Petka who told Vanga where to site the church, knew what she was doing. Near the building hot sulphurous springs rose in great steaming pools, a holy well where people were bathing under the eyes of a family of Gypsies who hoped to try their luck telling people's fortunes in competition with Vanga. The Gypsies were studiously avoided by the crowds who preferred to feed the geese which thronged the site.

"Well, that's Vanga," said Elias at last. "Now let's go to Petrich to look at the millionaires. There are more millionaires there than anywhere else in Bulgaria. They make a killing by smuggling goods over the border."

The market in Petrich filled with consumer goods almost unavailable in the rest of Bulgaria. "All this is contraband I promise you," said Elias. "The police are not interested in what happens here.

Everything is controlled by the Mafia. You see them changing money in the street? That is illegal. You should have a licence but it is the Mafia which says what is allowed."

"Well, you need a police force, and if the government won't pay them the Mafia must," I observed jestingly. Elias took exception to that.

"It's a question of morale not money. Right now the police have very little morale so they are corrupt. They get paid enough."

✳ ✳ ✳

Just inside Bulgaria, and an equal distance from both the Greek and Vardar Macedonian borders, Petrich is the ideal haven for criminals, and VMRO had by 1924 become nothing more than a criminal syndicate amusing itself with random killing, internecine feuds and plundering in three countries. It was also powerful enough utterly to destabilize Bulgarian politics. Even today Bulgarian law hardly runs. Until 1992 the town harboured a company which dealt in spare parts for Mercedes cars. All the parts came from stolen German machines which were dismantled in Petrich and brand new cars assembled out of the resulting pieces. The villains failed to keep up their "insurance" and eventually the police got them. The town is also the stronghold of the radical wing of UMO–Ilinden which feeds off the local distaste for the laws of Sofia.

In the bad old days just after the First World War, when the laws of Bulgaria came a poor second to those of VMRO in these parts and raids were continually being mounted on Greece and Yugoslavia (which is precisely why Greece invaded in 1924—*somebody* had to do something, and the Bulgarians themselves weren't up to it), life was cheap in Petrich. So cheap in fact that a murder could be arranged for $10 (which was then somewhat less than £3). This represented a considerable drop in the value of a life since the Balkan Wars, since on his visit Abbott encountered a man who "had been offered T£6 (about £5 8/-) if he would join the Exarchic fold … or a free passage to immortality if he should refuse." By "joining the Exarchic fold" the person in question, a Slav, would cease to be "Greek" and become instead "Bulgarian". The man had refused the offer and lived in constant fear for his life. At the time there were as many "Greeks" as "Bulgarians" in Petrich, but "a Greek will on no account speak to or shake hands with a Bulgar. Nor will a Bulgar patronise a shop kept by a Greek." In one telling incident Abbott overheard two men debating whether Jesus was a Greek or a Bulgar. The suggestion that He had in fact been Jewish was met with derision.

As we left the town the sun was setting, turning the peaks of the mountains pink against an azure sky and a valley the colour of wood smoke. "*C'est si bon!*" cried Maria, and it was.

Georgii the Historian

Back in Melnik my landlady took me to see Georgii Styanov, the town historian, in his eyrie in the museum house, where he sat in a plain office furnished with a table, a bed and a coffee pot to one side of the public rooms. Black-bearded, he was in his late thirties or early forties and looked every inch the master of the house.

"How can I help you?" he asked. "I read French but I can't speak it, so we'll have to speak Russian." I started by asking about the Greek icons in St Nicholas.

"We got our Christianity from Tsarigrad as you know, although the Apostle Paul passed through Macedonia. In fact, one of the earliest Christian basilicas is here in Melnik, on the citadel. After the Slavs came, Emperor Justinian, who was born in Ohrid, resettled Greeks in Macedonia and began to convert the Slavs to Christianity. Later Alexei Slav invited many Greeks here to bolster his own power and Melnik became a mostly Greek town, though there were some Armenians and Jews here as well. Alexei Slav built a monastery on the hill where they wrote Slav grammars in the Greek language, but you must remember the Greeks were only ever guests here. Melnik remained at heart a Slavic town. Its very name tells us that: *mel* is our word for these cliffs that you see around the town. After the Balkan Wars the Greeks left and that was the end of Melnik. This used to be a great centre of Christian art, culture, trade and religion, far more important than Sofia. The citadel here is as large as the Tsarivets in Târnovo." Târnovo was many times the capital of medieval Bulgarian states. Its citadel, the Tsarivets, is held up as a prime example of the glory that was Bulgaria in those days.

"Politics killed the town," added Georgii, "but as for the church, the Eastern Orthodox Church is one, even if we habitually talk of a Russian, a Greek or a whatever church. Christ is one, and ours is the Church of Christ, unchanged for centuries, though the Catholic

Orthodox Church [as he called the Church of Rome] has split into many new sects. What sense can it make to talk of an exclusively Greek Church when there is just one church? We have only had one major heresy—the Bogomils, who were very poor, spiritual people. Unlike your Church, which is legally-minded like the Romans were, ours is mystical. That is what makes it Eastern. We're not too bothered about outward appearances, which I think is why we've had so few heresies."

"But," I objected, "it *does* matter, because the Orthodox Church here is a national church."

"True. That is why there were so few converts to Islam even after 500 years unlike in Bosnia, where there was no national church. The Bosnians could never decide whether they were Catholic or Orthodox, and of course many of them were Bogomils. That is why so many of them became Muslims. The Turks were only guests in our country. Their religion was foreign, and in a very real sense to be Bulgarian is to be Orthodox but this modern division of churches by country is purely political. Take Vardar Macedonia. They have a 'Macedonian Orthodox Church', but they should of course be members of the Bulgarian Orthodox Church since there is no Macedonian people. Tsar Samuel had his capital at Ohrid, before the disaster of the Field of Eyes when Basil Bulgaroctonos, the Bulgar-Slayer, blinded so many. Ohrid was the centre of our religion long after it stopped being the centre of our state, but the Yugoslav authorities said 'you are not Serbs so you cannot join the Serbian Church, but we will not let you join the Bulgarian one either so there must be a Macedonian Church.' But you can't be a Macedonian, you can only be like me, a Bulgarian from Macedonia."

Georgii's assistant came in bearing a tray with cups of Turkish coffee on it. "It's that old question again," she said. "Is Macedonia part of Bulgaria or is Bulgaria part of Macedonia? I don't know."

"Whatever," commented Georgii. "The one thing that is certain is that the Greek claim based on Aleksandâr Makedonski is absurd. He has nothing whatsoever to do with modern Macedonia."

"Yesterday," I said, changing the subject, "I went to Rupite. Have there been many others like Vanga?"

"She's a one-off. You've seen her church you say? It's a travesty of Orthodoxy. She's not Orthodox. She represents something much older. It's a kind of catharsis for Orthodoxy in this region. That church is not

a monument to St Petka but to Vanga, an attempt to make a marriage
between Orthodoxy and paganism. That is wrong."
    "I've been told she talks to Marko." The two of them looked blank.
"You know, Marko Kraljevich the Serbian king." The penny dropped.
    "*Kralje* Marko! I can well believe it, but if she does she's certainly
not Orthodox! Personally I think she's mad."
    "Can you tell me something about Islam in Macedonia?"
    "There are very few Muslims. There was a mosque in Melnik at
one time, but not for long. There were never many Turks here, and Yane
Sandanski took care of the few there were. VMRO worked closely with
the Church in establishing Bulgarian schools, and Sandanski had an
especial dislike of Muslims. As far as he was concerned, anyone who
lived in Macedonia was a Macedonian—provided they weren't Muslim.
That is where he disagreed with Delchev. Of course Delchev came from
Aegean Macedonia, where almost half the population was Muslim. The
land there is much better than here, so more Turks settled there."
    "This word Pomak, it means someone who isn't a true Muslim
doesn't it?"
    "Exactly. It derives from *poloviŝte Musulman*, 'half-a-Muslim'.
That's why they don't like it. When the Turks came they brought very
few women with them so they married locals, many of whom never
properly understood Islam. Many of the Muslims still went to church
and venerated the saints, especially Elijah and St George, even though
you could be killed for it. On the other hand Christians began to call
the Holy Sepulchre in Jerusalem the Kaaba after the Muslim's stone in
Mecca and a person who went to Jerusalem was called *Hajji*, like a
Muslim who went to Mecca, so you see Macedonia is confused
religiously as well as ethnically. There are many sects in Islam and one
of them, the Bektashi, married Islam with Christianity. They were very
popular here, but now there are very few Muslims in our part of the
world. When you go to Bitola you will see that there are many there,
but we never had any use for them."
    It was lunchtime and Georgii led me along a narrow path through
the ruins. He pointed to a pile of stones.
    "That church was given by the people of the house just up there
(another ruin). There's another church just there. On the hill you can see
Alexei Slav's monastery, and the old Metropolitan Church of St Nicholas
the Miracle Worker. The new one's down there. In the days when there

were 35 Eparchies in Bulgaria there was a bishop in Melnik, but now there are only ten Eparchies and we fall under Nevrokop. That's the Church of St Anthony of the Desert, the founder of monasticism, and up there was a big house which belonged to a man who had a ceramics workshop and became very rich. All gone now. When the refugees came from Greece they settled in Gorna Dzumaya and Sveti Vrach, and Melnik just died. It would be good if we could get more tourists so that more of us would have jobs. Otherwise Melnik will die completely. There isn't the transport though. No-one comes here."

I climbed back up the steep path to the old acropolis, up the monastery Georgii had pointed out to me. The village was far below, and the sounds of goat bells and crowing cocks drifted up to me. At length I came upon a tiny basilica, perched on the very edge of the cliff. A heavy brass padlock was on the door and the iconostasis had been stripped of its images but inside were the dried remains of flowers and trails of congealed wax from long-dead candles. To the west the sun was setting behind Vanga's church in a brilliant array of pinks, golds and blues. All around me the mountains raised their peaks against a sky which seemed made of the very thinnest glass. It was perfectly still, and I sat for a long time simply absorbing the tranquillity. Perched in that high place, all but cut off from the world by sheer cliffs, the tragedies of this land seemed as nothing, and the gods came and whispered "See what We have made. This peace is eternal. Forget the sufferings of human folly, forget those man-made ruins, and live with Us." How could so beautiful a land have so troubled a history? Vanga no longer seemed preposterous, indeed I would not have been surprised if Macbeth's witches had turned up. So many religions have made the priestly function the prerogative of men that it seems almost inevitable that it should be people like Vanga who become the officers of the old faith once it has fallen from favour.

Far below a man and his wife were walking along a path with a donkey laden with wood. They were arguing and the woman walked several paces behind her husband.

I walked slowly across the plateau through the gathering dusk towards the citadel. A single spot of rain fell into a cistern sending perfect rings spreading. Under a stunted oak an unshaven middle-aged man wearing shabby blue overalls was picking mushrooms.

"*Dobre vecher*, Good evening," I muttered as I passed him.

"*Dobre vecher*," he responded, straightening up and gazing across a gully to the mountains beyond. "It's magnificent isn't it?" He was a goat-herd.

"Truly magnificent. Can I ask you something? Who is that church up there dedicated to?"

"To St Zona, but people also pray to the Mother of God there. The women go. Where are you from?"

"From London."

"And you speak Russian ... That is good. Russian and Bulgarian are much the same. You should have come on 31 August or 1 September. That is when we have a feast for St Zona. There is music in the village, we dance many *horas*, and the women come up here to the church. I don't know what they do—it is women's business. You know, there used to be 77 churches in Melnik and 5 monasteries. Three were up here, Rozhen makes four and there was another in the hills. Melnik was a big city like Tsarigrad, but that was in the time of the Despot Slav."

"Alexei Slav? I've heard of him."

"Of course you have. He built the fortress here. He was ... let me see. The grandson of Tsar Samuel. That's right. After the disaster at the Field of Eyes Alexei came here and built his castle, so a part of Bulgaria was still free of the Greeks. He was a great man." Alexei in fact lived in the thirteenth century, 200 years after Samuel.

"He sounds a bit like Kralje Marko. Have you heard of him?"

"Of course I have. He is our most famous Bulgarian hero, almost a god in these parts. Look, come here." He led me to the very edge of the cliff. "You see that mountain? That is Pirin. Over there, on the other side of the Struma is Mount Ograzden. I remember my grandmother telling me that Marko could step from one to the other." That gave him a stride of 30 miles. "He used to rule all round here, and some people say he still does. He lived in Štip, over the mountains."

"I thought he lived in Prilep."

"Of course he does! How could I be so stupid? Yes, it's Prilep where he has his castle. But that was in the old days. Why are you writing only about Macedonia? Don't you know that Macedonia is part of Bulgaria? We had all of Macedonia, but it was taken away from us by you British in the Treaty of Berlin in 1878, and again it was stolen from us in 1913 after the Second Balkan War."

"But now Vardar Macedonia is an independent state … "

"Not so. It is independent only of Serbia. Have you heard of the Carnegie Institute? There they have statistics from Russia, France, Germany, VMRO, even from the Serb Nastestvo Verkovich and they all say the people of Macedonia are Bulgarian. Now it should be Bulgaria again. An 'Independent Macedonia' is a nonsense."

✳ ✳ ✳

It was Elias who took me to Rupite, but I had also been offered a lift by a woman who wore too much cheap jewellery and had a penchant for wine. She claimed, in a thick Bulgarian accent, to be an American, and was fond of letting people know that she had *valuta*, hard currency. I was rather glad when she failed to show up, but I met her again by chance, holding court at one end of a long table in a *mehana*, surrounded by villagers who hung on her every word.

"I'm sorry about the lift," she said, "but it was late and I did not feel well. You've been anyway? What did you think? I didn't like it. It is not in the Orthodox tradition, and those icons—ugh! Here, would you like to try some of this? Be careful. It is very hot." She pushed a dish towards me which proved to contain fat little roasted chillies swimming in vinegar. They were incredibly hot. I could feel my eyes watering. An old man seated at the table smiled and said something.

"He says that to eat these and to drink wine is very good," I was told, though I noticed he was doing neither.

"I know you!" piped up a spherical bespectacled woman whose mouth was almost completely innocent of teeth. "You're the Englishman who writes with his left hand. Look everybody, watch how he writes. When I was at school they tied my left hand behind my back so I couldn't use it. I was never any good at school, but now I don't have to write any more, thank God!"

"She says," began the "American", swinging her pendulous earring towards me.

"I understood."

"So! You say you don't speak Bulgarian but I think you do. You must be very clever for one so young. Now Ilya, he owns the *mehana* and he is also very clever. Tell us about Melnik, Ilya," and Ilya, a thick-set old man with a shock of white hair and a bushy moustache, began.

"There were once 14,000 people living here, and 73 churches. See, here is a photograph taken in the old days, when there were many Greeks. Now there are just 300 people. The Greeks left. No-one knows why. But they were only guests anyway. After a while a guest has to go back to his own home."

He was interrupted by the Toothless One. "This song! They are playing my song: 'Do You Have Wine' it is called. *Da, ima! Ima vino!* Yes there is! There is wine! *Nasdravye!*" She swayed slightly.

"Look at her," said the "American", "she has drunk fifteen glasses of wine today, but how to tell?" It seemed fairly obvious to me. "Now *this* is a song that I like. It tells of how Macedonian women are the most beautiful in the world. In my country—I mean California—I listened to it all the time."

"Why did you go to America?"

"My family has a restaurant in New York. I married out there, but my husband was a very jealous man. He was 51 and I was 30. He wouldn't let me go to school, so I don't speak English so good, and he wouldn't let me learn how to drive. I had to have a driver. Even now I cannot drive. She [the Toothless One] is my driver here. And did you know," she said reverting to Bulgarian, "when I filled in my forms at the frontier I had to state whether I was a Bulgarian from Macedonia or a Macedonian from Bulgaria! What do you think of that? They have two churches, one for Macedonians from Bulgaria and another for Bulgarians from Macedonia!" The assembled company was scandalized. She went round each in turn: Ilya; the old man; Ilya's son, daughter-in-law and grandson; and the other woman. Without exception they averred themselves to be Bulgarians from Macedonia and expressed wonder at the concept of a Macedonian from Bulgaria.

"There can be no such thing," said Ilya.

"But," I objected, "I have been in many parts of Bulgaria, and although Macedonians always say 'I am from Macedonia', nobody ever says 'I am from Moesia' or 'I am from Thrace', so there must be a difference between Macedonians and other Bulgarians."

"Macedonians," riposted Ilya, "are the true Bulgarians. If history was correct Bulgaria would be a province of Macedonia and not the other way around. But history is never correct. The heart of Bulgaria is here: Cyril, Clement of Ohrid, Tsar Samuel, this is our true history. That is why the best music, the best dancing, is here in Macedonia. This is the true Bulgaria. It doesn't matter what the Greeks or the Serbs say. They do not know history."

"What do you drink in England?" I was asked apropos of nothing, "Whisky?"

"Beer mostly, but our beer is not like yours. It is more like wine, dark and warm." That took them by surprise.

"The best beer," asserted the "American", "comes from Germany. Heineken and Pilsner Urquell." I forbore from mentioning that the first is Dutch and the other Czech. "In all cold countries they drink beer," she went on. "I think the cold freezes their brains. That is why they don't drink wine. How can you live without drinking wine? Anyway, American beer is just water."

"How strong is your beer?" asked Ilya. When I told him he snorted in disgust. "That's not beer, that's lemonade! Son, bring me raki!"

The party was showing every sign of going on long into the night but I had to catch the 6 o'clock bus the following morning and so I left.

Part Two
"WELCOME TO SLAKA":
VARDAR MACEDONIA

When people say "there is peace and security" then sudden destruction will come upon them as travail comes upon a woman with child, and there will be no escape
— I Thessalonians 5.15

Nationalists Flex Mussels
— *Balkan News,* Athens, 13–19 November 1994

God is no Albanian—Proverb

Skopje and the Macedonian Church

Another train, another border, but how different it was to that between Bulgaria and Turkey. No fences, no tank traps, no cemeteries. One moment we were in Igoumeni in Greece, where the Star of Vergina rested on a blue ground, the next in Gevgelija in the Republic of Macedonia where the same symbol was backed with red. Two officials in field-grey uniforms entered the compartment where I was sitting. One pushed his cap far back on his head and said "Passport." The other adjusted the little pill-box hat, the kind air hostesses sometimes wear, on her immaculately coiffed brown curls, smiled and said "English?". Ker-chunk! went the mechanical stamping machine on the page in my passport, but the device contained no ink and consequently left no impression. The intention was there though and we could all swear truthfully that my documents *had* been stamped. The couple left and I stared through the window at oil tankers branded "Zit Skopje" standing rustily in the sun, stranded by the eighteen month old trade embargo imposed by Greece. Their counterparts, still for all I knew loaded with oil paid for with Macedonia's scarce reserve of hard currency, lined the tracks on the other side of the border, unable to move until a settlement to the Graeco-Macedonian dispute could be arrived at. Until then they would stay where they were, for years if need be.

Nothing happened. After a while it did it again, only for longer. A bee buzzed lazily into my compartment and lurched around in drunken flight for a while before escaping through the open window. Outside on the platform a dog uncurled itself and yawned. The trip-trap of high heels came down the corridor and another official poked her head around the door.

"Are you from Yugoslavia?" she asked.

"No, from England."

"Oh good!" She smiled, displaying perfect white teeth framed by the reddest of lipsticks, and went trip-trapping off again.

It was all a bit of a let down really. I had been fantasizing about being hauled off the train to buy a visa, an operation which was to have involved complicated transactions in a number of currencies and repeated visits to various offices where I would be made to fill in forms in triplicate, which after a few hours would procure me a beautifully squiggly Cyrillic document with a couple of postage stamps and a bit written in by hand for good measure. I would show it to my grandchildren at intervals of roughly a year and tell them for the umpteenth time about the impossible and short-lived Republic of Macedonia. The country was meant to be under siege, for God's sake, but nobody seemed to be taking the threat of imminent and bloody war with all its neighbours at all seriously, except perhaps for the old lady who came swishing her besom along the corridor.

"How far are you going?" she asked me.

"To Skopje."

"Then the Serbs can empty your ashtray after you get off." Was this a subtle form of chemical warfare? The train was one of those little anomalies which seem to have been overlooked by the powers that be. Despite world sanctions on Yugoslavia and Greece's personal embargo against Macedonia, it was travelling from Athens to Budapest via Skopje and Belgrade, one of two daily trains to link the Greek and Serbian capitals, a vital lifeline for the Serbs and anyone else who chooses to ignore the war in Bosnia.

✳ ✳ ✳

The Republic of Macedonia does not, in international law, exist, largely at the request of the Greeks, who found the concept offensive. There is, however a state clumsily known as the Former Yugoslav Republic of Macedonia. I've never really understood that 'Former'. The country is unquestionably a republic, it is inhabited in the main by South Slavs (*yug* means "south" in all Slavonic languages) and it is located in Macedonia. The Former Republic is usually referred to as FYROM for short. According to the *Balkan News & East Europe Report* it is inhabited by a tribe of people charmingly called the Fyromians. *Balkan News* is published in Athens. Nowhere else have I seen the word Fyromian in print and I have never heard it uttered, but you can see the logic. If the country is not Macedonia it follows that it is not inhabited by Macedonians, but by somebody else. Macedonians do not exist, remember.

The Republic of Slaka was invented by Malcolm Bradbury in 1983 and first described in his novel *Rates of Exchange*, which—like all good satire—is uncannily accurate in its portrayal of pre-1989 Eastern Europe. He described it thus:

> *Located by an at once kind and cruel geography at the confluence of many trade routes ... its high mountains not too high to cut it off, its broad rivers not too broad to obstruct passage, it is a land that has frequently flourished ... but has yet more frequently been pummelled, raped, pillaged, conquered and oppressed ... Its inhabitants have seen its borders expand, contract and on occasion disappear from sight, and so confused is its past that the country could now be in a place quite different from that in which it started.*

That of course was pure fantasy. No such country as Slaka could possibly exist outside the minds of professors of American studies at English universities. But the description perfectly fits FYROM, the most improbable of all improbable European countries, which was entering yet another confusing phase in its already hopelessly confused history.

✳ ✳ ✳

And so we rumbled on into the supposedly non-existent land of FYROM through fields which spread bright green as I had never before seen, between distant snow-capped mountains which lifted their blue bulk out of the flatness of the Vardar basin. A shepherd unconcernedly directed his flock towards Greece, past another making the return journey. A huntsman, rifle over his shoulder, stalked through a coppice with two rather daft-looking mongrels at his heels. At a wayside station Fatma and Osman had made their marks, presumably on the assumption that the place was so remote that none of their relatives would chance upon this evidence of their rendezvous. A bright sun suffused the landscape with a yellow light.

Eventually the valley narrowed into a gorge still known by the Turkish name *Demir Kapija*, the Iron Gate. Craggy white limestone cliffs loomed over river and railway before we popped like a cork from a bottle into a wide vale where the Vardar sluggishly curled itself into knots and poplars determinedly marched in dead straight rows towards low hills. I was reminded of some of the more pleasant parts of Anatolia, which may explain why so many Turks settled here. It was I believe Garrison Kieller who observed that emigrants tend to settle in places that remind them of home. From time to time we would pass a village of whitewashed houses, where, on a knoll just beyond the settlement, a new church was being built, dainty little structures, with none of the *braggadocio* of modern Greek churches. They were building churches in Bosnia too, before the war. In every village where a mosque had been restored or built anew, the Serbs were responding by building a larger and infinitely uglier church just to show who was boss, to stake a claim to the land that two years later was to be 'redeemed' for Greater Serbia. It would be impossible to accuse these demure Macedonian sanctuaries of nationalist intent though. They are too retiring, and besides there *were* no mosques to counteract, there was no *irredenta*, or at least not here. It seemed simply to be a case of the villagers feeling that they needed a church, and building one.

At length we rounded a corner and were abruptly presented with a gleaming white massif which strode boldly across the horizon from west to east, its peaks sparkling in the sunlight. This was the Šar Planina, the mountains marking the northern limit of Macedonia. Beyond, less than an hour's drive from Skopje, lay the troubled province of Kosovo, the scene of the definitive defeat of Christian power in the Balkans in 1389, where in 1989 Slobodan Milosevic fanned the flames of Serbian nationalism by invoking the Serbs' sense of historical injustice at the scene of that battle. Even then there had been rioting in the streets of Kosovo's towns and the police patrolled in armoured cars. When night fell in Prizren, a mere 20 miles from Skopje, the Serbian police force would huddle for safety in the bar of a hotel on the edge of town and watch the news from Belgrade while the Albanians flooded the town's restaurants and streets. On an earlier visit some young Serbs had asked me to take their photograph with the town's bridge as a backdrop. "We don't know how long there will be Serbs here," they had said. That was 1991.

As for the Albanians who make up 90 per cent of the province's population, they had said: "We don't want to leave Yugoslavia, we want a [Yugoslav] Republic of Kosovo. We are the third largest nationality in Yugoslavia—why should Macedonians and Montenegrins have republics when we have none? Milosevic is a Fascist, no better than Hitler or Saddam Hussein. Ramiz Alia is a good man. He will help us." Ramiz Alia, Albania's last Communist president, was deposed, and his replacement Sali Berisha has more pressing problems, such as keeping his own population from fleeing to Italy and Greece. Meanwhile the situation in Kosovo has continued to deteriorate, and the Albanians have taken a leaf out of VMRO's book and established an underground parallel administration complete with president, parliament, police and schools. The unfolding story of Kosovo could not but have a profound effect on Macedonia.

✳ ✳ ✳

Skopje was hot. Very hot. I trudged down a dusty avenue away from the station past shady men who whispered "Mister—taxi". Grim towerblocks with grimy yards, empty cigarette packets and people carrying peppers in string bags filled my vision. Battered Zastavas—the miniature Yugoslav Fiat—vied for possession of the road with the Gypsies' decorated carts and buses belching out black fumes. Amazingly, the Tourist Information Office was open. Inside was a young woman who spoke fluent English and wore hip-hugging blue jeans and a T-shirt with "I love Macedonia" written on it. She rang for a room.

"Are you a journalist?" she asked.

"No, but I write. I don't suppose you get many tourists here now."

"You'd be surprised. Last summer all the beds were taken. Mostly Americans, but there were some Canadians and Australians as well. Émigrés. We Macedonians live all over."

"Melbourne for instance," I butted in. "There are many Macedonians there. And Greeks, but they don't get on. I was there for the MOOMBA arts festival (held annually). The Macedonians had a boat for a parade on the river Yarra, but the Greeks sank it."

She tossed her peroxide curls dismissively. "Greeks! Always trouble. Two weeks ago they closed the border."

"But I came through it today," I objected.

"That's different. It's closed only to Macedonians and Greeks, so we don't infect them, as if we had some kind of disease. Mad! I have been to Greece many times. It is a wonderful country, but Greek people are the worst. Completely mad! They think we will invade their country, but even if we wanted to—which we don't—how could we? We are 2 million people. They are in NATO. What contest? But I'm not doing my job. I will give you some brochures. This one's in German ..."

"No problem."

"No? Then perhaps you will like this one. It is in Greek."

My landlord, a plump elderly man in a grey suit, came and collected me in his battered white VW Beetle. "English I like very good," he proclaimed as he pumped the choke and swung madly off into the traffic.

✳ ✳ ✳

Skopje. Or Skoplje, Skupi or Üsküb depending on what language, Serbian, Albanian or Turkish, you happen to be speaking at the time. Once you enter the former lands of Austria–Hungary or the Ottoman Empire, towns tend to have several names. The city has been catapulted from the sleepy administrative centre of an underdeveloped and forgotten backwater to the capital of an independent European nation overnight and it hasn't yet entirely come to terms with the change.

It's not the first time Skopje has been a capital city though. Shortly after the Serbian King Stefan Uroš II Milutin ascended the throne in 1282 Serb armies crossed the Šar Planina into Byzantine Macedonia. Under the influence of the city's mostly Greek population the Serbian court rapidly became Hellenized, a change recorded by two Byzantine ambassadors dispatched 30 years apart. The first, which visited the court of Milutin's father Uroš I in his ancient capital of Raška in 1266 found the Serbs to be revoltingly primitive (the Serbs in their turn considered the Byzantines revoltingly effete). By 1299 the luxury of the Serbian court in Skopje was "quite Byzantine". Serbia had taken over from Bulgaria as the major Slav power in the Balkans and the Serbian cultural world was entering its golden age.

That age was to be short-lived. Its apogee came during the reign of Stefan Dušan "The Strangler" (1331–55). Dušan conquered the whole of Macedonia except for Thessaloniki, and added Albania and Epirus for good measure. In 1345 he elevated the archbishop of Pec in Kosovo to the rank of "Patriarch of the Serbs and the Greeks" and the following year he had himself crowned in Skopje as Emperor and Autocrat of Serbia and Romania, Tsar of the Serbs and the Greeks. In his own words, he was "lord of almost the whole Roman Empire".

Dušan's son, Stefan Uroš (the fourth of that name and the last of an unbroken line of Serbian kings called Stefan which reached back to 1166 and Stefan Nemanja), rapidly lost control of his father's empire after the latter's death in 1355, and a number of petty principalities arose like those of Constantine in Kyustendil and Ivan Uglješa in Serres which the Turks easily mopped up before the final showdown at Kosovo Polje in 1389, when Tsar Lazar, last descendant of Stefan Nemanja, was defeated by the Turks. Lazar's son, Stefan Lazarevic, died in 1395 fighting the Romanians on behalf of his Turkish overlords. Serbia's medieval greatness may not have lasted long but it has cast a long shadow over the imagining of modern Serbs. Dušan's kingdom was centred on Skopje, and Macedonia continues to be referred to by many Serbs as "South Serbia".

Skopje owed its position as a citadel in part to the fact that after his defeat of the Bulgarians in 1014, Basil the Bulgar-Slayer made it the centre of the new *theme*, or military-administrative district, of Bulgaria. The Turks too designated the city as capital of one of the four provinces, or *vilayet*, into which they divided Macedonia, and much of the little that is pleasant about the city is their doing. On a rock above the old town stands the ruined citadel, the Kale, looking down grandiosely on the turbulent brown waters of the Vardar, which dry to a trickle in the summer. Homer described the Vardar as "the fairest of streams", a description which has done him no good in my eyes—

nobody in their right minds could possibly describe the Vardar as "fair". An old photograph of Skopje taken around the turn of the century shows the Kale not in its present ruinous state but surmounted by an impressive range of administrative buildings and barracks, a sanctuary from which the Ottoman administrators could look out over the mass of people below.

Behind the river is the jumble of streets that comprise the bazaar, punctuated here and there by minarets. An old stone bridge allegedly of Roman origin but Turkish to all intents and purposes tentatively stretches across the river to Ploštad Marshal Tito and the new town. The river is a dividing line between old and new, between a town that—if it put its mind to it—could be fairly pleasant, and the ugly mess of the city centre where the banks, parliament, and smart shops are. It was Skopje's misfortune to be almost completely levelled in an earthquake in 1963. A plan to rebuild the city was drawn up by the United Nations, but it was soon abandoned and Skopje developed as a depressing jumble of what passed for good architecture in the mid-60s. Especially distressing are a central post office which resembles a giant concrete crown roast of lamb and the Macedonian National Theatre which emerges from the river bank like an iceberg, a mass of smooth tatty white walls leant against each other at uncomfortable angles. Even before the earthquake, though, Skopje cannot have been an attractive place.

❊ ❊ ❊

By some irony, the old Turkish part of the town was largely unscathed by the earthquake. It was the Christian sector on the Vardar's right bank which was devastated, a sector which in that early photograph seemed barely to exist. Narrow roads wind between single-storey buildings which house tea-shops and money-changers, and past derelict *hamams* and *caravanserais*. Here and there the huddle of buildings is punctuated by a slender minaret, whilst above, on the hill where the Kale stands, floats the Mustafa Pasha Mosque, Skopje's grandest and one of its oldest, a symbol of an imperial grandeur and an Islamic certitude now long gone.

Just below the mosque the little church of St Spas, the Saviour, shelters half underground behind a high fortress-like wall. When it was built in the seventeenth century Christians had to be discreet about their faith and the church is sheltered in the secure embrace of a range of buildings—the priest's house, the school—which present graceful wooden balconies to the inner courtyard and blank walls to the street. It was in the womb-like security of places such as this that the idea of a return to Christian power was gestated. St Spas is a shrine still, but not to God. No priest swings his censer before the elaborately carved iconostasis, the work of the most famous products of the Debar school of carving, the brothers Filipovic. No peasant women come to seek succour from the hardships of their daily lives. As a place of worship the church is dead, but people still come here on pilgrimage, because in the courtyard, in a granite sarcophagus under a pine tree, lies the body of Gotse Delchev. His moustached face gazes down from a photograph hung like an icon on a wall under the wooden gallery that runs around the courtyard.

St Spas has become a shrine to the twin concepts of Macedonia's nationhood and its statehood. This place exists to give legitimacy to the Macedonian claim to be a distinct people, and hence to their right to a state of their own. The Macedonians have found a new mythic hero to emulate, neither a wandering Jewish preacher nor a feudal baron like Marko, but a socialist, a revolutionary—and a schoolteacher. There is not a town or a village in Macedonia without its Gotse Delchev Street, just as in the Soviet Union there was not a settlement no matter how remote without a Lenin Street. But human gods are neither immutable nor perfect. Lenin has been deposed and the Delchev myth, his demand of "Macedonia for the Macedonians", is not immune to nationalist manipulation.

As I sat in that peacefully sunny enclosure listening to the plashing of a drinking-fountain outside, a car drew up and a party of suited men appeared. One bore a television camera on his shoulder. Two others clearly had guns under their jackets. The fourth, a grey-haired man who carried himself with gravitas, approached the sarcophagus of the dead teacher and stood before it in silence, his head bowed as if in prayer while his bodyguards stood behind him and the cameraman filmed. It was only after the party had left that I realized who that sombre old man was. I recognized him from tatty election posters from the previous October which still hung from the walls of buildings, an avuncular old man with a half smile and gleeful eyes. Kiro Gligorov, onetime head of the Macedonian League of Communists, now president of the Republic and leading a coalition government largely made up of former Communists which holds 90 out of the total of 120 seats of the single-chamber parliament. Gligorov himself won the presidency with 77 per cent of the vote and the slogan "Independence, Peace, Democracy". Now he was seeking to prove that a leopard can change its spots by visibly associating himself with the new divinity.

That footage of Gligorov worshipping at the shrine of Macedonianism would doubtless be shown on national news later that night. Simultaneously, everyone in the country would be able to see the source of their president's political legitimacy. Unlike any other politician, he comes with the direct sanction of god. That is why political leaders perform such pilgrimages to places associated with their nation's sense of history and identity. They hope to assume the embodiment of the nation into themselves.

The Delchev myth was largely the creation of the Communists. It would hardly have been in the interests of the pre-war Belgrade government to promote his legend, but to the Communists he was the ideal hero around which to build their new Socialist Macedonian nation. Fortunately they rather than the Bulgarians had the body— Yane Sandanski never carried half the cachet in Yugoslavia that Delchev did. Here was the ideal rallying point of the newly emancipated people: modernist, internationalist, federalist, socialist, revolutionary. But in the Balkans the provision of a national hero is not in itself enough to call a new people into being.

At the foot of the Kale, behind the bus station and far from Delchev's tomb stands a brash and rather ugly church, St Dimitrii. Rebecca West compared it to "an opulent two-storeyed farm building", but externally at least, it looks more like a huge casket which some philistine has ruined by smothering it in grey undercoat paint. It is a solid, no nonsense kind of place, and until recently it served as Skopje's cathedral. A steady stream of people was passing through its doors, pausing to buy candles from a sour-faced priest who sat at a rickety wooden table in the porch.

It was Easter Saturday, and the people had come to pay homage to the two-dimensional effigy of the dead Christ which lay on a crêpe draped bier in the centre of the nave under the church's curiously squashed dome. As the worshippers came near the bier a second priest, short, round and jolly, the exact antithesis of his colleague, flicked holy water over them from a chalice in his hand using what appeared to be an egg-whisk. Eggs painted red or purple and crumpled 20-denar notes were left on the bier as each supplicant crawled, giggling, underneath and then stood around chatting and trying to distract the priest, who continued to flick water about merrily as if this was quite the best game. Again I was struck by the peculiarity of a church which can be at once intellectual, mystical and almost childish, not with the contrived childishness of Evangelical churches in the West, but with a spontaneous outpouring of *bonhomie*. This was not arduous religious ritual performed for the good of the soul and the discomfort of the body. These people were *having fun*. A party atmosphere was building up before the iconostasis and under the gaze of the little carved dove which peered over the edge of an improbably high pulpit. You would have to be fit to climb up there under the eaves, and when you arrived you would be all but invisible to the congregation below, but I could imagine the priest flitting up there in a trice with a naughty gleam in his eye just for the fun of flicking water unseen onto the people below. These people were enjoying their church. The fact that they were able to do so, that they were able to celebrate Easter in Macedonia in a Macedonian Orthodox church was due in part to the work of one man. His remains lie under a black marble slab at the back of the nave. Archbishop Dositej.

The old Bulgarian patriarchate based at Ohrid in Macedonia was abolished by the Turks in 1767. Just over 100 years later, when the new Bulgarian exarchate was established, the headquarters of the new church were not in Ohrid but north of the Stara Planina, the Balkan range, in the Danube Basin. The ancient see of Ohrid was thus up for grabs in the mêlée that accompanied the expulsion of the Turks from Macedonia, although the first demand for an independent Macedonian church had been voiced in 1891 by Metropolitan Teodor of Skopje. This left an opening for the creation of a Macedonian Orthodox Church with its spiritual if not its administrative home in Ohrid which could claim descent from that earlier patriarchate and thereby give "historical" legitimacy to the Communist claim that the Macedonians were a distinct people, neither Serb nor Bulgar, who deserved a republic of their own within the Yugoslav Federation. The establishment of such a republic would have the happy effect of limiting the political clout of the Serbs, but this was of course purely incidental to rectifying the historical injustice done to the people of Macedonia by the suppression of their cultural life.

That life was, of course, linked to the church. The cultural life of all Balkan peoples was, historically, linked to the church. In fact, a national revival was unthinkable without a national church. Bulgaria could hardly claim ecclesiastical jurisdiction over Vardar Macedonia when it had no territorial jurisdiction and, besides, the Bulgarian leader Georgi Dimitrov, who was himself of Macedonian parentage, agreed with Tito that there was a Macedonian nation distinct to the Bulgarian one. In 1951 Bishop Dositej preached a sermon in Macedonian when on a visit to Skopje (all the bishops actually resident in Macedonia were Serbs). In the same year Macedonian priests demanded that these Serbs be replaced by Macedonians, and asked for permission to use Macedonian for administrative purposes and Old Church Slavonic, the language of Cyril and Methodios, in worship rather than Serbian. Four years later, the Congress of Orthodox Priests' Federations, which was of course controlled by the Federal government, proclaimed that the church in Macedonia should no longer be referred to as "Serbian". In 1957 the Serbian hierarchy met the demands of six years earlier, only to re-appoint Serbian bishops in 1958.

Meanwhile Todor Zhivkov had come to power in Bulgaria and, after exhaustive scientific research, was able to proclaim that there was no such thing as a Macedonian after all. They were Bulgarians. This understandably irritated the Yugoslavs.

The League of Communists of Macedonia, whose very existence depended on there being a Macedonian people, hurriedly called a church conference in Ohrid which duly proclaimed the church in Macedonia to be autonomous and appointed Dositej Archbishop of Ohrid and Skopje and Metropolitan of Macedonia. At the time Dositej announced that the church "would remain in canonic unity with the Serbian Orthodox Church through her head, His Holiness the Patriarch". There was now a Macedonian people. And they needed to worship in the Macedonian Church.

The Serbs were not convinced. Their patriarch continued to call himself "Patriarch of Serbia", refusing to add "and Macedonia" to his title. In fact no mention was ever made of Macedonia in Serbian church circles—it remained "South Serbia". Finally, in 1966, Dositej was moved to announce "We have agreed to seek independence from the Serbian Orthodox Church. This decision was presented to the Executive Council of Macedonia which devoted a whole session to the question and notified us we were not mistaken." Putting its trust in the theological acumen of the League of Communists, the Macedonian Church proclaimed itself autocephalous (self-governing) at a council again in Ohrid and appointed Dositej archbishop of Ohrid and Macedonia.

For his selfless devotion to the cause of emancipating the enslaved Macedonian nation, Tito presented Dositej with the Order of the Yugoslav banner (with sash). Setting up the church proved the easy part. The Macedonian Orthodox Church remains unrecognized by all others. Not that it seems to trouble the Macedonians unduly.

One of the happier architectural experiments of the new town is the new Metropolitan Cathedral of St Clement of Ohrid, which stands among trees slightly set back from Partizan Units Avenue. For an Orthodox church it is immense, a perfectly smooth dome like a giant pepper pot with four porches nestling up close to it, linked by graceful concrete arches in a harmoniously curved composition. This is the nerve centre of Macedonian Christianity, the focus of the nation's spiritual striving, and its sheer grandeur speaks volumes for the way Macedonians feel about their faith. That faith has finally emerged along with the nation from the gloomy underground of St Spas through the clumsiness of St Dimitrii to something triumphal. No religious building in the Balkans is simply that, and St Clement's is a confident statement about Macedonia's nationhood. Inside an outsized iconostasis curves around the east wall and a giant Christ gazes down from the dome surrounded by His angels. Four cosmetic 'pendentives' have been added to hold the portrayals of the Evangelists that traditionally occupy this position in the corners of the dome (the church, being all dome, has no corners). Only St Mark has been painted into place so far. He sits with his lion by the shore of Lake Ohrid with the churches of St Sofia and St Clement behind him. There can be no doubt about the link between Orthodoxy and Macedonianness here.

The Muslim Quarter of Skopje

For all the Christianity of the Macedonians, their capital is still to a large extent a Muslim city. It is the Islamic influence that predominates

in the mind of the visitor. Mosques rather than churches are what catch the eye and the undistinguishedness of the new town—which could be anywhere in Eastern Europe—results in the old Muslim quarter giving Skopje much of its character.

Time and again I found myself returning to the maze of streets that comprise the old bazaar to sip Turkish coffee in the tiny squares where fountains played under plane trees or to eat succulent kebabs or spicy sausage in restaurants which had their menus written on the walls in Albanian and Turkish as well as in Macedonian. People drifted through these streets seemingly without a care, licking ice-creams or fiddling with their worry beads. Others refreshed themselves at the drinking-fountains that cluttered the narrow polished stone streets, a legacy of the Muslim obsession with water.

Nobody was in a rush to do anything much save sit in the sun and chat with friends. Boys scurried here and there carrying trays of tea, or hawked cigarettes, their voices huskily crying "Marl-boro! Marl-boro!" Shops offered imported pornographic videos and day trips to Tirana. I found just one Islamic bookshop, carrying titles with Albanian names and a single Macedonian edition of *The Beauty of Namaz.*

The Muslim theological seminary (*madrasa*) had just had its graduation day, and the photographic images of the new *'ulema* were displayed on a board in the bookshop window, with a tri-lingual text naming each one. They were all young men in their 20s, looking very self-conscious under the red fez and white turban they were entitled to wear for the first time as qualified experts in the esoteric mysteries of *hadith* (traditions of the Prophet), *tafsir* (Qur'anic exegesis) and *fiqh* (jurisprudence). They would go on to become the imams of Macedonia's mosques, responsible not only for performing the rites of Islam but for ensuring the next generation of Albanian and Turkish children grew up in the faith of their ancestors in this Christian land. I wondered what they had learnt in their studies, the intolerant Wahhabi creed or one of the more generous interpretations of the Islamic message. I hoped the latter; Islam in the Balkans has seldom been fanatical. Historically, it has been not Muslims, but Christian nationalists expressing their nationalism through their Christianity who have been responsible for inter-religious strife in the region.

Nothing stays the same for long. On my first visit to Skopje in 1991 those narrow streets winding past mosques and solid old *caravanserais*, or *hans*, as these old warehouses-cum-inns are known in the Balkans, had been the haunt of Gypsy metal workers, who hammered out horseshoes and bent over lathes under the watchful eye of Marshal Tito. They had without exception described themselves as Turks—Gypsies were discriminated against, and since all Muslims were commonly referred to as "Turks", the temptation to adopt that name must have been overwhelming. Besides, it was just possible that another of the periodic arrangements with Turkey allowing Turks to leave Yugoslavia for the "mother country" would be arrived at, and anyone calling themselves a Turk would be eligible for an exit visa. Many Muslims had already proclaimed themselves Turks and taken advantage of similar opportunities.

Today those workshops have vanished, and in their place are jewellers and travel agents, interspersed with restaurants whose glazed charcoal grills project into the street so that potential customers can see what's cooking and teashops whose all-male clientele sit all day in a blue fog of cigarette smoke playing backgammon. Where once buildings were tumble-down to the point of imminent collapse and the streets were muddy and unswept, there is now a smart—or relatively so—

shopping street paved in pristine stone flags polished smooth by the passage of people's feet. Where the metal workers have gone I have no idea, but the old bazaar is steadily going up market.

Take any one of the narrow streets that snake through this area, and sooner or later you are bound to emerge in Skopje's main marketplace, the Bit Pazar, whose name in Turkish literally means "flea market". That name, to a Westerner, is misleading, for this flea market does not specialize in brass candlesticks and old regimental badges being picked over by only half-interested punters. It is the main market of the city, always chaotic, always crowded. Long metal trestles stretch away groaning under the weight of piles of fresh vegetables or consumer goods of dubious provenance. Anything and everything is available here, from jars of honey and crushed chillies to satellite dishes and exhaust pipes. Every language imaginable, Arabic, Greek, Turkish, Finnish, appears on the packaging of radios or toothpaste, whisky or children's dolls. Every language, that is, but Macedonian.

Macedonia itself produces very little in the way of consumer goods, and what is sold in the Bit Pazar is what is brought home by returning migrant workers or spirited over the border by organizations with names such as the "Macedo-Iraqi Import-Export Company" (which advertises itself with a fine line in calendars which depict trucks and scantily clad women), or "Skopje–Rotterdam B.V." Everyone is shouting, the stallholders to attract the attention of customers away from neighbouring stalls selling exactly the same produce: "Come buy my fine cucumbers!" The potential buyers, their faces set in scowling expressions of disdain, berate the mothers of people who could display such shoddy produce and have the nerve to bestow on it the honourable name of cucumber. Meanwhile buses move slowly along the main road along one side of the site, roaring as if in agony and belching out acrid black fumes which mingle with the smell of charcoal and grilling kebabs.

I took refuge from the disorder of the market in the overgrown garden of a mosque where yellow wildflowers all but engulfed the simple white gravestones. The octagonal domed *türbe* of some saint or other emerged from the undergrowth, cracked blue tiles falling from the frieze around its drum. Groups of men sat around the *sadirvan* or on benches under the trees, chatting, smoking, reading the Qur'an. More arrived slowly, in dribs and drabs, taking their time to greet acquaintances. It was coming near to the time for the noon prayer. The imam strode past in his turban, treading with a light but determined step. "*Salaam Aleikum*," he greeted me before entering an out-house, followed by a string of supplicants. A spindly old man with sharp creases in the trousers of his light brown summer suit and a fez on his head turned a craggy face surmounted by bushy white eyebrows towards me, and after a measured scrutiny turned back to face the *türbe*, holding his hands up before his face in an attitude of prayer. Conversations were subdued. People moved as if in slow motion, gently gliding back and forth to the sound of the water splashing from the ablutions fountain. Here in a small pocket amidst the chaos of modern Skopje a tiny fragment of the elegance of Ottoman culture at its best had survived the modern age. One by one the minarets of the city began to issue the *ezan* and the people gradually filed into the mosque.

After about 20 minutes they began to emerge again and go off about their business. A few asked "Who are you? What are you doing?" as they walked past me, only mildly curious, though some paused to whisper to their neighbours "He's from England!" Soon two young men were standing before me.

"Hello," said one, a solidly built man of about 25. A fine down of beard covered his cheeks and chin, and he had brown eyes with which he looked at you directly. "My name is Bayram [Holiday]. This is Fetih [Victory]."

Fetih nodded his jovially ruddy face and smiled.

"I am learning English," Bayram confided. "So is Fetih. Do you speak English? It is very important that we learn, because otherwise how can we be European?" I introduced myself, and Bayram continued in his gentle, lilting voice:

"You don't work for the UN, do you? I thought not. All the UN people do is drive around in their big white cars and spend their money everywhere. They don't really care about us. You would never meet a UN person at a mosque—not even the Egyptians. What are you interested in, religion or politics?"

"Both. Sometimes they go together. How many Muslims are there in Skopje."

"The city is half-Muslim and half-Christian—Macedonian Orthodox. Most of the Muslims are Albanians like us, but there are a few Turks."

"Gypsies?"

"I don't think so. If there are they don't live in houses. They must live in the country. Besides, we must not call them Gypsies now. We must say *Roma* for some reason, but they're still Gypsies just the same. This is something the government has done for some reason, perhaps so they think that they are different. They have their own political party now."

"Do you think that now that Macedonia is independent it is better than before?" Fetih turned back to me.

"In some ways it is better, in some worse," he said. "You know about Kosovo? We have no Serbians here now to tell us what to do. Look at Bosnia. But now there is little work. This is a very small country, only two million people. What can we do? Over all life is better though."

"But I heard there had been trouble in Tetovo." Tetovo, an overwhelmingly Albanian town west of Skopje had been the scene of violent clashes two months earlier between police and demonstrators demanding an Albanian-language university. An Albanian youth had been killed, 28 injured and the leaders of the protest, including Fadlil Suleimani, the "rector" of an illegal underground college, arrested. Western commentators began to issue dark predictions of further ethnic violence and even civil war.

"You have heard about our university then?" asked Bayram eagerly. "Yes, we must have a university, otherwise how can we better ourselves? Now they are trying to make a political issue out of it by saying we can't have one."

"Why do you think that is?"

"Because Muslims do all of the dirty work. If I go to university my place is in an office, not in the fields. They want to keep the office jobs for themselves. There should not be violence or shouting—Macedonians and Albanians should talk to each other, should understand each other. This is a civilized country."

✳ ✳ ✳

I walked on through dusty streets shaded by plane trees, past the "Nur International Dragstor [*sic*], Telephone, Currency Exchange". A sleek grey Volvo, its Tirana licence-plates decorated with a black double-headed eagle, jostled for space in the road with a bus from Istanbul.

Backstreet coffee shops were filled with men playing cards while women amply swathed in raincoats and black headscarves pounded the hot streets with bags of shopping. Up a dirt road I came across a low mosque with gleaming copper roofs. Through plate glass windows I could see the newly refurbished prayer-hall, but a stumpy minaret showed the building to be older than it seemed. A young boy stood watching me sullenly, a finger in his mouth. I asked him whether the mosque was new.

"Yes, it is new," he replied before running off, embarrassed by the stranger who asked stupid questions.

The main road was dominated by a huge and totally square mosque capped with a pyramidal roof. I turned off the road and drifted past houses built of concrete and mud brick till I was near its encircling wall. Some teenage boys, seeing me, cried out "Hey, foreigner! Take our photograph! *Shqiper!*" and flapped their arms. *Shqiper* is what the Albanians call themselves. The name means "Eagle". "Would you like to see our mosque?" one of them asked.

In the courtyard of the mosque two men were sitting under the canopy of the *sadirvan* resting their feet in its cold water. A third man in an olive-green suit and wearing a white lace skull-cap on his head came up to me, fingering his worry beads.

"Where are you from?" he asked, his weak grey eyes searching my face. His own face was kindly enough, with its wrinkled brown skin and bushy white moustache, but I couldn't help feeling that he had some sadness about him, some sense of loss.

"I don't speak English or German," he apologized, "but I understand your Russian. Let me show you our mosque."

He went in and switched on the lights while I struggled with the laces on my boots, to bare my feet. Inside the building was wonderfully cool after the searing afternoon sun. The walls seemed to have been adorned with marble. The whole place was Spartan, bare, just a box with a wooden ceiling on which had been painted some calliagrams, with the name of Allah, Muhammed and his four immediate successors, the "Rightly Guided Ones".

"This is the oldest mosque in Skopje," I was told, "more than 470 years old. It is named Yahya Pasha after its founder. Now there is no more Yugoslavia so our boys do not have to go to Sarajevo, they can study in the *madrasa* here. Many people come here to pray. Things are so much better here now than they were. Are there problems between Christians and Muslims? Of course not! This isn't Yugoslavia!"

We shook hands as I left. "Have a nice time in Macedonia," the old man said.

I continued through the back streets of little concrete villas with kilims hanging over their balconies. Everything seemed perfectly peaceful. There was no hint of the war raging not far away in Bosnia. From a nineteenth-century Orthodox church loudspeakers were blaring forth hymns in honour of Easter. People came to light candles in front of the bier in the nave with its cross decorated with a towel and a pair of socks. Vaguely I wondered whether prayer at Easter was sovereign for cold feet. Outside in the courtyard, sheltering under a juniper, a tethered sheep quietly munched grass seemingly oblivious of the fate that was to befall it on Easter day. I hope it enjoyed its last meal.

Rifa'i Dervishes

I got lost wandering through those roads away from the centre of town. Each was much like another, similarly decrepit, similarly dusty, always lined with plane trees and little shops.

After a while I stopped on a patch of waste-ground by a ruined lorry which had come to rest leaning heavily on a flat tyre as if it had finally given in to despair and was resigned simply to rusting where it stood. Behind the lorry was a low, apparently derelict building whose rough whitewashed stone wall was relieved by narrow windows protected by iron grilles. A black painted metal gate with the Islamic star and crescent moon welded onto it was open, revealing a courtyard beyond, and to one side of the gate a stone plaque clung to the wall. "Historical Nation Monument," the plaque read, " *Tekke* of the Rifa'i". It was a dervish meeting house. Inside the grass had grown up to knee height. Wooden doors and shutters that had once been painted green hid inner secrets from me. Here and there gravestones beautifully carved with Arabic script leaned against one another like a party of drunken ghosts. A fountain trickled carelessly, watering a tiny patch of watercress. Above it another plaque declared that it had been donated some years previously "to the Sufis of Üsküb" by two Turkish men.

A door creaked and a boy of about twelve with long brown hair, round eyes and a faint down on his upper lip emerged. He looked at me expectantly.

"Do you speak English?" I asked him in Macedonian.

"No," he replied, "I only speak Macedonian. If you like I will get my father. He speaks German, if that is good."

For the first time I noticed that the courtyard was connected to a second one which was filled with growing vegetables and flanked by a small house with a veranda along one side into which the boy ran.

"Daddy," he cried, "an Englishman to see you!"

A portly middle-aged man whose grey polyester jersey was slightly too small for him emerged. Seeing me he crammed a white fez with a black turban, a kind I had not seen before, onto his head.

"What can I do for you?" he asked in German.

"I'm writing a book about religion in Macedonia," I replied. "Can you tell me about the dervishes here?"

"Sit down," he said, indicating a bench and slowly levering himself into a sitting position. Leaning on his knees he examined me along the length of his beaky nose, wheezing from time to time. Then he wiggled his eyebrows and asked,

"Where are you staying?"

"In private accommodation—not a hotel." He nodded his approval.

"What do you know about dervishes?" He sucked his teeth, scanning me.

"I've done some reading in England. Also I have visited some *tekkes*, some *türbes*. I saw Mevlana in Konya, as well as Shams-i Tabriz. I have seen Haci Bektas in Anatolia, I have been to Bokhara ..."

"Bahauddin [Naqshiband, who is buried near Bokhara]—very good."

"Yes. There is also a *tekke* of the Naqshibandiyya near where I live in London."

"Dervishes of the Naqshibandiyya? They must be from Cyprus."

"Yes." Actually I think the members of that *tekke* are Pakistani, but if he wanted Cypriots, Cypriots he should have.

"What are the *tariqat*?"

"Naqshibandi after Bahauddin, Mevlevi, Bektashi, Qadiri ..."

"And in which countries are there dervishes?"

"Turkey, Afghanistan, Chechnya, India ..."

"What is the *tariqa* in India?"

"Chishti."

"Very good. Come this evening between seven and eight. There will be many dervishes here and we will make *zikr*." I had passed the test. I was in.

* * *

Dervishism, or Sufism as it is sometimes called, is probably the one phenomenon within Islam that, along with "fundamentalism", has generated the most research, the most literature and the most confusion. The very fact that "dervish" and "Sufi" are often used as synonyms points to this confusion. The two phenomena are distinct, but because the former is to a large extent derived from the latter this distinction has often been overlooked, not only by Western and Muslim scholars, but as often as not by the dervishes themselves. Typically Sufism is called "mystical Islam" or some such thing. Its name is said to be derived from the word *suf*, which in Arabic means "wool"—a reference to the woollen robes Sufis are supposed to wear or to have worn. Sufism is regarded as something dependent on Islam, in fact in some ways it is seen as a reaction against the formal text-based religion taught in such centres of learning as Cairo's al-Azhar. As a result Sufism has often been described as "popular Islam" or "parallel Islam" (when it is not being characterized by Muslim scholars as anti-Islam), and any religious activity not specifically enjoined by the Qur'an has been attributed to the activity of Sufis, in part giving rise to the belief that the survival of religious and magical rituals in Soviet Central Asia was due to the presence of Sufi adepts. Sufis are supposedly secretive and fanatical, jealously guarding their secrets. They are said to be divided into "orders" each of which follows the teachings and rituals laid down by a particular teacher, usually sometime between 1100 and 1500.

If anybody cared actually to *ask* the Sufis, which few bother to do, they would quickly find that none of this is the case. What Sufism actually *is*, though, is a much harder matter to define. In fact it is impossible for somebody who is not himself or herself a Sufi. Although the content of Sufism remains constant, its form is continually changing to meet the needs of the age, and this makes it hard to pin down except in the most general sense: "it is a teaching".

What *can* definitely be said is that there exist several organizations throughout the Muslim world and beyond, which are formalized into groups and which believe themselves to be, and are popularly believed to be, following the teachings of particular people who undoubtedly were Sufis, such as Rumi. These groups borrow Sufi terminology by the spadeful as well as assiduously studying the writings of Sufis from the past (despite the fact that Sufis will tell you that these writings were written at specific times for specific purposes and are not to be extrapolated from uncritically). All these groups claim a direct line of spiritual descent through which the original teaching has passed into the modern age, and there is no reason to doubt that this is indeed the case—but the teaching has remained static. The group has become a cult. Sufis are particularly scathing of cults of any kind whether or not they are religious, seeing them as hindrances to human potential rather than aids to spirituality. However, as one Sufi commentator has written, "they have continued to ransack the Sufi tradition for materials to support their own weirdery."

That comment was directed particularly at western groups and "mystics" such as Gurdjieff, but groups remain in the Muslim world which have not only adopted half-understood aspects of Sufism, but believe themselves to be Sufis. The same Sufi intellectual quoted above has described these organizations, for which the word *tariqa* (literally "the way") is commonly used, as

> *groups of Muslim religious zealots who gather for communal prayer-exercises which stimulate them emotionally and sometimes have a cathartic effect ... these coteries are often in reality groups of fanatics using the Sufi form. Some are plainly hysterics. Others never have heard of any other form of Sufism.*

These are the dervishes, a group who have been around almost as long as Islam itself. It is these on whom most scholarship has focused, albeit often unknowingly. Their "communal prayer-exercises" can take many forms, all of which are known as *zikr*. In the nineteenth century it was briefly fashionable to categorize dervish sects, or *tariqat*, as "whirling" or "howling" according to whether their *zikr* took the form of a dance like that of the Mevlevis or of chanting. Lucy Garnett, whose book about dervishes in the Ottoman Empire—first published in 1912—is fascinating as much for its inaccuracies as for anything else, particularly associated "howling" with the Rifa'i *tariqa*.

Confusion sets in when it is realized that Sufis too practise *zikr*. The difference is that while dervishes seem to do it to induce states of ecstasy which are interpreted as proximity to the divine, Sufis claim that the exercises fulfil an entirely different function, that of *metempsychosis*, changing not *what* a person thinks but the *way* that person thinks. Unlike the ecstasy of the dervish, this change is intended to be permanent. A dervish must continually repeat the *zikr* to achieve his high, rationalizing it as a form of worship. The Sufi may or may not perform it, depending on whether his or her teacher considers it necessary to the achievement of the desired change. Psychological literature is filled with discussions of the effect of chanting, breath control, music and dancing on the brain. Religious literature is filled with information on the use of such activity as a form of worship. It was this that I had been invited to witness. It is this which is the essence of dervishism, and this in particular is what many "orthodox" Muslims are objecting to when they complain that "Sufism" is un-Islamic or anti-Islamic.

✳ ✳ ✳

That evening I returned to the *tekke*. A few men were milling about, but it was the boy who led me through a low door and into a green-painted corridor. "In here," he said, motioning me into a dimly lit room. Beautiful kilims lay on the floor and on the divan which ran around three walls of the room. By the fourth wall, where the door was, a wood-burning stove spluttered and hissed, a kettle on top hissing gently in harmony with it. Green curtains covered the few windows, blocking out all light from outside. On the wall hung pictures of the Kaaba, a child-like representation of Rumi's tomb in Konya and some calliagrams. I recognized the name of Allah and a decorative design I had seen before, the Arabic writing contorted into the shape of the hat and turban of the Mevlevi dervishes, Rumi's followers. The boy motioned me to sit on the divan next to a sheepskin. "That is the sheikh's seat," he told me, pointing to the fleece.

Opposite me sat an old man wearing a tatty grey jacket. Some six feet tall, he seemed to have been sitting there forever. A voluminous beard flowed from his chin to halfway down his chest. On his head was a skull-cap with a tartan scarf wrapped tightly around it which made his ears seem abnormally large, matching a beaked nose which projected in front of him. He was trying to be solemn, but his eyes were sparkling and smiles constantly played across his lips. "*Salaam Aleikum,*" he murmured, placing his right hand on his heart. "*Marhaba. Wilkommen.*" A mischievous grin flicked across his face. "I am a sheikh. Not *the* sheikh, but a sheikh. Do you speak Turkish? Or Arabic? Or Albanian? I'm Albanian, but one language is much like another really. They are all the same. We are all the same." He hummed a snatch of a tune to himself. "I'm called Dervish by the way. Dervish by name and dervish by nature!"

He took a cigarette in his long fingers and sucked hard, expelling the smoke slowly with a soft cry of "*Hu!*" which seemed to have come from somewhere deep inside him.

Gradually I was introduced to the other dervishes. Most of them were young, in their 20s and 30s, though a few were older and there were a couple of boys not yet in their teens. As each came in he bowed, hand on heart, to the sheikh's seat before taking his place on the divan.

"Do you speak German?" someone asked me, and simultaneously I heard "Where is he from?"

"Yes, I speak German," I said in that language and again in Russian for good measure. "I'm from England."

"What did he say?" piped up a wizened nut of a man in a reedy voice, "Holland?"

"No!" came a chorus of voices. "England! Bree-tan-ee-yah!"

A spokesman was elected. He was aged around 30, with a round swarthy face, lank black shoulder-length hair and a droopy moustache. He had a slightly wild look, as if he had just emerged from Genghis Khan's horde. On his head was a white skull-cap with orange and gold embroidery. He spoke excellent German, far better than mine. Twenty people spoke to him at once, but he managed to condense their words into a single sentence:

"What is your work?"

"I teach in London University."

"What faculty?"

"Religion—Islam." I threw in a few technical terms in an effort to look impressive. They were baffled.

"But why study Islam if you are not a Muslim? Are your parents Muslim? What do they think of you learning Islam? Don't they mind?"

We were interrupted by the arrival of the sheikh, the same man I had spoken to that afternoon. I now understood the significance of the turban—it indicated his sheikhly status. Everyone stood up until he had lowered himself onto his sheepskin. He sat for a moment leaning against some cushions, looking aloof and fingering his rosary. Then he spoke.

"*Wilhelm! Das ist Ihre Name, nicht so?*" he addressed me in German. The circle of dervishes stared at me, eyes agog. My status had risen enormously. I was on first-name terms with their sheikh. He transfixed me with his eyes. "What do you want to know?"

I should have been prepared for that but I wasn't. I asked the first thing that came into my mind.

"How many dervishes are there in Skopje, and to what orders do they belong?"

"Ach, this is trivial!" he replied. "Have you heard of Alexander Popovic at the Sorbonne? He has a good friend, a Belgian, who made a study of this *tekke*. Do you speak French? Then I will bring you his book. It contains all the answers to that kind of question. Ask again!"

"Put on the spot like that it's hard to think of anything," I said feebly.

"Then your mind is like a pond full of fish. You must catch just one fish and bring it to me. I will get the book. That will help you to think." We all rose again as he left. Twenty pairs of eyes looked at me expectantly.

"How can I go to England?" a hollow-cheeked man asked me suddenly.

"You can't. You'd never get a visa," I replied. "There are Bosnians in England, but there's a war there. There's no war in Macedonia." As a joke it was a terrible effort, and it went down like a lead balloon.

"I am from Kosovo," the man persisted. "Do you know what is happening in Kosovo? I cannot live there. I must have a visa for England. Why can I not get one?"

"No war," his neighbour reminded him.

"No, I want the Englishman to tell me. Why not?"

"Look," I said ungraciously, "I'm not the prime minister, I don't make these decisions. Anyway, why not go to Albania or Macedonia?"

The sheikh swept back into the room, his eyes ablaze.

"We will not talk politics here! This is a place of God! You may only talk about religion!" He glared at me accusingly, then threw down a book. "Read this," he said resuming his seat on the sheepskin. The others began to ask him questions, addressing him respectfully as *Sheikhbaba*. They spoke in Macedonian, with Turkish words creeping in from time to time.

I picked up the book, a slim volume entitled *Les Rifâ'îs de Skopje, Structure et Impact,* and flicked through it. The *tekke* had at one time been in Kyustendil, just over the border in what is now Bulgaria. In 1878, when Kyustendil was incorporated in the new Bulgarian principality and Turks were no longer welcome, the present sheikh's great-grandfather had removed it first to Veles, where there was a large Turkish community, and then to Skopje, still the Turkish city of Üsküb. When that city fell to the Serbs in 1912 the *tekke* had stayed put— obviously the dervishes were tired of trying to outrun history, but ironically it was that decision which saved them.

Had the *tariqa* again uprooted itself and fled to Ottoman territory it would ultimately have fallen foul of Atatürk's reforms, which resulted in the suppression of dervishism in Turkey. To Atatürk dervishes were obscurantists, not worthy of a place in the modern Turkey he was building, relics of a time that he was condemning to the dustbin of history. Their leaders were a source of religious authority alongside the *'ulema,* and whilst the latter could be brow-beaten into doing his will, the dervishes could not. Said Nursi, a member of the Naqshibandiyya, had even had the effrontery to raise the tribespeople of the east in rebellion against him. Dervishes were useful only if they were dead— Haci Bektas' statement that "a country that does not educate its women will never advance" obviously chimed with Atatürk's new ideology.

Ironically, the Bektashi *tariqa* was the one most associated with the Ottoman authorities—by the early nineteenth century it had among other things become a kind of trades guild for the janissary corps.

The sheikh was leaning back looking at me disdainfully again. "Now speak," he commanded. "Where have you seen Sufis?"

"I have never seen *zikr* before," I confessed, "but I have spoken to people in Konya. Also I have been to Hacibektas."

"Where is Haci Bektas? In which town?"

The fact that the saint had been dead these 500 years was irrelevant. I had been to see him in person, perhaps even gained some of his *baraka,* his blessing, from doing so.

"In Hacibektas," I replied.

"But in *which town?*"

"You misunderstand. The town is named after the Master."

The sheikh smiled. "This is good," he said. "And you have been in Konya. How do Mevlevis make *zikr?* What do they wear?"

I described their curious whirling dance, one hand stretched up and the other down to transmit, it is said, the divine *baraka* from heaven to earth (though that sounds like an old wives' tale), and their garb of skirt and tall felt hat.

"Can you tell me something about *baraka?*" I asked. "As you know, when a Sufi dies, a *mazar* is often built," I used the Persian word for "tomb", "In Central Asia I have seen people—not dervishes—rubbing their hands on these *mazars* like this …" I rubbed my hand against the wall behind me. Powdery green paint came off onto it. It illustrated my point perfectly. Pointing at my hand, I said, "This is the *baraka*. It goes onto their hands, and then they rub it off onto their faces."

Baraka is less of a "blessing" than a divine energy. It comes from God. Saints have it. Prophets, of course, have it. Dervish Sheikhs also are believed to have it. Like energy, it can be neither created nor destroyed, but it can be transmitted. One way of transmission is by association. When a saint dies his *baraka* remains with his body, but it can be transferred by close proximity to that body. As a result the tombs of saints have often become places of pilgrimage.

"That is the Naqshibandiyya. Here people often pray at the *türbeler* [using the Turkish word]. Sometimes they even go to pray at churches. It is normal. Let me tell you some history. You have heard of Ahmed Yassavi, Mevlana Rumi, Burhanuddin Naqshiband. All these people came from Khorasan, now Afghanistan, Iran, Turkmenistan, Uzbekistan. This is where Sufism is from. Later, it went to Spain but there was a big war with the Christians and in the time of Harun ar-Rashid it went to Baghdad. In this time the Iranians worshipped fire and the Turks were Shamanists. The dervishes went to the Turks in Central Asia and mixed dervishism with Shamanism and brought the Turks to Islam, so the true Islam of the Turks is dervishism."

The gist of what he was saying I had heard many times before, but I was less sure of his chronology.

"I have read that there may be links between dervishism and Shi'ism," I prompted.

The sheikh answered my question by saying, "That is absurd. Wherever you have read that dervishism and Shi'ism are the same, it was a very bad book. There is no link. Shi'is are not true Muslims. They worship fire. Khomeini worships fire, like all Iranians from ancient history."

He was annoyed again, and found some pressing business to see to. Moments after he had left, the stove collapsed sending a shower of sparks onto the carpet and clouds of pungent smoke into the room. The offending article was hastily removed. I felt guilty, as if by some unknown mechanism I had been responsible for the collapse. A small brown trickle of tea dribbled across the floor.

I jotted down a few notes.

"Are you writing in Arabic?" asked a voice at my elbow.

"No. I just write with my left hand."

"Strange. I've never seen that done before. It would be useful for writing Arabic though. I always smudge the ink."

"How long have you been a dervish?" I asked.

"Thirty years. I began when I was 31."

"Why did you become one? Is it better than going to mosque and making *namaz*?"

"Of course it is!" exclaimed the Mongolian-looking character. "When you make *namaz* it is all just movement, just ritual. You do it automatically, but you might be thinking not of Allah but of something else—of what you will do next, say. When I do *zikr* it comes from my heart, I give my whole body to Allah. I think this is the true Islam. It must come from inside, not from a ritual."

The sheikh returned. "You have been talking about *zikr*," he said. "You know of Martin Luther, the great Protestant? Why did the Catholics make war on him? Because Protestantism comes from the heart, not from the bishops. Dervishes are like Protestants, because *zikr* is from the heart, not from the *'ulema*. You see," he held up his rosary beads, "I have 99 beads here. God has 99 names. The first is Allah." He ran his fingers down the beads, stopping about a third of the way down. "This one is Hu. These are the most powerful names. So we say 'Allah-hu'. Now it is time for *zikr*."

✳ ✳ ✳

A lighted candle was placed in the middle of the floor and a black cloak draped around the sheikh's shoulders. Then the lights were put out and the group knelt in a ring around the candle, focusing on its single hypnotic flame.

"Allah-hu!" exclaimed the sheikh, and they began to sing a hymn, their strong voices filling the room rhythmically.

Then they started to chant: "Ya ... Illah-hu ... Ilallah ... A*ll*ah ya ... A*ll*ah ya ... Ya illah-he i*l*allah, ya illah-he i*l*allah ..."

Slowly the chant gained momentum and volume. I could feel my heart beat beginning to fall into the rhythm of the words. The stress on i*l*allah became more and more pronounced, until suddenly the volume decreased and the chanting came in breathy pants rising from somewhere deep inside them. An old man, the one who had thought I was Dutch, began to sing a hymn over the top of the subduedly incessant sound and occasional shouted instructions from the sheikh which directed the speed and intensity of the chant. From time to time he simply shouted out "Ya Allah!"

The words of the man next to me were coming out in sobs now as the dervishes began to sway back and forth on their haunches. Casting an eye at the sheikh I could see tears streaming down his face. Faster and faster the chant went. Some of the younger dervishes were swaying as if possessed, unable to control their movements. Skull-caps began to fly off.

At a spoken word from the sheikh, they stopped and began to exhale long draughts of air. "Hu ... hu ... hu ..." Then the sheikh started them off again.

"*Ul*-lah ya Al-lah, *Ul*-lah ya Al-lah ..."

Again the chant started off slowly, gradually picking up speed and intensity before abruptly becoming hushed, breathily insistent. My head was beginning to swim, my heart beating exactly in time with the chant. The old man's song seemed to be coming from somewhere a very long way away, and it was boring itself through my skull. Involuntarily my lips began to form the words.

"Allah! Ya Allaah!" cried the Sheikh. "Hu, Hu, ya Allah! Hu, Hu, ya Allah!" continued the dervishes irresistibly, faster and faster.

There was nothing but the chant, nothing but those two words, Allah Hu.

Skopje had vanished.

The room had vanished.

All we were left with was a small point of light which flickered faintly, and Allah Hu.

At the last moment, just when the momentum seemed unstoppable and we seemed condemned to spend a timeless eternity locked in the sacred words, the sheikh said "Ya Allah", drawing out the last syllable and in an instant we were back with the calming breathing exercise of "Hu … Hu … Hu …" The sound of the exhaling dervishes itself filled the room.

We were not finished yet. That calming exercise was the basis for the next chant.

"Hu … Hu … Hu … *Hu!* Hu … Hu … Hu … *Hu!* " the first three words drawn out, the fourth short, abrupt.

Again I involuntarily found myself swept up in it.

An amazing transformation had come over the dervishes. Before the *zikr* started they had been alert, jovial, civilized people. Now they seemed wild, fanatical, possessed. Something darkly elemental had emerged, something uncontrollable and threatening. Who knows what people in this state would be capable of doing?

To my relief they stopped. The Mongolian began to sing a hymn, punctuated from time to time by subdued murmurings of "Allah-hu Akbar." It was refreshingly normal.

Then the chanting started again briefly before the sheikh began to lead them in responses. The word *haq*, meaning "truth" and one of the names of God, was mentioned frequently. Each statement carried the same reply, eagerly expressed by the worshippers. I didn't catch what it was, except that it ended with the name of Muhammed.

After a while the sheikh began to delegate others to say or chant the initial words the congregation was responding to, calling them by name. Sometimes they uttered just a couple of words, sometimes whole stanzas. One of the dervishes was reluctant to take his turn but the sheikh insisted. Another replied "Nothing" when he was asked what he had to say and the sheikh passed on. Then they rose and turned towards the door, the direction of Mecca, and chanted a prayer.

The *zikr* ended with a final cry of "Hu! Hu! Hu!" and everyone resumed their seats.

✳ ✳ ✳

I felt exhausted, but when the lights were put back on the dervishes appeared no different to before the *zikr*, just a group of men who had come to drink tea and have a chat. The menace of that bizarre atmosphere generated by the chanting dervishes had passed as if the last hour or so had never been.

The sheikh hung up his gown and took a crumpled banknote from his pocket, which he handed to the boy Rifat, his son.

"Go and get some *lokum*." he said, resuming his customary seat. We sipped glasses of tea and nibbled the *lokum*. I've never liked Turkish Delight, but etiquette demanded that I take my share.

A couple of the dervishes asked permission to leave, which was granted to them. They approached the sheikh with a curious gait, taking three paces forwards and then pausing, the toes of the right foot touching the side of the left. Each in turn kissed the sheikh's hand and then retreated backwards, stopping in the doorway to bow before disappearing.

"I know about England!" somebody announced. "They have Naqshibandis from Cyprus there. Their sheikh is called Nazim." He leapt up and took a photograph off the wall. It showed a man with a bushy black beard whose white robes matched his turban. "This is Sheikh Nazim!" There is a Naqshibandi *tekke* in the Turkish sector of Nicosia. I don't know whether it is still used, but it is well maintained. I had been shown a photograph of the local dervishes taken sometime in the 1920s. Sheikh Nazim must be the grandson of the commanding man who had stood centre-stage in that photograph.

"Where are the Qadiris?" somebody else asked me.

"In India."

"I know all about the Qadiris," exclaimed Dervish, springing to his feet with amazing agility for a man who must have been at least 70. "They make *zikr* like this. They have a fire in the middle and they go around it like so." He danced lightly anti-clockwise around an imaginary fire. "They have bare feet, not even socks, and they walk through the fire. They never get burnt." He sat down again, beaming. Everyone was staring at him incredulously. "Strange people these Indians," he added by way of explanation. The sheikh chuckled indulgently to himself, clicking his beads.

The ancient who had sung during the *zikr*, a shrivelled old man who looked almost as if he had been dried to a paper crispness by the wind, was ordered to sing again. His cracked voice came out hesitantly at first but once started there seemed no way of stopping him. Words of praise for Allah spilled from his mouth and flitted hauntingly around the room with no seeming source, at least not in any human agency. The old man was completely motionless, his eyes half closed and his lips barely moving.

"This is our oldest dervish," I was told. "He is 80 years old and he has been a dervish for 70 of them. A very special man."

It was almost eleven by now. I could see there were things the dervishes wanted to discuss with their sheikh without my presence, so I requested permission to leave, citing in justification the fact that it was the eve of Easter, and as a good Christian I should be making my way to church. The sheikh clasped my hand strongly.

"First you will see the *semahane*, the proper one which we use for special occasions. Come back any time if you want to ask more questions."

The wild-looking youth led me into another room, where we were joined by Rifat and a few others. The hall smelled damp, and was only dimly lit. The back wall was painted green and near to the *mihrab* a row of pikes leaned against the wall. Some rolled-up flags rested in one corner. Hanging up was an array of sickles, daggers, swords and maces. Begging bowls also hung there, a reminder of the times when mendicant dervishes would roam the land performing minor religious or magical ceremonies and living off charity. The word "dervish" in fact means "poor". The youth took one of the maces off the wall and swung it. Chains flew out dangerously from its rotating head. The shaft was a foot long and ended in a sharp steel spike.

"On *really* special occasions," he said, "we use these. You put it here, here and here." He made as if to stab himself through his tongue, cheeks and lips. "You can put it through your leg or your side if you want," he added as an afterthought. Suddenly those Indians didn't seem so strange after all. In fact they seemed positively normal.

"Doesn't that hurt?"

"Not at all. You don't feel a thing."

"Show him the sword!" exclaimed a youngster. A long cruelly

curved sword was removed from its scabbard. Its blade was honed to a razor-like sharpness. The man with his hand on the hilt seemed to by enjoying holding it, and waved it around alarmingly.

"Careful!" he was admonished, "There are children here. What we do with this, is two people hold it, one at each end, with the blade turned up, and the third sits on it. He feels nothing."

I was reminded of the Indian fakirs. The practice of performing in a state of ecstasy feats which would ordinarily be harmful or even fatal is quite widespread in the world's religions, though the means of attaining that ecstasy vary. Sometimes it is self-induced, through controlled breathing, chanting or drumming, all of which can alter your heartbeat and the supply of oxygen to the brain. Sometimes the ecstasy, or "standing outside yourself" is the result of taking hallucinogens, and it can become an end in itself. If it is possible to attend the same *tekke* for 70 years one wonders what spiritual progress is actually being made, but perhaps "spiritual progress" is not the point of dervishism. *Namaz* can be very formal: dervishism is a far more spontaneous expression of love for Allah, an expression that engages the emotions as much as it does the mind and which allows for different vehicles through which to express the single truth that there is but one God and that Muhammed is His messenger.

Easter Celebrations

I walked back slowly through the now deserted Bit Pazar, past the shuttered shops. Muslim Skopje had gone to bed, but the Christian city was just coming to life. Crowds of people thronged outside St Dimitrii holding candles aloft or, leaving, cupping them carefully in their hands lest the sacred flame go out before they got it home. The courtyard before the church was ablaze with tiny spots of light from the candles, and the stentorian tones of the priests within boomed forth from loudspeakers hanging under the eaves. For the Orthodox, Easter is the most important day in the calendar, it's what Christianity is all about, the promise of resurrection and of eternal life. It is not the birth of Jesus that is important but his death. Without Easter, Jesus would be just another of the many itinerant mystics who crowded Palestine at the time, all of whom have now been forgotten.

Outside St Clement's the six lanes of Bulevar Partizanski Odredi had been closed to accommodate the masses which had gathered.

Upright middle-class families, groups of teenagers, all of Skopje spilled across the street, sitting on kerbs beside forests of candles rooted in their own wax. The voice of Mihail, Archbishop of Ohrid and Macedonia, an outspoken nationalist, thundered from banks of loudspeakers. I could only understand a fraction of what he was saying, but it was a homily on Macedonia: "The Great Macedonian People is reborn! The Orthodox Church is its Head! We have never, we will never allow ourselves to be crushed!" I looked around me. Nobody seemed to be paying the slightest attention to the Episcopal ravings. I was reminded of music festivals in England—you might not think much of the band, but the point is to be there.

I fought my way into the church. People were still desperately throwing money and eggs at the symbolic bier and a priest was flinging holy water about. The building was almost insufferably close as a smog of incense rose into air heated by human bodies, candles and powerful television lights. Near the door a great tray full of lighted candles suddenly dissolved into a sheet of flame as they all melted simultaneously and their wax merged to form a giant torch. Caretakers hurriedly flung buckets of water over it, making the marble floor treacherously slippery. There was a minor war going on in the doorway as worshippers tried to force their way in past a returning tide of people carrying lighted candles. Uneasily I remembered Curzon's description of Easter in the Church of the Holy Sepulchre in Jerusalem half-way through the last century. The heat and smoke of the candles was so intense that "one poor Armenian lady, seventeen years of age, died where she sat, of heat, thirst and fatigue". As the asphyxiating masses rushed to the door for a breath of fresh air carnage had ensued, hundreds being crushed or trampled to death.

Once inside, people wandered around waving their candles and chatting, renewing old acquaintances. Everyone was dressed in their very best, the young women sporting chiffon sleeves and very short skirts, the young men, with their gold earrings, wearing carefully pressed denim shirts. Nobody took the slightest notice of the archbishop, who stood in the open Royal Doors of the iconostasis in his golden crown and flowing white beard surveying the chaos and looking slightly bemused. Around him fussed a body of priests and monks like workers tending to a queen bee. Everyone was getting in everyone else's way. From the balcony a bored choir gazed down on the mass of

members of the congregation. Midnight drew near. The archbishop's minders elbowed their way
towards the door, a bevy of clerics in their wake sweeping the hapless
hierarch along with them. The bier was withdrawn, people still making
last-minute attempts to crawl beneath it. The assembled ecclesiastics
began to circle the church anti-clockwise, a monk holding an icon of
the resurrected Christ aloft. I fought my way outside, crushed between
the crowds, as the Holy Horde arrived at a platform which they
mounted, clustering around a microphone. A female choir to one side
burst into song as the clerics performed further incomprehensible
rituals which nobody watched. Then, as midnight struck, the
archbishop intoned the words which everybody wanted to hear.

"*Hristos Voskrese!* Christ is Risen!"

"*Vistima Voskrese!* He is Risen Indeed!" thundered the crowd, and
a rippling, scrunching sound filled the air as thousands of eggs were
cracked against one another. Christ was risen. Life could begin again.

I struggled away from the church, past the people selling popcorn
and roasted sunflower seeds. The further away you got, the more
Partizanski Odredi resembled the fringes of a music festival. Bundles of
young people sat by miniature pyres of candles, strumming guitars.
Couples retreated to bushes thoughtfully provided by the Municipality.
Wax flowed everywhere—two weeks later the road was still slippery
with it. The smart set retreated to the neon-lit pizza houses lining the
street and looked down disdainfully at the crowds below. It had been a
long day. Slowly I walked home.

It seemed that all Skopje had had the same idea as me and had chosen
to spend a blisteringly hot Easter Day at Matka. I took a local bus
painted red and white in honour of the Coca-Cola Corp. through
congested dusty suburbs and a clutch of Muslim villages where men
were beginning to gather outside the mosques for the noon prayers.
One large body of devout Muslims caused a considerable traffic jam as
they ponderously moved *en masse* up the only street to the mosque.
Hot-looking women in scarves and raincoats ambled along the road,
taking no notice of the bus's horn. No-one was in a hurry to do

anything much. The land lay perfectly still. Occasionally we would pass a café where two or three men sat listlessly before half-empty bottles of beer. The Vardar basin shimmered in the heat, all colour bleached to a dusty brown, whilst looming through the haze the snowy peaks of the Šar Planina could just be made out.

After a while the bus left the main road and headed for the mountains, following a tributary of the Vardar towards a cleft in the rock. At the bottom of steep white slopes studded here and there with stunted trees a river ran crystal clear. People paddled or tried their luck with fishing rods. On the far side, under some trees, a cow-herd lay flat on his back while his beasts stood by looking glum. Further up the slope a hubbub of merry voices rose from the open-air terraces of a couple of restaurants where chickens were turning lazily on spits.

A little behind the restaurants, in a grove of beech trees, stood the Monastery of the Nativity, its wooden balconied courtyard not dissimilar to that at Rozhen, sheltering a tiny cruciform church. The dome rested on a tall drum and, seen from the right angle, the windows, surmounted by a wavy lead eave, gave it a slightly surprised look as if it found it hard to credit the crowds which had flocked here. Inside it was gloomily dark, barely large enough to hold ten people. Smoke-blackened frescos gazed down on trays full of lighted candles and a plate of Easter eggs. In honour of the day an extra icon had been laid out. "The Resurrection of Christ", it said in Greek. The frescos just predated that arrival of the Ottomans and of the mosques further down the valley, the time of Marko. Their inscriptions were written in Church Slavonic. When I emerged from the building I found the courtyard had been taken over by a Scout troop. Bronzed, supple young men and women lounged about or laid a table with a feast of bread, salad and roast lamb. Speeches were made to applause, and the lamb was formally presented to the leader of the troupe.

I followed the crowds further up the gorge, past white cars with "UN" stencilled on their doors. A uniformed German and his Polish counterpart were deep in conversation. The stream of people led me through precipitous walls of rock to a dam where a path branched across the river signposted "The Church of St Nicholas". I took it, and was soon labouring up a steep slope through the scrub with the hot sun beating down on me. The stunted trees offered no shade. Just as I thought I had got to the top the path plunged down again briefly before recommencing its ascent. One slip would have sent me plunging into the artificial lake far below, 200 feet down. My temples were hammering and I was gasping for breath, the sweat running off me in rivers while I cursed the pig-headedness which made me turn off the main path.

At length I came across a spring. Ice-cold water gushed from the hillside. An icon and a few rags tied to trees, just like those I had seen in Turkey and Armenia, marked the place as holy. I praised the goodness of the Lord and the sagacity of the monks as I drank deep draughts of that water, then took off my boots and plunged my feet into

the pool that had formed. Bliss! But I had come so far, and I could not turn back now. On I went, eventually emerging on a small plateau studded with pines where stood a tiny church of red brick and white limestone. An architectural gem, but I had an uneasy feeling that it knew it and felt rather smug, especially after having tempted an unwary foreigner to mortification of the flesh on the way up to it. I sat down and leaned my back against the sun-warmed nave and smoked a cigarette. Above my head two stone lions fought to the death. A bird twittered irritatingly from a tree. A low murmur of voices drifted to my ears and somewhere a bell clanged. Tentatively I peered over a ledge. Below me, seemingly 100 miles away and shimmering like a mirage, another minuscule church rested by the side of the lake. A rowing boat dallied on the water. Blue smoke curled up from a restaurant or a bar of some kind beside a terrace. People were sitting at tables drinking something cold. I never got off a mountain so fast in all my life. Down below, next to that second smug little church which oozed "I told you so" through every brick, I gulped down a cold beer.

Tetovo

I wandered through Tetovo, past the elegant *konaks* the Bulgarians call "National Revival" and I call "Turkish". Plaster flaked off to reveal a timber frame and bricks of baked mud. Balconies sagged as if ready to give up their uneven struggle with gravity. Posters written in Albanian and English suggested the citizens vote for Abduladi Vejseli of the People's Democratic Party, not to be confused with the other PDP, the Party of Democratic Prosperity, which also appeals to an Albanian constituency. The Prosperous Democrats have been accused—usually by Macedonian nationalists—of propagating Albanian separatism, but whether this is true or not they form the largest Albanian party and have at least brought an end in Macedonia to the murderous blood feuds, described by the Albania author Ismael Kadere and the English ethnographer Edith Durham, with which Albanian society was once rife.

Shop signs were written in three languages in these backstreets; Albanian, Macedonian and Turkish. Those few entrepreneurs who were not offering "Import–Export" suggested that you fly abroad by obscure airlines or they promised undreamed of delicacies from the grill. A carpenter was fashioning wooden rakes and saddles for your mule. The coffee shops were full, spewing pungent blue tobacco smoke into the street, and little boys darted here and there with trays of the life-giving liquid. In a fishmonger which rejoiced in the name "Barracuda" an enormous block of frozen mackerel, probably imported from Bulgaria, dripped fishy water over the concrete floor. A picture framer displayed examples of his work in his shop window—an embroidered calliagram with the single name Muhammed and the Albanian eagle on a blood-red field occupied ornate gilt frames. Another street was lined with shops specializing in wedding dresses, both the European-style white confections and more traditional attire, tight waistcoats and bodices, baggy *salvar* and wide skirts. Most of the old houses in the central part of town had been torn down, but over a low wall I caught sight of classic Turkish *konak*, all lath and plaster, slowly sinking into the mud. Starched white laundry hung over the balcony. Like the Šarena Dzamija it was painted all over in a naïvely provincial style. A date painted under the eaves in Arabic script showed that the work had been done in 1320. That would be of the Islamic era—lunar years since the flight of Muhammed from Mecca to Medina to escape his persecutors. I did a quick calculation. Roughly, the date was shortly before the First World War, a last testament to the dying Balkan Muslim empire, a time which had been swept away as surely as the similar houses with which this must have once shared the street.

I heard the sound of wild drumming and followed it down a muddy alley till I arrived at a locked gate from behind which came women's voices raised in jaggedly harmonious song. Willing myself not to, I peered over the gate. A wedding party was being made ready. The bride sat in her wedding dress surrounded by a flock of ululating women. Over her white wedding dress she wore a black waistcoat with two double-headed eagles embroidered on it in gold, a compromise between old and new. The party would go on late into the night, the groom's friends dancing to the sound of a shrieking saxophone, white handkerchiefs held over their heads.

I was looking at a bristling moustache and a fierce pair of eyes. Discretion proved the better part of valour.

Someone had too much money and, I guessed, a guilty conscience. A large new mosque squatted in the road like an alien visitor, its bulbous dome and Egyptian-style minaret testifying to a benefactor in the "Import–Export" business. Around it lay the ruins of the mosque it had replaced, shattered as if the new building had been dropped on it from a great height, simply crushing its predecessor. The old mosque must have been rather cosy, a simple structure of mud brick painted pale green on the inside and simply decorated with calliagrams. Its replacement, a vast domed hall which was bare save for ostentatious brass chandeliers, seemed soulless by comparison.

To my surprise in this famously Muslim town, I found myself face to face with the Church of the Virgin. It stood on a bluff by the river at what seemed to be the point where the hill became too steep to build on. It had recently been whitewashed, and its roof was clad with new sheets of copper. Two faded red flags fluttered from the porch. One was the national flag, marked with its gold star, the other bore the unimaginative legend "Macedonian Orthodox Church". Behind the church an old man was sawing wood.

"Excuse me," I said in Russian, "I'm from England and I'm writing this book about religion in Macedonia ..."

Slowly he straightened up, pushing a greasy blue cap onto the back of his head. He looked at me myopically for a time. Then he spoke. He was almost completely incomprehensible. I understood that I should return at five, when the church bell rang ("Bong! Bong!" the old man said to make sure I had got the point). The priest would be there then. I could talk to the priest. The priest knew all about religion. He returned to his wood. Conversation was evidently not his forte.

✻ ✻ ✻

I crossed the river and climbed past another newly whitewashed church, hoping to photograph the Church of the Virgin. A wiry tanned man in a blue suit that had obviously seen better days followed me wheezingly up the path. On his head he wore the white hat of the Albanians. I *salaamed* him as we met. He stopped to catch his breath and slowly straightened his back from the stoop that had propelled him up the hill.

"Where are you from? London? Do you speak German?" He leaned towards me conspiratorially, smiling to reveal perfectly yellow teeth.

"Let me tell you something. Macedonia is just a great pile of shit!" He gestured to indicate the exact size of the pile in question. It was large.

"Why do you say that?"

"Well, the Macedonians control everything. Here in Tetovo perhaps 8 per cent of the people are Christian, 2 per cent are Turkish, 2 per cent Gypsy. Everyone else is Albanian. All the villages are Albanian as far as Gostivar." He swept his arms up in a gesture that encompassed the entire basin, "but everything is controlled by Christians. The police, everything! All Macedonians. They beat us with their clubs, do anything they like. Where is justice? Where are there laws like this? Albanians have nothing! If you go to Switzerland there is no problem about language, about religion, about anything. Why not here? Did you see the demonstration? We must have our university. Without that we are not true citizens in our own country. We must be able to speak our own language. But the politicians, they are Mafia, even worse than the Communists. What are you doing here?"

"Well, I was actually taking a photo of this church."

"If you like. It's Orthodox though, not Catholic. There are Catholic Albanians, but not here: in Albania. Here we are Muslim."

"I've been told there's a danger of Islamic fundamentalism. Is there any—like in Iran or Saudi Arabia?" He didn't understand me.

"We are all Muslim, like the Saudis and the Iranians. We believe the same thing. There is just one Islam."

"What about dervishes?"

"Oh! There are lots of them! That's the heart of our religion. There's a *tekke* here, but the Communists turned it into a hotel. Tito was a very great dictator, and he tried to kill dervishism, but he couldn't of course. It still goes on."

I had seen the *tekke* once, even stayed in it. A walled compound on the outskirts of town, its single gate is guarded by a high watchtower. Inside, a lavish garden surrounds an open pavilion for the *zikr*, an elegant wooden structure with finely panelled ceilings which is divided by a lattice screen into two areas, one for sitting and one for dancing. The dervishes who had occupied it had obviously been far richer and far more influential than Skopje's Rifa'is, but now it was merely a relic gradually going to seed on the edge of a town few people had heard of and nobody visited. A large and raucous wedding party had made it impossible to sleep.

"So you say there are problems with the Christians?" I persisted.

"Of course. You look over the town." I looked, and saw a forest of minarets. One of them proved to be a chimney. "That's the textile mill. It employs 6,000 people, and they're all Christian—brother, sister, mother, father, grandparents. No work for us. It's bad. Just a pile of shit. Shit upon shit. And now they've got our rector locked up. Things must change, and soon. Please tell everyone in England. I must go now, so goodbye. Remember Tetovo!" Slowly he struggled on up the rubbish-filled gully.

I went back down the hill, and found myself in the Christian quarter of town; after the business of the bazaar it seemed almost deserted. People sat on the steps of their shops and stared at nothing as

I walked the cobbled length of Gotse Delchev Street. It was the only street in Tetovo in which all the signs were monolingual. No doubt Albanians and Turks never came here; even if they had they would have had to speak in Macedonian. But then there was no reason why a Muslim ever should come here. It felt like a ghetto. The Christians were clinging to their hillside, keeping aloofly apart from the threatening Muslim town below. Far up the hill above them two small villages shot minarets into the sky. In the long run, Christian withdrawal from the Muslim environment could only be counterproductive. The Christians could not run the town from their eyrie for ever. Although living in their own country they were doing so almost as colonists, simply storing up trouble for themselves. That trouble was just about to spill over.

As rain began to fall I ducked into a coffee shop which two turbaned imams were just leaving, laughing. "Do you have Turkish coffee?" I asked in Macedonian.

"No. Espresso."

"Then I'll have espresso." It was brought, silently. I sat, ignored, longing for the friendliness of the Bulgarians who would never have left an eccentric who spoke the wrong language badly, and wrote with the wrong hand, alone. People came and went. Nobody spoke a word, but glances were cast in my direction.

I rose to pay.

"*Zwei,*" said the man at the till. I couldn't believe my ears. Normally coffee cost far more than two denars. I offered him a ten-denar note. He took it.

"Another."

"*Zwanzig? Dvadeset?*"

"*Da,*" he replied sullenly, "*Dvadeset.*"

❋ ❋ ❋

Tetovo made me depressed. I took the bus back to Skopje. Some policemen got on and began to lord it over the other, mostly Albanian, passengers, who silently turned their faces to the windows and stared out at the driving rain. The conductor overcharged me for my ticket. The driver put on a tape and the words of John Lennon's *Imagine* washed over us: "Nothing to kill or die for, and no religion too."

Mafia Politics

Two pieces of graffiti daubed on a wall in Tetovo had caught my eye. One read *Vojvodi—Zakon*, literally "Warlords—Law". The other was the single word *Vujche* written in Latin script, followed by the Serbian cross with its Cyrillic "S" in each quadrant. The letters stand for "Serbia alone is its own Saviour". Back in Skopje I asked my friend Vahram, who worked at the OSCE mission, what the graffiti meant.

"I've really no idea," he told me. "*Vujche* means 'Uncle' in Serbian. If you find a Christian village around Tetovo, chances are it's inhabited by Serbs. Who the uncle is I can't say. Milosevic perhaps, or Serbia as a whole."

A thin-faced man with the regulation moustache looked up from his work of filing press cuttings. It turned out that he was from Slovakia.

"That *Vojvodi—Zakon*," he said. "On the wall of the House of Culture? I noticed that, and I don't really understand it, but you should know that the two words were written in different hands. It's as if someone was saying 'We need warlords' and someone else replied 'No, we need laws'." He smiled. "Laws are what we all need in Eastern Europe. That and being taken seriously by the West. I'll count you as an exception because you visited our countries under Communism and you seem to understand us, but in general the West doesn't know and doesn't want to know what we think. You just wade in and tell us what to do. Naturally we don't like it."

✳ ✳ ✳

Spots of rain were beginning to fall again. In Ploštad Marshal Tito a small group of people was hanging around with Macedonian flags. This was the famed "General Strike". It wasn't much of a demonstration. A portly old woman swathed in black was haranguing them, waving a tightly furled umbrella threateningly.

"Macedonia doesn't need loafers like you!" she screamed. "Go and find something useful to do!" Her efforts were met with stares of blank incomprehension.

I spotted some UN agents milling about, a Russian, a Swiss, a couple of Canadians. Gradually the square began to fill up. Placards appeared: "Kiro—executioner of Macedonian intellectuals!"; "When will you pay our pensions?" Two banks of speakers hummed into life and then began to blare forth strident nationalist songs.

I walked a short way across the old stone bridge over the Vardar and turned to take a photograph. Two men in their mid-30s, clean shaven and with neatly trimmed hair, came up to me. One of them said something.

"I don't speak Macedonian."

"Do you speak English? What newspaper are you from?"

"None."

"Ah! Freelance. My name's Ljuptso." Though accented, his English was faultless. He hunched his shoulders inside his leather jacket and turned towards the square.

"This is a very bad turnout," he remarked, puffing on a Camel, "There should be three times this number of people. It's the weather. And fear. And indifference." He glanced up at me.

"What's the strike about? I've seen a sign saying 'Down with the Communist Mafia.'"

"That is a very good sign. This is a protest against the government about wages, about lack of work. This country is run by a Mafia. They call themselves Socialists, but they're just making money. The biggest capitalists around. Socialists are supposed to care for the working people, but not these. With them it's just take, take, take. The son of the labour minister is only eighteen, and he drives a BMW, but my friend here has not had work for two years. They say they're privatizing everything. Well that's a strange thing for Socialists to do for a start. Just five industries have been sold so far, and four of them were bought by members of the government or their relatives. How does someone on an official salary of 400 Deutschmarks a month find the money to buy an industry capitalized at $20 million?"

"Are you saying politicians are corrupt?"

"Corrupt? That's your word. I'm not saying anything."

"Shall we say good businessmen then?"

"Yes, by accident. And by accident all the business goes their way. Did you see that boutique just behind the post office? It was bombed the other day. Somebody put a stone through the window, purely by accident. Unfortunately we have exploding stones here in Macedonia. I expect they weren't paying their protection money. If you want to do business, to trade say, you must have a permit from the government, and for that you must pay *baksheesh*. The question is not 'How much capital do I need', but 'How much *baksheesh* must I pay?' Terrible. You can't live off your salary so you need another line of business just to survive. Even the police. I was at school with one minister. He was a right shit even then. He drives a top-of-the-range Mercedes. Policemen, hardly paid enough to live, say 'What must I do to have a Mercedes?', so corruption is endemic in this country."

"Perhaps it's the legacy of the Turks. The Ottoman system was very corrupt."

"Don't come at me with that one! That is bullshit-baloney. I have trouble with my ulcer when I hear it. We can't go on blaming the Turks for everything. Sooner or later we must realise that no-one is responsible for this mess but ourselves. Until we do that nobody will do anything about it."

"Do you think there'll be war?"

"Yes. Not now, not next week, but sometime. Things are very bad now and they're not about to change. The government can do whatever it likes and no-one seems to care. They've lost all faith in the politicians, because they just see one giant Mafia."

"People say the same in Bulgaria."

"But at least the Bulgarians have a state. Here people say that the state must become established first, that democracy will take a long time. Bullshit-baloney." He was fond of that expression. "They just don't care. Yesterday a factory was closed with 12,000 put out of work. That's a lot of people in a country of 2 million. Where are those 12,000 today? They haven't come to demonstrate have they? The old people are the worst. They've lost the most, but they just take it lying down. They just say 'At least there's no war. At least we're not starving'. But this is Europe. People do not starve in Europe. This can't go on. I was talking to a policeman just now and he told me they were meant to break up the demonstration by force, but he said 'How can I hit my brother?' That is why the police have stayed away. I expect they're manning road blocks, preventing people coming here." It was true, I hadn't seen a single Macedonian policeman in the square.

"Yesterday I was in Tetovo," I observed. "There was a big demonstration, for the university."

"That's just politics. They've got their teacher training college here in Skopje, but they say they don't want that, they want a University of Tetovo. Rubbish. They don't want a university. Besides, who ever heard of a state university using a language other than that of the state? If I go to university in Germany I study in German. You don't have special Pakistani universities in England do you? No! There is a single system. This is normal. If they want to study in Albanian they can go to Albania to do it. That is their country, where they have their universities. I suppose you saw a lot of people in those white hats. Muslims. Muslims don't go to university, they just do whatever they're told. The first thing Khomeini did was close the universities. To have a university you must first be democratic, and Muslims aren't democratic. That is why there was a big demonstration. Someone said 'Go!', so they went. Did you speak to anyone?"

"A couple of men."

"There you are you see. You can't speak to a Muslim woman. They shut their women up. Undemocratic. The whole thing was probably put on by the Albanian Mafia and the government, so that if they need to they can make some nationalism and nobody will notice the mess they've got us in. That's what the Serbian government did. Everyone in Serbia was making nationalism, no-one was making policies.

"Nobody will make nationalism yet, not while America is involved. America is very close to Albania. They want to open it up for American businessmen, and soon maybe Albania will join NATO. The Albanians won't do anything the Americans don't want them to do. Same with our government. America is clever. They give just one fish a day," he held out an imaginary fish in his fingertips, "but they won't teach anybody how to use a fishing rod.

"How do you like Skopje, anyway, apart from all this?"

"Very nice."

"Meet any girls?"

"I'm married."

"Bad luck then." The two men melted into the gathering crowd.

I wandered through the throng waiting for something to happen. People, almost all men, stood around in groups of five or six. Each was easily identifiable. Pensioners, besuited businessmen, students with their banners, bearded and pony-tailed intellectuals. Clouds of blue tobacco smoke rose above the square. Someone touched my arm and asked for a cigarette. I gave him one, and lit it for him.

"Thanks. Where are you from? London? What do you work in, radio, television or press?"

"Press," I told him. I didn't see him again. Before long I bumped into a group containing my two recent acquaintances. Ljuptso introduced me to his friends as "The Man From Reuters".

"People are very frightened, that's why they haven't come," one of them said. Another opined:

"Everything is backwards in this country. Communists are businessmen. Government ministers join strikes against the government, strikes which the trades unions tell their members not to join. Who ever heard of a trade union that told you *not* to strike? We pay for state television and private television is free! Absolutely crazy. How are we ever going to be like Germany if we always do things the wrong way round?"

"State television is just propaganda for the government anyway," put in Ljuptso. "It's not the BBC. There's no free press either. And people *believe* the rubbish they hear. In the villages the people are very ignorant, they have no experience of the world and the only information they get is from the government. Whoever can control the press is a very powerful man because he controls what most people think. Here are some old people. Let's see what they say." Two dapper white-haired gentlemen were standing nearby. They shied away slightly when I was introduced as a journalist.

"You see," said Ljuptso, "they're afraid. They don't want to talk." They didn't look very frightened. Afraid of whom, anyway? And why was Ljuptso not afraid? One of the men decided to speak.

"He says it is all your fault for allowing Macedonia to be divided in the first place, in 1912. He says that now nobody can trust the government and that he wants his pension. Next time he will not vote. They are all as bad as each other."

The man's friend agreed, nodding his head sagely. Across his cheeks bright red capillaries had cast a net as if trying to hold his face together. Removing his beret, he said, "I blame the Turks."

Ljuptso shrugged despairingly.

"You see," he said, "Blaming the Turks again! When will we grow up? It works like this—maybe 60 per cent of the population is loyal to Macedonia as a state. The government knows that, so it just hands out more and more money to the army to buy its support. Who needs votes when you have an army? But that is not good enough. We need the rule of law. There are no laws now, the government just does whatever it wants, working with the Mafia. The police must take bribes because they are not paid enough. Taxes always go up but we get nothing for them. Now they say they're going to tax the markets, the Bit Pazar and the others." I had a feeling that was one tax which would prove impossible to collect. "All the money goes straight into the politician's Swiss bank accounts. They all have them. They're just sucking everything they can out of the country and at the first sign of trouble they'll leave. Then just VMRO will be left to fight for us."

"Do you think so? VMRO in Bulgaria …"

"I know what the Bulgarians think. This is a Bulgarian newspaper I'm reading. We're never going to join them. During the war they were as bad as the Serbs. In Vardar Macedonia it's just us or the Albanians, and they're getting strong simply through demography. They have much higher birth-rates than us, and maybe 200,000 people have come from Kosovo. That's too many for a small country like us to swallow. We're beginning to get indigestion."

"Do you think the census results were fair?"

"Yes. The Albanian claim that they make up 40 per cent of the population is absurd. Some people boycotted the census at first but the results came in in the end. It's just that a few Albanians like to say that all Muslims in Macedonia are Albanian. And what of the Turks, Pomaks, Roma? You've been to Tetovo …"

"The shop signs there are written in Turkish and Albanian as well as in Macedonian."

"It should not be so. They should only be in Macedonian. Well, I don't mind about the Turkish …"

"You just don't like Albanians."

"Don't get me wrong. I'm not a nationalist. So long as you agree to abide by the laws of the state anyone can live here. That is not the problem, but half the Albanians in Tetovo have no papers. *That* is a problem.

"Ah, this man used to be the prime minister until they sacked him, in the time of the 'Government of Experts' after independence when politics was put on hold for a while for the good of the country. Let us talk to him."

A jovial-looking man with a shock of white hair was advancing through the crowd preceded by his paunch. He wore a neatly pressed light grey suit and a crisp white shirt adorned with a sober tie.

"When did they sack him, and why?" I asked Ljuptso.

"Two years ago. I think he was too honest. He used to be professor of economics at the university. Just the man who ought to be running the country. Economics is our biggest problem. We need an economist to sort that our, not a politician."

I was introduced, Ljuptso addressing the former prime minister as "Professor". He had a gentle but firm handshake and I trusted him immediately.

"The main problem," he said ponderously, looking first at his shoes and then at me, "is the economy. Everything else, the social unrest, comes from that. Partly it's the Greek blockade but mostly it's the government. The economy's in a mess and they won't do a thing about it. So I'm supporting this strike for the pensioners, for the workers, for the unemployed ..." And building up a constituency. That was as far as he got before a party of large bearded men descended on him with cries of pleasure. Their claim to his time was infinitely greater than mine, so we left him engaged in hugs, kisses and debate.

The speeches were beginning and I took leave of Ljuptso. "One last thing," he said, "everything good comes from the West, yes? But west of us is Albania."

A stern-faced man with a luxuriant black beard ascended the platform.

"Friends!" he thundered into a microphone. "Brothers! ... And Sisters!" That last was an afterthought. "Workers! Trades Unionists! Welcome! [*applause*] We have called a General Strike! Against the Governing Mafia! [*hurrah*] They tried to stop us! [*boo*]" His words rebounded off the buildings on the far side of the square and came back to him. I wandered through the mass of people, taking photographs. Apart from a small claque at the front of the crowd the audience seemed only mildly interested in the proceedings. To my surprise an elderly Albanian was present, his eyes screwed up in concentration on the speaker's words. People continued to cross the bridge into the square, barging their way through the demonstrators with their shopping. The clouds began to break up and sunlight flooded the square intensifying

the blood-red of the students' banners with their glittering gold star. The Star of Vergina. Alexander's star.

Away from Marshal Tito Square Skopje was functioning normally. As a "general strike" the demonstration was a failure. The buses still ran, kebabs were bought and consumed and the little boys still paced the streets shouting "Marl-boro! Marl-boro!" hoarsely. No-one really cared. There were better things to do. I bought a handful of kebabs stuffed into bread and munched them on my way to the British Embassy, where I needed to register.

❈ ❈ ❈

The vice-consul was busy. I sat in the waiting room and leafed through the pamphlet on "Britain's Ethnic Minorities". It was adorned with photographs of Trevor MacDonald OBE and the late Norman Beaton and maintained that Britain was a paradise of multiculturalism and racial tolerance. I decided not to read the FCO's publication about the Channel Tunnel. I never was very good with propaganda. It's not their fault I suppose. Their job is to promote "Britain's interests", and that involves selling the country to gullible foreigners.

After a short time the vice-consul joined me. She was an effervescent woman with blonde curls. She handed me her card. "Thank God *someone's* writing about Macedonia. I'm sick of writing FYROM on forms, although I have to. FYROM doesn't really mean anything, it's just something we have to do. Leaving aside the diplomacy, as soon as you write "Former Yugoslavia" it puts people off. Businessmen ring me and ask whether Macedonia is safe. It's safer than London, for God's sake. This is the only city in Europe where I feel that I can be out on my own after dark. And there's none of the Mafia problem that you get in Bulgaria or Russia. Cars that go to Bulgaria simply don't come back. Even the Macedonian government returns one or two lighter. Here only the French have had trouble. Someone got some bolt cutters and chopped the driver's door off one of their cars. The driver was in it at the time. Where else are you going apart from Skopje? Ohrid? Good idea. If I have to stay in this country and I can't go to Greece I always go to Ohrid. In fact I'm trying to persuade the ambassador to let me set up a consulate there during the summer.

"This country potentially has a lot going for it, but some of our European partners don't see it like that. I still find it hard to believe that the embargo's continuing. I thought that would be resolved in weeks not months. I knew nothing about Macedonia when I was posted here, but now I find it quite hard not to go native. Breaking the sanctions on Yugoslavia is illegal of course and we can't condone it but it's hard not to feel sorry for the Macedonians. They simply can't *afford* to enforce it strictly.

"Did you see their strike, by the way? Not the world's greatest political manifestation was it? They sent us an invitation. In fact they sent everyone an invitation, addressed to mothers, workers, students and so on. They obviously hoped to appeal to any group you might care to name."

"What do I do with this registration form?" I asked.

"Well it's actually meant for long-term visitors, so people can contact you via us if necessary, but I'll take it anyway. You've got my card. Ring if you need help. That's what I'm for."

Evangelism
A neat square building nestling under plane trees and adorned with a simple wooden cross proclaimed itself to be an Evangelical church.

Sunlight filtering through the leaves created a dappled effect on its white walls. Outside two girls were sitting behind a table piled high with books. I introduced myself to them in Russian.

"You can speak English to me," said the elder, a pretty young woman of about seventeen whose light brown hair tumbled playfully down to her shoulders.

"Are there many Evangelicals in Skopje?" I asked.

"Quite a few. This church is Evangelical-Pentacostalist. There are also Methodists, Congregationalists and Baptists. The Methodists are the oldest. They've been here over 100 years but we're very new."

"And what are relations like with the Orthodox? In Bansko the Evangelicals told me that there were many problems because the Orthodox regard them as a cult like the Hare Krishnas."

"But in Bulgaria there was a big explosion in Protestantism," she replied. "That annoyed the Orthodox, but it never happened here. After Communism people are fairly uninterested in religion. They just say 'Oh well, I suppose I'm Orthodox' and leave it at that. Most people only go to church two or three times a year. Some young people have become interested but the old, say in their 50s, just don't care. There are some problems, but they are quite low level. You see ... do you know Protestant theology?"

"I'm Protestant", not that that necessarily implies any knowledge of theology.

"Then you know that Protestantism is very close to Orthodoxy. We read the same Bible. We both believe the same thing really, it's only our rituals that are different. We do things one way, they do them another. What's the problem there? You see this book?" She held up a sleek red hardback, *My First Bible*. "It's a children's Bible. We had 100,000 of them, but we gave 30,000 to the Orthodox because they need them too." Christian goodwill or a form of protection money? The survival of their church depended on good relations with the powerful Orthodox Church.

"Are there any Americans here?"

"Not yet. I think 30 couples will come in the summer. I don't know what they will do. If they only work in our church it will be fine, but if they try to convert the Orthodox there will be trouble." Sixty spirit-crazed denizens of the Bible Belt trying to gather up Macedonian souls for Jesus. There would be trouble.

"I will introduce you to someone who speaks really good English," the girl told me. "He was in England. Come."

We left the stall in the capable hands of her ten-year-old companion and passed through an iron gate into a courtyard partially shaded by a grapevine. Beans were growing in neat rows around the edge. A young man dressed in a scruffy pair of jeans and a T-shirt greeted us. He was splattered from head to foot in lead oxide paint. After the Evangelicals in Bansko he seemed refreshingly normal.

"Where's Krste?" the girl asked him.

"Inside."

We climbed some steps to the back door of the church past a window with broken wooden slats.

"Someone tried to break in last night," I was told. "Krste? Where are you?" A burly man of about 25 with soft eyes emerged from a small room containing an iron bedstead and a computer. "Just a moment," he said, and disappeared again.

"And this," said the girl (I never caught her name) with a flourish, "is our church!" An entirely bare room, innocent of decoration of furniture save a stack of amplifiers and speakers in one corner. She was very proud of it.

"We use these folding chairs in the corridor, but now we are having our Big Clean, so we have taken everything out."

"This seems a very new building. The one in Bansko was old."

"No, it's an old building but this Church has only been in Macedonia for four years so it's new to us. There is much work to do." Krste reappeared and the girl introduced us.

"Take a chair," he said, "I am glad to see you. I love your country. I have been there twice, first to Warrington to learn English, and then I went to London to a course on 'Christianity in the World'. England is so good. Except for the weather. But I have a friend there, also a Macedonian, who found the English very strange. He told me this story. First you must know that his name is Dragan, which is a very common name with us. Once, he went to church and it was a good service, he was enjoying himself, so he introduced himself to his neighbour. 'I'm Dragan', he said. 'Of course you are dear', she replied. I had to explain to him what 'dragon' means in English."

"I think I would have reacted the same way, or prayed to St George. You know he's our patron saint."

"Yes, I know that. When I was in London there was a concert given by a Serbian pianist. I took my landlady along. She was a sweet old lady who had a big Edwardian house in Chiswick. I'm so glad to have stayed in a real English house like that. Everything was old, or even if it was new, it was made to look old. Anyway, everyone was at the concert, even King Aleksandr [of Yugoslavia]. Afterwards there was an exhibition of Serbian icons. I had to explain them all to her: 'This is St Clement, this is St Petka ...' When we got to St George, she said 'Ah, you don't have to tell me who *this* is!' Here comes our pastor."

The pastor was a great bear of a man, the proud possessor of a beautifully rounded stomach and a mischievous grin.

"Can't stop now," he said, "Lunchtime! You will eat lunch!" He began to gather up bundles of collapsible chairs in his arms and carry them outside. We joined him and sat under the grapevine. Tender young leaves were just beginning to sprout. Behind me a line of apricot trees did sentry duty. Out of nowhere three young men materialized and sat with us. We men sat at one table, the girls from the bookstall were joined by another and sat to one side. Salad was laid before us, and bread.

"Now we will eat real Macedonian food," declared the pastor gleefully rubbing his hands. A huge tray was brought and set down on the table in front of him. It was lamb pilau. It could have been prepared anywhere between Belgrade and Bengal. Almost nothing "Macedonian" is unique to that country. The Pastor was not satisfied.

"Where's the brandy?" he demanded. A mostly empty bottle containing a pale yellow fluid was proffered. Produce of Croatia. Then one of the young men, the one covered in paint, had a brainwave. He vanished into the cellar of the church and re-emerged clutching an unlabelled bottle whose contents were completely colourless.

"Home-made!" he declared proudly. "It's *sljivovitsa*. What's that in English?"

"Plums," I said.

"You obviously know all about our country if you know what *sljivovitsa* is. Most Westerners have never heard of it." On more than one occasion I have had cause to wish that *I* had never heard of Balkan plum brandy. It can do nasty things to you.

"It's not plums," the man on my right objected. "It's peaches."

"It's apricots," said Krste, "from our trees." One sip and I knew what it was. It was white spirit or something very like it. Two sips and

I could feel the blood rising to my face. The boy who had brought it dabbed a few spots on his acne and fled from the table screaming. The pastor let out a great bellowing laugh.

"He shouldn't have done that!" He jabbed a fork in my direction. "What does he do?"

"I'm writing a book about Macedonia. I'm sure it *is* possible to understand this country." His laugh escaped again.

"Then you understand nothing!"

"I try. I was in Bansko, there's an Evangelical church there ..."

"That's one of the old ones, founded by missionaries from Solun [Thessaloniki]. Methodists." The acne sufferer had returned to his seat.

"Miss Stone?" he ventured.

"The one who was kidnapped by Sandanski and his men?"

"What's the use," the youth complained. "He knows it all already."

"You know there's a town in Bulgaria called Sandanski?" I asked.

"Never! There's a village here called *Yane* Sandanski. But then the Bulgarians have named a town after Gotse Delchev. They do that kind of thing. That's all history though."

"I suppose so, but VMRO is very popular in Bulgaria now."

"It's not the real VMRO. They're supremacists. They agree that Macedonia is an independent republic, but they claim it's an independent *Bulgarian* republic. But we are Macedonians. We do not feel anything else about ourselves, and that can't be taken away from us. Delchev came from Aegean Macedonia. He didn't feel Bulgarian any more than we do and when he said 'Macedonia for the Macedonians' he meant all the people of Macedonia regardless of language or religion."

"I think Delchev was a great man."

"Yes, but he died too young," said Krste, resuming control of the conversation.

"Do you think Ilinden would have succeeded if he hadn't been killed?"

"Ilinden wouldn't have *happened* if he hadn't been killed. He knew we were not yet ready. He was probably killed by the supremacists. There were so many *vojvodas*, each with his own *cheta*. That was the weakness of VMRO. The Great Powers wanted Ilinden to fail so that the Macedonian movement would be crushed. This is the fate of Macedonia. But we can truthfully say that we had the first republic in the Balkans, the Kruπevo Republic. OK, it only lasted for twelve days, but it was a republic, and it was ours.

"We are just a small piece on a chess board, being moved by others. Even now if war comes it will not be because of internal politics. All the countries around us are playing games but we are too small to play a game of our own. Take Greece. They are right. Macedonia is Greece, but it is also here. It is also Bulgaria. There is nothing we can do about other people's games, but I will tell you a joke. We used to say 'Why is Macedonia so backwards? Because the Turks were here for 500 years.' Now we say 'Why is Turkey so backwards? Because the Turks were *here* for 500 years!'"

A police helicopter flew low over the church and circled a couple of times. The pastor held his arms up and spluttered in imitation of a machine-gun.

"*Politsija!* Swine!" he shouted. "There're looking for our burglar. It's the second time we've been done. They're after our computer. I went to the police station this morning to report the break in. Five other people there. Two burglaries, two car thefts and a three-year-old gone missing! We never used to have crime like that. And what do the police do? Fly helicopters."

"We only seem to get bad things from the West," observed Krste gloomily. "But when I was in London I heard bad things all the time. London is a big city, but there is communication so you know what's going on. Things could happen in the villages here that I would never hear about."

"Tell me something," I put in, "I've been told there are no troubles with the Orthodox. Is that true? It seems strange, given the links between religion and nationality."

"I don't know who could have told you that. Of course there are problems, especially because the Macedonian Orthodox Church is not recognized by any others. If you leave the Orthodox Church you are seen as being a traitor to the nation. To reject that church is to reject Macedonia, not only as a country but as an idea. But we are all Macedonians! I do not think of myself as any less of a Macedonian just because I'm Protestant. Are you married, by the way?" I showed him Shaoni's photograph.

"Is she Japanese? Indian! When I was in London we went to Southall to see the Indians. We went to a mosque, a Hindu temple and a Sikh temple. The Sikhs gave us really good food because part of their religion is to give food to strangers, but we had to take our shoes off and cover our heads. Ugh! But the Indians in London are wonderful. They have good financial minds, and they are so helpful! I know that if you want directions you should ask an Indian. Their food is too spicy though."

"Are there really Muslims in England?" I was asked. I said there were, and then had to dodge the inevitable question about Salman Rushdie.

"Can you tell me about Kralje Marko? I'm going to Prilep in a couple of days' time."

"Now there's someone for you!" said Krste. "He's such a hero. They say that in the Prilep Museum they have two skulls. One big one, that is the skull of Marko. And a little one. That is Marko when he was a child. In fact he fought for the Turks against the Christians, but by doing that he kept his independence for a while at least, so he is remembered for saving Macedonia from the Turks. An inside-out story."

"Do you think I should go to Strumitsa?"

"Do I? Of course I do. I come from Strumitsa! The most beautiful town in the whole world." According to the old *Rough Guide—Yugoslavia*, Strumitsa is "a garrison town and one of the ugliest places in Yugoslavia", but as an elderly Romanian German once told me, "the bells sound sweetest from your own steeple."

"What interests you about Strumitsa?"

"Well, firstly the battle ..."

"Poor old Tsar Samuel! That was the end of *him*! There's still a village called Vadeochi near Strumitsa. That means 'to put out eyes'. Nasty. What else?"

"And Vanga."

"The witch? What's she got to do with it?"

"She was born there."

"I never knew that, perhaps because of my background as a Protestant. I don't like any of that kind of thing. People go to get their fortunes told, but it can't be right."

"You know there's a new church there, with Vanga's picture on it?"

"Never! That's horrible. No, I don't want to think about that kind of thing at all. Let's change the subject. You know that strike yesterday? Well, there's a man who comes here, he's a plumber, a gardener, everything—a jack-of-all-trades, I think you say. *He* says they promised to pay people to turn up, but they never showed a single denar."

One of the girls brought us little plastic beakers brimming with coffee. Krste took a sip and grimaced. "God this is sweet! Very Oriental though."

"That's what they call it in Russia, you know. *Vostochnoye kofye*, Oriental coffee. In Greece they call it 'Greek coffee'."

"Do they? How silly. At least we're honest about it. It's Turkish." He paused ruminatively. "That's why she made it so sweet. She sells coffee in the markets—that's her job. Most of the traders are Muslims, and Muslims *love* sweet things. Will we see you on Sunday? There's a service in English at nine for the Internationals. If that's too early there's another at eleven, but it's in Macedonian. You might find it interesting, but drop in anytime if you want."

Kumanovo

Kumanovo lies just east of Skopje, a half hour's drive through gently rolling countryside along the now almost deserted E-75, the motorway linking Belgrade with Athens. It's an unprepossessing place, as dustily forlorn as any town could reasonably hope to be, a centre of depressing concrete high-rises surrounded by a jumble of ramshackle older houses and shops which drift into mud-streeted suburbs where the corpses of old cars gradually rust away amidst piles of horse shit and clumps of nettles. Sullen, scruffy youths loiter with nothing to do and old men will sit for hours playing backgammon over a single glass in the gloomy tea shops. Kumanovo is a flashpoint.

The town is just a couple of miles off the motorway and straddles both the road and the as yet unfinished railway linking Skopje with Sofia. As well as being an Albanian centre, Kumanovo has a large Serbian population. The Serbian cross which adorns the flag of Radovan Karadzic's Bosnian fiefdom defaced a number of walls. On one wall someone had painted an outline map of "Greater Macedonia" and marked the city of Solun, adding the inscription "VMRO". But the writing had been scratched out and the map exorcised by the addition of that cross, the symbol Serbs use to mark out their territory, like dogs cocking their legs against streetlamps.

No-one knows exactly how many Serbs there are in Macedonia—some say 44,000, they themselves claim 300,000. Unlike other minorities, they have no special rights, no schools or broadcasting. They never technically counted as a minority because of the dominance of Serbia in the old Yugoslav federation. Moves are under way to change their status, but who could forget the chilling claim of the Serbian warlord "Arkan": "Where there are Serbs, there is Serbia"? Serbia will go a long way to bring all Serbs into one country, and many Serbs still regard Macedonia as no more than "South Serbia". After all, did not the Serbian King Milutin cause the monastery of St George to be built at Staro Nagornichane, just outside Kumanovo. It has been claimed that Vojeslav Šešelj, a Serb who makes Milosevic seem a paradigm of rationality, has been agitating for the creation of a Serbian Autonomous Region in the area around Kumanovo. That was how the Croatian war started. When the chief of the general staff of the Macedonian Army publicly stated that Serbia posed no threat to Macedonia's security he was promptly removed from his post. Were the Serbs ever to take hold of Kumanovo Macedonia would find itself almost completely cut off from the outside world.

But Kumanovo seemed more Albanian than Serbian, at least on first sight. Beaked-nosed men stalked the street wearing skull-caps. Women in pantaloons and raincoats flitted here and there. Shop signs, especially those for tea shops and pastry shops were written in Albanian. Before long I was swept up in a crowd that led me through those semi-derelict streets past what announced itself in both Albanian and Macedonian to be the "Bayram Shabani Ordinary School" and on to the market. A large space was partly roofed in and crowded with a mass of people, Christian and Muslim, who were frantically buying and selling fruit and vegetables. Or socks. Or scythe blades. I toyed with the idea of buying an enormous jar of richly dark honey in which pieces of the comb floated but rejected it as impractical. The jar was heavy and the lid didn't seem to fit properly. I doubted it would last the journey back to London. Behind me a wizened old woman was pouring her home made raki, colourless brandy, into the bottles proffered her by her customers. The German author Günter Grass once tried to sum up the difference between Eastern and Western Europeans thus: in the West we have plastic bags, in the East they have string bags. We throw things away, they re-use them. Nothing in Eastern Europe is disposable, whether it is a shopping bag or a history. You can always take it out again and adapt it to a new use.

✳ ✳ ✳

I left the marketplace and wandered around those poverty stricken backstreets. The two confessions, Christian and Muslim, seemed about evenly spread in their little compounds or apartment blocks. You would pass a tea shop with its sign written in Albanian, and then come upon a *nekroloz* adorned with a cross. Some still bore the red star that indicated a now officially banished faith. Here and there a car with Bulgarian plates was parked outside a house, its owners visiting relatives or engaged in "trade".

In another street I found the "Mother Teresa" Foundation for Aid to Kosovo. Mother Teresa is of course herself an Albanian but there was something deeply cynical about using her name to lend respectability to an organization whose "aid" was almost certainly politically motivated and not purely humanitarian in nature. There was also some irony in an aid agency most probably run by Muslims and delivering its aid to Muslims adopting the name of a Catholic. But then the King Zog Foundation would have had no cachet in the West.

Kumanovo had links to Serbia, Bulgaria and Albania. Did it, I wondered, have any links to Macedonia? I followed a trickle of men down a muddy lane. A man with a resignedly defeated look, his straggly moustache surmounted by a pair of round black eyes, was being drawn towards us by a broken down nag. He hardly seemed alive.

One of the men I was following wore an imam's turban, the tassel of his fez neatly tucked into the folds of white cloth enveloping his head. Sure enough, I was being brought by degrees to a mosque, a curious structure of dark stone which rested its hulk in a small garden. Lean-tos huddled higgledy-piggledy up to its walls, giving the impression that a once-grand building had gone to seed, that, like a rose which has not been tended, its roots had reverted onto the stock to which it was grafted.

A large crowd had gathered by the time I arrived. Men sat on benches around the *sadirvan,* smoking and talking quietly. A stocky man of about fifty came up to me, his neat white toothbrush moustache counterpointing the lace skullcap he wore. He stood for a while, just looking at me.

"*Salaam Aleikum,*" I ventured.

"*Marhaba,*" he replied. "Where are you from?" I told him, and began to question him in Russian. He had a softly mellifluous voice. "Kumanovo is about 35 per cent Muslim," he told me. "Albanian. We have had problems with the Christians in the past, especially over that mosque that the police pulled down, but now the difficulties are very small. Everything is normal." The *muezzin's* voice burst from the minaret.

"There is the *ezan*," I observed, "you must go and make *namaz*." He smiled at me.

"You know Muslim words? If you like you can come in and watch us pray. Only you must take off your shoes."

He took my arm and led me to the porch of the mosque, waiting patiently while I did battle with the laces of my boots. Inside, racks were filled with the shoes of the worshippers who spread themselves out and began to pray, bobbing up and down and prostrating seemingly at random. The imam's sweetly melodious voice made itself heard: "I bear witness that there is no God save Allah. I bear witness that Muhammed is the Messenger of Allah."

The men bunched up. Some entered the main prayer-hall, the others stayed in the lobby and lined up shoulder to shoulder into two neat rows facing Mecca. Then the imam spoke again, the sometimes harsh and guttural sounds of Arabic falling musically from his lips in what was half-song, half-chant. There was a moment of silent prayer, then the imam announced "*Allah-hu Akbar*, God is Most Great."

As if by magic the congregation of over 200 became a single organism. At each repeated cry of *Allah-hu Akbar* they moved as one, praying silently or listening to the imam's chanted prayers. They stood. They kneeled. They prostrated. Resting their weight on their heels they sat back with their hands held in front of their faces and mouthed the words of the prayer. You have to be fit if you want to be a Muslim. All over the world people were doing exactly the same thing. The strength of the claim "Islam is one" came to me forcefully. The only sounds were the imam's voice softly repeating *Allah-hu Akbar* and a rustle as the congregation adopted a new attitude of prayer. Everything was ordered and peaceful. There could hardly have been a greater contrast than that with the *zikr* of the Rifa'is.

The ordered ranks broke up again and the imam chanted some more while the people told their rosaries. I noticed only a handful of young men in the crowd. Most were dignified men of middle age or more whose beaten faces had an air of having endured great hardship. As the congregation broke up and began to file out of the building I noticed that three men were wearing imam's turbans. One, who had led the prayer, was tall and erect and wore a smart suit and a full white beard. Another was a gnarled, bent man whose ears stuck out and who could have been aged anything between 60 and a 100. The third was about 40, and had a merry, rotund face and fluid lips which broke into a smile often.

My mentor motioned me to stay where I was and vanished into the throng. When he returned he was leading a sharp-eyed young man who was wearing a baggy green suit and a purple shirt with button-down collars. He took my hand.

"Hi," he said shyly, "I hear you're from England. I speak some English. I learnt French at school, but I got English from films and music. Everyone listens to English music. Come outside and we can talk."

We sat on a bench by the *sadirvan*. An excited group of men clustered around watching me. It was assumed that I was a journalist. Everyone wanted to shake my hand. The young man introduced himself as Agim. He worked for a privately owned Albanian-language radio station.

"Too many people are only interested in money," he said. "You must make time for spiritual things. Prayer is important."

"Are many young people interested in Islam? Most of the people I saw here today were old." He laughed.

"That is true. Young people *are* interested in Islam but their knowledge of it is very low. Also they are put off because the outside things of Islam—prayer five times a day, fasting—can be difficult. But true Islam is not in these things, it is in the heart."

"Does he like Islam?" someone asked. I replied that though I was a Christian I had studied Islam at university and was very interested in it. Agim translated.

"Then," the man commented, "you are like those English Orientalists who understand Islam so well, like Montgomery Watt. I have read some books about Islam written by English people and they are very good. You have Islam in your heart, not on the outside."

It was the turn of a tall bearded man to speak. He was the mosque's caretaker. Agim turned to me: "He would like to make a gift to you. It is a small book in English about Islam."

The caretaker went into a store room where I could see piled logs, and returned bearing *The Muslim World League Journal, Shawwal 1414—April 1994.* "Bloodbath in Hebron!" screamed the cover. The magazine was published in Mecca. It contained articles on "Sayings of the Prophet Muhammed (peace be on him) explaining the importance of repayment of debts"; "The Irresistible Charm of the Qur'an": "Stress in the Twentieth Century" and "Discrimination: a Threat to Islamic World Order ('Everywhere Muslims are discriminating against each other ... the sense of discrimination is a deadly disease ...')". Finally there was a feature on a new Islamic information centre in Tirana: "The Centre is using the Albanian, Arabic and English languages but may also consider the use of other languages ... the Centre gives emphasis to Islamic issues with a view to reviving the Islamic Faith in this part of the world."

"I have a friend who works there, named Yusuf," said Agim, "though he actually comes from Elbasan in central Albania." I had heard of Elbasan; its citizens had been convinced that Edward Lear was a Russian spy who was planning to sell them to the tsar. Lear found the city riddled with dervishes. "Knowledge of Islam in Albania is very low," said Agim. "There is much work to do."

"When I was in Bulgaria I heard that people came from Turkey and Arabia to give Qur'ans and books of *hadith.* Does that happen here?"

"A little." Agim gestured towards one of the company. "This man is my very good friend. He is from Turkey. A very good man. There is a Muslim organization in Skopje—there used to be two but the League of Muslim Youth is closed now—but there are no formal links to groups outside Macedonia."

"And what about relations with the Christians? I heard that there had been problems. The police destroyed a mosque."

"There were problems, yes, but the police never totally destroyed that mosque, they only took down a bit that we had built on while we were restoring it. We didn't have planning permission to do the work, but this is the only mosque in Kumanovo and we need another. Now we have permission, and work has started again." It all seemed perfectly civilized, but who grants or withholds permission, and on what basis is the decision made? Had any of those new churches I had seen been given "planning permission"?

The caretaker offered to show me the interior of the mosque. Struggling out of my boots again I followed him into the main prayer-hall. It had recently been renovated, with fresh calliagrams on its walls and a shiny new wooden *minbar*.

"This is the oldest part of the mosque," I was told, "dating from 1332. The mosque was built by a Turk not an Albanian. His name was Sinan Pasha, and the mosque was named after him. All the stuff outside was added later, over 500 years." I didn't believe it. That would have had it dating from the reign on Stefan Dušan.

"Are there dervishes in Kumanovo?" I asked. Agim and the caretaker found the idea faintly amusing.

"Certainly not! We are Sunnis. Dervishism and Sunnism are two separate things. We have nothing to do with them."

In the garden was a grave sheltered by a green-painted iron cage. "This is the grave of a very important man. He lived more than 100 years ago and he was very rich, but when he died he gave all his money to the mosque, so he has a special grave." His family must have been furious, but his way to heaven had been smoothed. It would have been still smoother had he given his money away before he died, but nobody's perfect. An old man who had stuck with us pulled the grass away from a tombstone and squinted at the Arabic numerals at its base.

"1330. That is two years older than the mosque."

"No its not," I said, "That's a *Hijri* date. Muslim calendar." The three consulted among themselves for a while.

"You're right," said Agim. "Add 600 years. It's still old. You see—written in old Turkish, Arabic script."

"Can anybody still read that?"

"Not really. To write, yes, but not to understand."

A thought struck me. Perhaps the mosque *had* been built in 1332, *al-Hijra*, from Muhammed's flight from Mecca to Medina, rather than in 1332 in the Christian calendar. The Muslims had forgotten not only their alphabet but their calendar. The anonymous "very rich man" could conceivably have been Sinan himself, but the people who were reaping the benefit of his *largesse* had been deprived of their historical memory. Or was it their history? The Albanians only began to move west from their mountain fastness in the nineteenth century. Sinan was a Turk, but there are no Turks in Kumanovo now. In a sense, the town's Muslims were squatting.

Agim and I drifted along the road outside the mosque.

"What kind of programmes do you have on your radio station?" I asked.

"A bit of everything, news, music, information on culture, that kind of thing. We need to teach our people about our culture so they know what freedom is, and we will not be *really* free until we have our university. There are two private radio stations here and a TV station, and they do this work. Again, there used to be more, but not everybody had a licence. That building just there is Radio Kumanovo, the state radio. They say they have Albanian programmes, but it's only for two hours a week. That's nothing like enough. There are many Christians here in town, but all the villages are Muslim. We fill the gap. People listen to us."

"What do you think of the Albanian political parties? Do they really represent the people or are they just for the politicians' benefit?"

"Hard to say. There are three parties, with 26 seats. They are in opposition, but what is wrong with that? Everyone is in 'opposition'. What is most important is to teach the Albanian people the meaning of the word 'freedom'. The Macedonians simply don't understand what we want."

"But the biggest problem surely is that there is no work in Macedonia." He misunderstood.

"You can't work with Macedonians! They are very hard to make friends with, not like us Albanians. They are a shut-in people. They do not trust."

Serbs and Croats

On a low hill just outside the town stood a war memorial. The war was as messy in Macedonia as anywhere in Yugoslavia, but further complicated by rivalry between the Yugoslav and Bulgarian Communist Parties and uncertainty as to who exactly was meant to be "liberating" Macedonia. Many Macedonians did not regard Bulgaria as an occupying power, and initially the resistance movement was limited, but on 2 August (Ilinden) 1944 the Anti-Fascist Assembly of National Liberation of Macedonia met for the first time at the monastery of Prohor Pchinski just outside Kumanovo. The assembly was led by Metodije Antonov, known as "Chento", and had close links with the Communist Party of Yugoslavia (YCP). Later, another of its prominent members, Vladimir Poptomorov, defected after falling out with the YCP on the Macedonian Question and ended up as foreign minister of Bulgaria. Chento was to find himself on trial after the war for failure to follow the party line.

Prohor Pchinski had been back in the news within the last few years. On Ilinden 1990 about 100 members of the newly formed VMRO–DPMNE had held a rally there, calling for its transfer to Macedonia from Serbia. They were promptly attacked by Serbian police. The previous year supporters of the Skopje football team Vardar had been chanting "Prohor Pchinski is Macedonian" and "Chento" from the terraces. A hand-made wooden sign pointed the way to the monastery but I didn't want to risk it.

On the hill outside Kumanovo a Heroic Woman stood in effigy bearing aloft a sheaf of corn and looking out over the town. Grass grew through the cracks in the paving stones around her and some faded red roses adorned her plinth. On either side of her two plaques bore images of Partizans going to war and returning as heroes to be greeted by their womenfolk. Behind, amidst beds of pansies, the names of those heroes had been inscribed on polished granite. I looked for Muslim names among the Kiros and Aleksandrs, but found precious few: Naif Bektas, Arif Arifi, a handful of others. Perhaps the Albanians had been supporting the Italian-run Albania that was occupying Kosovo and half of Vardar Macedonia. Now they were calling for their "freedom".

✳ ✳ ✳

The British vice-consul told me that new radio and television stations were founded almost every day and as regularly closed down again by the authorities, who were making up the broadcasting regulations as they went along—controlling the media had never been an issue under the Communists and, as with so much else, the necessary legislation simply did not exist. Nor did anyone seem in any hurry to introduce it. The stations were mostly terrible.

"There's a new 'experimental' TV station, but the 'experiment' seems to consist of broadcasting Serbian pop videos. Not in my home!" she shuddered.

"It's an acquired taste."

"And not one that I intend to acquire. Horrible!"

I've come to quite enjoy Serbian music, even if it is mostly rubbish. I must have been in the Balkans for too long.

* * *

One hot day I climbed the hill on which the Kale stands. From within its ruined walls the city could be seen in its entirety spread out along the Vardar with the towerblocks and neon signs across the river opposite me—Christian Skopje—and at my back the maze of the old bazaar with the rounded domes of old *hamams* and pointed minarets from which streamed green banners. From up here the sound of the traffic below was muted, remote. All around snow-capped mountains held the city in a protective embrace. A few Muslim families were picnicking on the grass amidst the blossom of cherries and apricots. The sound of the *ezan* warbled forth from the minaret of Skopje's grandest mosque, the Mustafa Pasha Camii, losing itself among the plane trees that are such a feature of the city.

Seated by the *sadirvan* facing the simple domed structure a man in his 50s was enjoying the garden and the view over the city. He wore a light grey jacket and a silk cravat. He was obviously not a Muslim. In fact he looked British. I asked him.

"In a way," he replied. "I'm actually Croatian, but I'm a British citizen. I thought I'd enjoy Islamic Skopje while it's still here." He worked for a London newspaper.

"Our paper's running a report on doing business in Macedonia," he said. "I've been given special permission to call the country by its constitutional name, Republic of Macedonia, not FYROM."

"The Greeks won't like that."

"No. They'll probably seize all the copies of that issue, perhaps make trouble for our correspondent in Greece. Do you think they'll withdraw advertising?"

"The government may not, but individual businesses could well do."

"Ah! The Greeks, the Greeks! What are they doing in the EU? They have no place there. It's meant to be for European co-operation, but who do they ever co-operate with? They're always messing up my work.

"We're doing Macedonia a big favour running this report, trying to get people to invest here. The Macedonians are great traders, but at the end of the day you can't have a purely service economy. Someone must pay for the services and that means you have to produce things to sell. "

"That's why they need Western businesses to invest, but why would anyone bother? If you want to move into the Balkans there's Greece or, better, Bulgaria. Who needs Macedonia? How's Croatia anyway?"

"Not bad, but for two things. One is Franjo Tudjman. I shouldn't say this because I'm a Croat, but I cannot support him. He has many bad policies, especially in Bosnia. The other is the UN, protecting the Serbs and splitting our country. There is a lot of Serb propaganda in the West. Our view never gets heard. What have the Serbs lost in Croatia? Some privileges, some people lost some power, but nobody was *physically* threatened. These thugs, these *vojvodas* stirred the people up in rebellion. We could have crushed them at the outset, and we should have done, but now Tudjman wants to be friends with America, so the UN divides our country.

"Part of the problem is that Tudjman was in it with Milosevic from the start to divide Bosnia. That was a big mistake. We should have combined with Izetbegovic to fight the Serbs like we should be making alliances with Albania and Macedonia against Yugoslavia. Think of it. We're celebrating 50 years since the war against Fascism, yet Britain, America, the West, are supporting Serbia, whose policy is Hitler's: 'We need *lebensraum*! We must protect our nationals beyond our borders'—like Sudetenland. They even have their own Jews—the Muslims. Have you ever thought of making a study of the mosques the Serbs have destroyed?"

"You mean like in Mostar or Banja Luka?" I asked, naming two Bosnian towns.

"There yes, but also in Serbia. Five hundred years of Muslim rule, and there are no mosques left in Serbia to show for it." There's a mosque in Belgrade, in the middle of a housing estate of buildings that tower over its minaret, and I had to point out:

"There are mosques in Novi Pazar."

"You have seen them there? But that is Sandjak, not Serbia proper. We should all combine to fight these Fascists, but the UN is protecting them in my country and it is worse than useless in Bosnia."

"Well, you know it's not *there* to do anything ..."

"And what is the point of an army that does nothing? They should pull out, and then we can sort out our problems by ourselves. Shall we carry on this conversation over a coffee?"

We walked down to the old bazaar and sat under a tree outside a smart café, smarter than I would have chosen. My companion ordered Turkish coffees, speaking his own language. I could see the waiter mentally doubling his price as he assumed an obsequious aspect. I asked for a glass of water with mine.

"Can you drink the water here?" asked the Croat suspiciously.

I sat back and lit a cigarette while a small boy pestered us to buy his Marlboros.

"*Ne pušim,* I don't smoke. I told you already." snapped the journalist irritably.

"They understand your Croatian?"

"Of course. Everybody had to learn that bastardized language Serbo-Croat. It was based on the Bosnian dialect actually—half-way between Belgrade and Zagreb. They say the 'best' Croatian is spoken in Herzegovina, which is why 'we must control the province', but there is no such thing as pure Croatian. It is more a group of dialects. The Tudjman government has been trying to 'purify' the language, but I will give you an example of that 'purification'. In Serbian and Serbo-Croat you say *chas* for 'hour', as in 'what hour [time] is it?'. In Croatian we do not do that, we have another word so the word *chas* was taken out of our language. But we have a colloquial expression, *chas!,* which means 'just a minute!'. It seems we cannot have even just a minute any more."

"Do you think there'll be war?" I asked him.

"I hope not. If there is it will not be of the Macedonians' doing, but the work of outside forces. You take the Albanian situation. I am sure there are *agents provocateurs* involved. I have a friend who used to work at Priština University. Now, the first trouble in Kosovo was in 1981 just after Tito died. My friend told me 'Why should we make trouble? We already had everything we wanted, but people came from the outside.' It's the same here, the trouble is caused by Kosovo Albanians who are far more radical than those from Macedonia because of the oppression in Serbia. And who knows who is being paid by Milosevic? There are plenty of Albanians who would be willing to work for him for some future promise. It's so easy to destabilize the Balkans if you really want to. Look at Greece. I don't know if this is true, but I've heard that their foreign minister, Karamanlis I think his name is, is actually a Slav, but you won't find anyone more virulently opposed to the concept of Slav Macedonians. He knows which side his bread is buttered."

There's nothing like a conspiracy theory. Apart from anything else they absolve the theorist of any responsibility for the situation he finds himself in. The Balkans have always been rich breeding ground for theories of dark, shadowy plots against various individuals and groups, if only because there have in the past been a superabundance of such *actual* plots. In the nineteenth century any European travelling through the region was a spy, probably working for the Russians. Many of them actually were, if not working for Russia then for Britain. Later, every political figure was involved with some revolutionary group and engaged in secret war with every other politician. Again, many of them actually *were*. It became all but impossible to distinguish a conspiracy theory from a genuine conspiracy, and the expression "Balkan Politics" entered the English language to mean "Byzantine, but even more obscure". The Western belief that the politics of the Balkans is impossible to understand and almost certainly not worth the effort involved was born. Relations between north-west and south-east Europe have been hampered ever since.

My companion changed the subject.

"So you're writing a book about Macedonia. Are you dealing with any of the other countries?"

"Not directly, though of course there's reference made to them. So many of people's attitudes in this country are conditioned by the Bosnian war that you have to bear it in mind, but it's best to stick to a small area. To tell you the truth, there's been a lot of rubbish written about Yugoslavia recently especially, with respect, by journalists."

"Absolutely. It's the way journalists work. Sometime you can even tell which newspaper cuttings they've stitched their reports together from. There's one book in particular [he mentioned a book by a well-known English journalist] that is almost complete rubbish but new journalists coming out here for the first time treat it like the Bible. They pass it around on the plane. Like most English journalism it's very pro-Serb. For instance he claims that the Krajina Serbs were 'driven' into secession by Croatia's use of Ustaše symbols. Complete rubbish!"

I am no great enthusiast of most of the work of the author of the book in question, and the view is certainly simplistic, but it is not *complete* rubbish. The Krajina Serbs never wanted Croatia to leave Yugoslavia in the first place—which they demonstrated by voting first for the (federal) Communist Party and then by boycotting Croatia's referendum on independence which returned a 93 per cent vote in favour. Serbs did well out of Yugoslavia. They were in general over-represented in the institutions that mattered—the army, police and Communist Party. They had been used to dominating the country and stood to lose this power. In the words of Reneo Lukic, a Croat, the Serbs were left with the choice "either to [lose] political power and to recognize the new realities or to adopt the policy of open confrontation with the Croatian government." The use of symbols by that government that had also been used by Ante Pavelich's Ustaše during the war made it almost inevitable that they would choose the latter. The Yugoslav army began to arm the Croatian Serbs.

The Ustaše came to power in Zagreb on 10 April 1941, days after the German invasion of Yugoslavia, and ruled over a Croatian state that was comprised of virtually all of modern Croatia and the whole of Bosnia-Herzegovina, only just over half of whose population were Catholic Croats. In May that year Croatia became a monarchy under the Italian Prince Aimone of Savoy, Duke of Spoleto. Though he was crowned as Tomislav II he never visited his kingdom.

It was not long before the killings started. Serbs were given the options of conversion to Catholicism, emigration or death. It is estimated that in 1941 alone, 350,000 Serbs in Croatia and Bosnia died out of a total of 1.9 million. A further 200,000 to 300,000 converted, but in the end the Ustaše was compelled to create a "Croatian Orthodox Church" to deal with the remainder.

The killing was perpetrated not only by Catholics but also by Muslims, and for a while an anarchic barbarism reigned as each side mounted raids on the other. The Croatian politician Machek recalled in his memoirs that he had asked one of his gaolers, when under house arrest, whether he did not fear going to hell for his crimes. "For my past, present and future deeds I shall burn in hell, but at least I shall burn for Croatia," the man replied.

Unsurprisingly, as Tito's Partizans began to organize, they found that much of their support came from Serbs living in Bosnia and Croatia, and for most of the war their activities were largely restricted to those areas.

Then, in 1991, Croatia was reborn. Pavelich was rehabilitated, as was Archbishop Stepinac, the Catholic prelate who initially supported the Ustaše. The chequered shield of the Ustaše reappeared on the Croatian flag, and a currency called kuna, like its wartime predecessor, was inaugurated. Shortly afterwards Alija Izetbegovic accepted that his efforts to hold Yugoslavia together had failed, and against his better judgement—for he must have known what was coming—he led Bosnia-Herzegovina to independence. Both countries were immediately recognized by Germany. History seemed to be repeating itself, and the Serbs defended themselves in the only way they know how—by fighting. Ratko Mladic, whose first name means "Little War" and who later went on to make a name for himself as the butcher of Bosnia, was the officer in charge of the garrison at Knin, which for four brief years became the capital of the "Serbian Republic of Krajina". A native of Herzegovina, both his parents had been killed by Croatian Fascists during the war.

It is no use either Croatia's President Franjo Tudjman protesting that the symbols of the new state have deep roots in Croatian history totally unconnected to the Ustaše. The swastika is a symbol thousands of years older than Nazism, but in Europe it can have only one connotation. Even in the swastika's Indian home I can hardly suppress a shudder when I see it painted on temples or lorries. Symbols matter.

"It seems to me," I ventured, returning to Bosnia, "that the whole situation has descended to the level of *vojvodas* again, answerable to nobody but themselves but each with their own *cheta*. Even people nominally loyal to Izetbegovic are not controlled by him."

"What was that word you used?"

"*Cheta*. As in *chetnik*."

"I'm sorry, I didn't realize you were using our Croatian word. It looks like that, yes, and of course the whole thing is a mess, but even before the war people in Belgrade were saying that no-one's in control. That's an idea that's got into the Western mind, and it's a very convenient one, because if nobody's in control, no one person is responsible. It's an excuse for doing nothing. What would happen if Milosevic or Mladic were tried *in absentia* for war crimes and found guilty? How could we negotiate with them then? And who would be left to negotiate with?" Three months later Mladic *was* charged with "crimes against humanity", specifically with genocide. He now had every reason not to call a halt to the Bosnian war.

"Could it be the case that, though Milosevic and Karadzic say they hate each other, it's just a show for the benefit of the international community—to make it look as though it's a civil war in Bosnia, without Yugoslav involvement? After all, it's easy to say one thing and to do another. They could still have links."

"I hadn't thought of that but it's possible. You see, the Serbs have a great inferiority complex, perhaps the greatest in the world. For centuries everyone ignored them. They had their little revolts and their internal politics and nobody cared. Now they find the eyes of the world on them. For the first time since 1389 everything they do is important. Naturally they love it, playing at being the big shots, so they jump this way and that to keep the world watching them, to keep everyone following what they do. But you wait until this new road's built. You know they're building one from Durrës on the coast of Albania through Skopje and Sofia to Istanbul, a new Via Egnatia. When that's finished Serbia will be irrelevant. It only matters now because of the transport links through it. Serbs are good-for-nothings, all show and no work. All the profitable businesses were in Slovenia and Croatia. Serbian industry just sucked money out of the federal treasury. They're not workers. They're about to lose everything, so they're just stealing as much as they can."

The perennial complaint of the wealthy. The poor are poor because they won't work. As happened in the Soviet Union, it was the rich republics of Yugoslavia which broke the federation, refusing to subsidize the poor any longer. The poorest republic, the one with the most to gain from all that Croat and Slovene industry, as well as from the added security of being a part of a much larger whole, was Macedonia. Like Tadjikistan, the Soviet Union's poorest republic, Macedonia was the last to leave the federation, and then it did so largely to avoid becoming embroiled in the Bosnian war. The movement started in 1991 with the founding in the Bitola army base of the Secret Macedonian-Revolutionary Organization (Officers). Its demand was simple—Macedonians would not fight against Croats. The catalyst for the movement was an incident earlier in the year when Yugoslav People's Army (JNA) troops were on the streets of Split on Croatia's Dalmatian coast. A Croatian mob attacked an armoured personnel carrier. A soldier, a conscript rather than a regular, was hauled from the machine and strangled to death. That conscript was a Macedonian.

Ironically, it was to Split that the Roman Emperor Diocletian retired to engage in the entirely harmless pursuit of growing cabbages, having wearied of persecuting Christians. He left behind him a Rome divided into four parts with two emperors and two vice-emperors. Before long Rome was split by civil war and emissaries were sent to Split to beg the old man to come out of retirement and restore the order and unity of the empire. He refused. Cabbages were preferable to politics.

Macedonia needed Croatia as a provider of subsidies and a market for Macedonia's agricultural products. So in truth did Serbia, but the Serbs are too proud a nation to allow of dependence on anyone. Nobody needed poverty-stricken and remote Macedonia—it was the only republic from which the JNA withdrew without a shot being fired.

✳ ✳ ✳

It was time to get out of Skopje. The city had become oppressive. Spivs roaring down the avenues in their German cars, some of which must have been provided by that "collective" in Petrich, were just showing off their money while they still had it, crowding the Casino of the Grand Hotel with their molls. The thrill of seeing buses from Istanbul lined up in the vacant lot outside the hotel soon wore off. People walked around with a dazed air as if recovering from a concussion and not entirely sure of what was going on. Skopje was a temporary city, restless, uncertain of its future and of itself. The only place I felt comfortable was a bar out in the suburbs near where I was staying, out past the so-called "Audi-Porsche" franchise, where I would go in the evening to eat grilled meat and write up my notes over a bottle of Skopsko lager. I sat in the gloom in one corner, the elderly owner sat in another, chain-smoking and reading that day's issue of *Nova Makedonija* while youths from the student flats across the way came in to use the telephone and dilapidated buses filled with women bearing string bags staggered along the pot-holed road. Outside, under the intermittent street lighting, dogs would be scavenging in the rubbish bins. The old man and I rarely spoke to one another.

Most of all I needed to get away from the overbearing presence of the Internationals. Those white UN cars forever dashing off on some errand or arrogantly parked outside the most expensive restaurants and most exclusive bars, their helicopters forever beating the air with urgently thudding rotors, gave Skopje the feel of living on the edge, as if everyone knew that disaster was imminent. A Chinese family that had set up a restaurant in the bazaar found itself catering mainly to off-duty American soldiers who spoke too loudly and defaced the menus, correcting the English spelling and substituting "scallion" for "spring onion". The agencies carry themselves with a self-important swagger which is almost all show. Some, like the UNHCR or the OSCE appear to be doing something to stabilize the situation, but most—UNPREDEP especially—are simply there because they are there. They serve no function besides salving the conscience of a self-obsessed West and lining the pockets of the petty criminals who supply them. You can't escape them, Skopje is too small a city for that. Before long I caught myself assuming that every half-glimpsed white car belonged to the UN and was surprised each time I found it did not. They swarmed like flies around a dying but not yet dead corpse, just waiting to lay the eggs of future "peace-keeping missions" in the rotten flesh. But it was the flies, not the flesh, that stank.

Prilep

I travelled to Prilep on the train from Skopje, from the new station that replaced the one preserved as a monument to the earthquake, its clock eternally stopped at 5.20 when the disaster struck. Four carriages did service for what had once been an express from Belgrade. They quickly filled as we meandered back down the Vardar valley past green fields baking in the sun. Families still in their Sunday best and fresh from church could be seen driving their horse to plough. Skopje may have been given over to gangsterism and a blue-bereted international Mafia every bit as distorting to the economy as the local wide-boys but rural life seemed to be going on as it had always done.

Except in times of cataclysm such as war, rural communities are far less susceptible to the breakdown of government than cities. Water comes from the well, fuel from the hills or out of the back of the family cow, food comes from the garden and from the orchard. Ceausescu

173

knew that, and so he bulldozed the beautiful wooden villages of Romania and rehoused the population in agro-industrial complexes, solitary towerblocks rising from the vast flatness of the Banat and the rolling hills of Bukovina, "villages" where water came from a tap and food from a shop. For the first time in history the Romanian peasant was entirely dependent on the state.

By Western measures—measures linked to disposable income— these solidly labouring villagers glimpsed from a passing train were poorer than the citizens of Skopje, yet it was not *their* world that had been turned inside-out. Yugoslavia never collectivized on a large scale, especially not in the south and east, where an army of peasant land-holders ensured that there were no big landlords against whom the Communists could turn their wrath. The small farmers kept their small holdings, living just above subsistence level, and consequently felt less of the shock of the change of governing ideology than their urban cousins. Seventy per cent of land in Macedonia is privately owned, and from it 90 per cent of the country's food requirements are met. These were the people who would vote for Gligorov and his cronies and not suffer from any alleged misrule. Macedonia is one of the few states in Europe with a largely rural population, perhaps not well educated and liable to follow the voting proclivities of the local mayor and chief of police (both of whom are in the pocket of the government) while the new opposition parties, dependent on an urban industrial elite, never organize in the villages that hold the keys to power.

We left the river at Titov Veles and swung towards darkly forbidding mountains, jagged as sharks' teeth. A barracks slipped by. At first its deserted watchtowers and broken windows made me think it had been abandoned, but lounging under trees in slovenly battledress were a few soldiers. This was the ARM, Macedonia's fledgling army, a force of 20,000 whose leader delights in the rank of vice-admiral. After all, if land-locked Hungary could have a full admiral as head of state between the wars, why could Macedonia not have a vice-admiral? Both had earned their rank serving in the Adriatic fleets of countries which no longer existed. The ARM looked incapable of anything, let alone of fighting, but when the time came they would doubtless fight bitterly and bloodily to the very end against overwhelming odds, crawling like mites over those sharks' teeth and waging guerrilla war as their grandfathers and great-grandfathers had done.

Habitation grew scarce as we climbed towards the mountains. Meadows studded with poppies rolled away to the distant slate-grey walls, and from time to time herds of goats could be seen sprinkled across the landscape. At long intervals the train stopped briefly outside tiny villages, clusters of whitewashed, red-tiled buildings strung out along dirt roads. People struggled on or off the train with cardboard boxes tied with string, fighting their way along the crowded corridors. In each village a new church, the classic cross-in-square, was being built, the unrendered concrete and brick starkly grey and pink against deep green fields. We sat in silence as the train rumbled on, listening to a five-year-old girl reading out loud from a primer to her father.

The valley narrowed, growing rockier and more sparsely vegetated. A river rushed by in a roar of angry white foam. From the sagging wooden balconies of tumble-down *konaks* in a solitary Muslim village children waved as we drifted past. Noticeably poorer than their Christian neighbours and unable to run to a new mosque, the villagers had nevertheless clubbed together to restore their old one, all save the minaret. A beautifully carved new wooden veranda faced the railway and freshly painted mystic symbols decorated the walls. There could be no Albanians here, and it seemed unlikely that they were Turks. They must have been Pomaks, or Torbeshi as Slav Muslims are known in this part of Macedonia, but as to why there should be this isolated Muslim village in a sea of Christianity there was no clue, unless it was to be found in the name of the next village we stopped in. Bogomila.

✳ ✳ ✳

Bogomil, whose name means "God-lover", is thought to have been a priest from Macedonia. We know little of the sect that he founded and which bears his name, and what little information we do have stems from anti-Bogomil writings. Bogomil was active during the reign of the Bulgarian Tsar Peter who introduced Christianity to the Balkan Slavs He taught a radical dualism which held that matter was the creation of the Devil and should therefore be avoided as much as possible. It followed that the Creator God of the Old Testament was evil, since He brought matter into being, as distinct from the God of the New Testament. Since Jesus was divine, He cannot have had physical form but only the appearance of it. "Matter" included the sacraments of the

Church, which were rejected, leaving only the Lord's Prayer. It seems that the Bogomils were divided into two classes, those sympathetic to the teaching and a body of "the elect" who were celibate, vegetarian, teetotal, and given to roaming the Balkans with a bag containing a copy of the New Testament as their only possession, for which habit they became known to the Greeks as the Phundagiagitae, or "bag-men".

Bogomilism caught on like wildfire in the new Bulgarian Empire, to the extent that Plovdiv became an almost entirely Bogomil town, and it even spread to Constantinople, where a monk by the name of Basil was burned at the stake for teaching the heresy. By 1211 Tsar Boril complained that the devil had "sowed all the Bulgarian lands with heresy". Well might he complain. As early as 970 the priest Cosmas noted that "they slander the rich, they hate their emperors, they mock their superiors and they insult their lords." However, he admitted that the clergy of the time were largely ignorant, drunken sloths and were largely responsible for their own undoing.

Anna Comnena, daughter of the twelfth-century Emperor Alexios I, put the blame for the heresy entirely on the Armenians, and it has often been claimed that Bogomilism was an offshoot of the Paulician heresy with its roots in Asia Minor. On the other hand modern scholars, particularly Communists, have seen in this medieval hippy movement a revolt against the aristocracy of both Bulgaria and Byzantium. It is true that Bogomilism seems to have appealed most to peasants, but that by itself does not make it a form of class war. In fact Cosmas paints a picture far removed from one of militancy: "the heretics are lamb-like, gentle, modest and silent … they keep away from the sight of men and outwardly they do everything so as not to be distinguished from Orthodox Christians."

The *Dictionary of the Middle Ages* has another explanation for the origin of Bogomilism: "Recent missionaries have observed that certain newly converted people, by exaggerating the role of the Devil, have spontaneously arrived at a dualist Christian cosmology." It was among the recently converted Slavs of the Balkans that Bogomilism developed. Bogomilism survived Byzantium, retreating into the mountains and spreading west, notably to Bosnia. What is certain, though, is that it did not survive Islam. Perhaps the Muslims of that village in a remote part of Macedonia near the town of Bogomila had once themselves been Bogomils.

✳ ✳ ✳

As the train plunged down through tunnels towards Pelagonia three people in their early teens took over some vacant seats in the compartment. They looked Turkish. The eldest spoke to me.

"I'm sorry, I don't speak Macedonian."

"I think you Englishman?" he said, a beaming smile lightening his face. "Please, can I see your book?" It was *Roughing It* by Mark Twain.

"Have you heard of Mark Twain?" I asked him. "A very famous American writer. But this book is very old, it is difficult. People do not speak like that now."

"I see. This bit I understand I think." He read a passage about "taking ship for Albany". I think he took it for a reference to Albania.

"I learn English five years," he confided, "but before I only talk in school. You are first English I find. I want very much go England. Please, how is London?"

"Very big."

"I want much see Oxford Street. You take me please London?"

"That would be difficult."

"I see. Soon I go Germany. I have aunt Germany."

"*Dann du sprichst Deutsch?*"

"Little. But please I want speak English. This man," he indicated the louche youth seated opposite, "my cousin. He learn French."

"*Et tu parles bien français?*" I asked him. He didn't understand.

"Please," continued the first boy, "you make pen-pal? I give address, you give?" We swapped addresses. I gave him the Ladbroke Grove address I usually pass out on such occasions. I have no idea who, if anyone, lives there but whoever it is they must be getting an awful lot of letters from obscure corners of the world. The boy's name was Asan Memedov.

"You're Muslim?"

"My mother. But I am orphan. My father dead, and many problems because my mother not work. Many people not work. Today I go see grandmother–grandfather in Prilep, but night to Veles. London big house?"

"Many big house."

"Our house two room. I have four brothers, also Mother is there."

I tried to draw him on politics or inter-faith relations. Of the former he said only "much poor", of the latter "not big problem". We rolled on across the plain.

"Ladbroke Grave!" announced Asan suddenly. "This is house of dead people, yes?"

"No, *Grove*. *Grave* is *mazar* in Persian, *türbe* in Turkish. *Grove* is like *ulitsa*."

"I understand. By this hill are many *groves*." We passed a cemetery.

A man in a grey suit and a mane of white hair who had a bulbously fleshy nose and who had sat opposite me in silence all the way from Skopje leaned forwards and addressed Asan: "Who's he?"

"Someone from London. He says he's a writer."

"He looks very young to be a writer. What does he write about?"

"About Macedonia." I interjected.

"What? Religion, politics, economics, mentality?"

"All of them, but mostly about mentality. Most people in England have never heard of Macedonia."

"Then it is good that you write. Are you going to Bitola?"

"No, Prilep."

"Then you must be interested in Kralje Marko. All the world knows of Kralje Marko! Look!" He pointed out of the window to a hill like a heap of pebbles, each perfectly rounded and smooth yet firmly anchored to the bed-rock. "That is Marko's monastery. The God-bearing."

"That is Mother Jesus Christ," explained Asan. Everyone peered out. Sure enough, clinging to the very uppermost part of the crag, a line of white buildings could just be discerned, inaccessible, free of Turks. Ten minutes later we were in Prilep, crawling around the foot of angry looking mountains.

"See!" exclaimed Asan, "Markov Kale, Marko's Fortress." Ruined battlements spilled down the hillside. "And here, lower down, Monastery Archangel. You will go. Varoš district. Very good, very old. In Prilep only bazaar interesting."

We shook hands outside the station. "I am very happy meet you," Asan declared. "You good man. I like you. No, I *love* you, very much! You have my telephone number in Titov Veles. When you are there you will ring? I come!"

✳ ✳ ✳

Prilep produces cigarettes. And beer. In their leisure hours its citizens smoke and drink, though sometimes they just sit as immobile as the statues that adorn their town, sculptures so abstract that sometimes it is only from the fact that they are mounted on plinths that you can tell they *are* sculptures. What little does happen in Prilep happens slowly. After Skopje it was a relief to come to this sleepy market town on the very edge of the Pelagonian plain.

The brewery was founded by a German in 1924, a fact of which the present management is extremely proud. The label on the bottles, printed entirely in German, proclaims "Kronenbier Export Pils. Produced with German Technology. Seventy years' love of beer." The cigarettes, by contrast, are stuffed into little red packets touchingly labelled "Filter Jugoslavija". They must have had an awful lot of those little red packets left over when Yugoslavia collapsed.

Actually, something *was* happening in Prilep. People were getting married. In droves. The smartest reception in town, being held in the only hotel, could be heard several blocks away, the sounds of wild music, clapping hands and stamping feet hanging like blossom in the acacia trees all along the main street. Every restaurant played host to a raucous party. At the Church of the Virgin, one of those half-underground basilicas built in 1838, the priests were still hard at it at six in the evening. A constant supply of wedding parties, decked out in their finest and armed with flowers and video cameras traipsed in and out of the building, barely giving the celebrants pause for breath. Perhaps it was something in the water that had prompted this sudden rush for wedlock, or the fact that the snows had finally withdrawn from the mountains.

In the courtyard of the church stood a freshly erected marble tomb. On the side, picked out in yellow paint was the Star of Vergina. It contained the remains of one Pere Tošev, 1865–1912, another VMRO hero fallen in the Balkan wars. If the Serbs came, how long would this tomb last? I wondered. Heroes have a habit of mutating into enemies or disappearing without trace in the Balkans. An elderly woman lifted a young child onto the tomb to pick the flowers of a lilac tree that shaded it. At long last Macedonia, a multi-racial, multi-confessional country in the Balkans, was being born out of the ashes of defeat.

Near the Church of the Virgin another, lavishly domed, church stood sentinel over a river which was in reality little more than a stream.

With the sun shining on it its cream walls, brown roofs and lead domes, bunched together in that pepper-pot configuration I knew so well, it stood out proud against the slatey blue of the sky and of the surrounding mountains. Already the wood for next winter had been chopped and neatly stacked along the wall ringing the compound in which the church stood. Two old men were grazing their goats in the lush green grass along the river and a horse clopped lazily by. Unhurriedly, the church bell clanked its appeal to whoever was interested, and a handful of people filed inside. A scene of perfect peace. Yet storm clouds were gathering over the mountains, darkly black against the vivid blues and yellows of the dying day. There was a stone plaque over the church's door. Carved in Greek, it read "Greek Church of the Transfiguration, 1871". The Greek for "Transfiguration" is *Metamorphosis*. It was a stark reminder that the peaceful scene I was witnessing was not timeless, but very recent. Always lurking in the background was the centuries-old struggle between Greek and Slav for supremacy in Macedonia. Fewer than 70 miles due east was the site of the Battle of Strumitsa and the monastery of The Putting out of Eyes, *Vadeocha*. Samuel's army must have stumbled blindly through Prilep on its way west to Ohrid.

Macedonia itself has undergone metamorphosis, from a Socialist Republic of Yugoslavia to a sovereign state, struggling for breath in a small pond already overcrowded with larger fish. I was uneasily reminded of Kafka's man–beetle, at first treated with condescending kindness by his family but ultimately capable of inducing only revulsion and condemned to being shut in a back room never to be referred to, a problem too big, too baffling, to be faced. Nobody deserves that fate.

Kruševo

The little town of Kruševo is depicted on the new blue ten-denar note. To get there you travel along narrow roads across the flat expanse of Pelagonia. Scattered villages shy away from the road, self-absorbed and compact, though a couple of times you pass through a square where a handful of young men are lounging around outside the Café-Bar Malibu. The belfry of the village church has been made taller and now sports a clock, but where the plaster has fallen from the walls of houses you can see bricks of baked earth beneath.

Out into the country again and storks are standing watch over herds of goats. A man calmly grazes his cattle on the runway of Prilep airport, where they share the grass with a biplane of Second World War vintage, the Star of Vergina proudly emblazoned on its tail. By a river families are picnicking and russet hawks rise from the verges as the bus passes. In the distance stands a solitary minaret, but a sign points to a dirt side road, inviting you to the Monastery of the Saviour. "VMRO is the Saviour of Macedonia" someone has written on a wall.

Then the bus begins to climb, falteringly finding bottom gear, and winds up the side of a mountain. Pelagonia, all that lush grassland, falls away. The mosque is a mere speck now, and through the blue haze are dimly discernible the mountains that guard Prilep. To the left, nestling among pine trees far below, is the monastery, a bright splash in the dark green. At last the bus rounds a corner and Kruševo comes tumbling down the mountain towards it, a jumble of solidly square houses.

Kruševo, a resolutely Christian town, was a collection of the forbidding *kâštas* also found in Bansko, though here called *kucas*, and Turkish-style *konaks* dating from the 1860s. The latter, beautiful wooden structures with overhanging upper storeys, ornate balconies and many windows, each sit in their own compounds behind a low stone wall in the company of a well and a pile of chopped wood. Large sums of money had recently been lavished on many of the houses and they stood spick and span under gleaming coats of blue and white paint. I was reminded of the countless similar small mountain towns in the north of Greece. Behind the main church a tiny triangular marketplace was a hive of activity but before long I found myself walking alone through the narrow cobbled streets that wound seemingly at random around the houses. Dogs lounged in sunny patches and looked at me in only mild curiosity as I passed. From a yard came the light tap-tap of a hammer as somebody shod a donkey. Far away a cuckoo was calling. Old people sat motionless outside their *kuca*s, following me with their eyes. Kruševo, quietly prosperous, was minding its own business. The only indication of its claim to fame—or to notoriety—was the name painted above a number of shops and businesses. Ilinden.

In 1903 two-thirds of the population of Kruševo was Vlah, and the remainder, all Slavs, supported the Greek rather than the Bulgarian Church. Nevertheless, it was here that the VMRO established their revolutionary government following the Ilinden uprising. From a robust *kuca* commanding a fine view of the town, the two roads approaching it and the Pelagonian plain they flew the Bulgarian flag and proclaimed the Kruševo Republic, issuing a statement to the effect that the uprising was directed against the sultan, not against Muslims. The telegraph was cut, along with the Bitola–Thessaloniki railway and bridges were destroyed. At the time the Ottoman army was otherwise engaged in Kosovo, where the Albanians were revolting, but as soon as troops were available, the rising was brutally put down. The revolutionaries had forgotten the first law of Balkan politics—gain the support of outside powers. Bulgaria gained independence on the backs of the Russians. Greece had Britain, thanks in large part to the efforts of Byron who helped them principally by dying and thereby drawing Greece to the attention of romantically minded and classically educated Britons. VMRO had no-one. Although the Great Powers had long been hovering over the decaying remains of the Ottoman Empire, the events of 1878 had made it quite clear that they would not countenance a new Slav state in control of Macedonia. Britain especially, terrified as it was of supposed Russian ambitions towards India, was frantic to prevent the emergence of a state which it was assumed would be little more than a Russian puppet, bringing that country perilously close to control of the Bosphoros.

Inevitably, the revolt failed, but if H. N. Brailsford is to be believed the leaders of VMRO seem to have been prepared for its failure. Brailsford worked with Edith Durham with the British Relief Fund distributing aid to the villages devastated by the Turkish reprisals after Ilinden, an experience he later wrote about in his book *Macedonia: Its Races and their Future*, a work produced with the aid of the *Manchester Guardian*. It is an impassioned book, filled with anger at the Turkish administration and the West's seeming indifference to the suffering Brailsford saw in Macedonia. He wrote of "an old priest lying beside a burning house speechless with terror and dying slowly; a woman who has barked like a dog since the day that her village was burned". Brailsford refers to the Slavs of Macedonia as Bulgarians, but makes a clear distinction between them and the Bulgarians of Bulgaria; indeed he claims that one part of the reason for the uprising's being called only in the *vilayet* of Manastir (an area which roughly encompasses the southern part of FYROM and the western part of the Greek province of Macedonia and which did not at the time abut Bulgarian territory) was that VMRO wanted to avoid the possibility of the uprising being laid at the door of Bulgarian agents. They wanted it to be clear that it was a purely Macedonian movement.

The second reason Brailsford gives for the limiting of the rebellion to the *vilayet* of Manastir is that VMRO *knew* they were likely to fail. They were 5,000 men, poorly trained and more poorly armed against three times that number of Turks. The chances were that only Slavs would join in the revolt: the Vlahs would bide their time until it was clear which side was winning before they came out for or against; the Albanians and the Greeks would clearly be opposed to the creation of a Macedonian state and the Muslims were an unknown quantity. Brailsford reproduces a letter sent to the Kruševo insurgents by the headman of a nearby Muslim village begging that the villagers not be harmed, and in fact VMRO seems to have been remarkably restrained, though the *cheta* in the hills near Kastoria did wantonly kill a few Greeks and Muslims. Knowing that failure would provoke terrible retaliation, VMRO, Brailsford claims, tried to limit the damage to a single *vilayet*. The aim, it seems, was not necessarily to throw off Turkish rule, but to provoke atrocities on such a scale that the Great Powers would feel forced to intervene, as they had intervened to create Bulgaria after the notorious Batak massacre. If that was the case, it was a terrible miscalculation.

Reprisal was every bit as brutal as had been anticipated. Kruševo was almost entirely razed; ironically, although they had taken no part in the rising, it was the Vlah quarter which bore the brunt of the Turks' anger. The following winter 3,000 homeless Slav Christians emigrated to America. Yet the powers did nothing. Those VMRO leaders who had survived went into hiding for a while, protected by villagers who seemed to bear no grudge at the hardship the rising had inflicted on them. It was as if the peasants *expected* to be slaughtered when they rose. Brailsford reported solid support for VMRO even in villages which had been completely destroyed, and VMRO leaders could openly walk the streets of Manastir and even Thessaloniki safe in the knowledge that no Slav would betray them.

After the failure of Ilinden VMRO split into a bewildering number of competing factions and waged vicious war on itself and on anybody else who happened to be handy. The underground "government" became a criminal organization engaged in extortion and smuggling, but one faction did succeed in a genuinely political act—the assassination of King Aleksandr of Yugoslavia in Marseilles in 1934, carried out with Italian assistance. At the time, Mussolini's Italy and its ally Hungary under Admiral Horthy were trying to undo the Versailles settlement by destabilizing Yugoslavia. Italy coveted Dalmatia—which had in fact been promised to it by way of a bribe for joining the First World War on the side of Britain and France in defiance of her treaty obligations to Austria-Hungary. The Hungarians would not have objected to the return of the Voivodina and probably much of Croatia as well. Who better to do the job of splitting Yugoslavia than disaffected Croats and Macedonians? Aleksandr, proclaimed Rebecca West, was "not surprised by his own murder"

✳ ✳ ✳

The pre-Ilinden VMRO was idolized by the Communists under Tito, since its existence showed not only that there was a Macedonian people, but a revolutionary one at that. Just outside Kruševo a monument was erected to commemorate the uprising. A cobbled road leads up through fragrant meadows until it comes to a kind of amphitheatre studded with brass plaques bearing the names of events: "Solun Congress 1896"; "Kruševo Republic 1903"; "Rila Congress 1905" and then a litany of names, all the usual heroes: Dimo Hadzi Dimov, Yane Sandanski, Gjorge Petrov, Dame Gruev, Gotse Delchev …

The path continues, and there it is, huge and hideous and the size of a large house, a concrete golfball studded with lumps which contain stained-glass windows. It looks like an especially nasty bacterium grown to monstrous proportions, or perhaps a spaceship from a bad science fiction film whose occupants, improbably, have landed on this Macedonian mountain demanding to be taken to Mr Gligorov. That impression is heightened by a ramp leading up to two huge brass doors in its side, doors such as only a giant would need. The structure is awe-inspiring in its unpleasantness. A family of Macedonians was gazing at it in admiration. The father, a man of about 45, dressed in a smart green

blazer, asked me to take their photograph with the monument as a backdrop, handing me an antique Zeiss camera.

"Everyone!" he shouted, "This is Mister William from England!"

"Manchester United!" came the reply.

I wandered a short way down a dirt track away from the Thing. Delicate yellow and purple wildflowers that looked like miniature pansies smiled up at me. The hill fell away steeply down to the plain, and the mountains on the other side were just visible through the haze, their snow-capped peaks gradually diminishing till they became lost somewhere near Bitola 20 miles to the south.

A bush shook and spat near me. Then a wizened old man appeared, trousers tucked into boots, a wiry grey moustache projecting from his upper lip. He seemed bent double by the weight of the spade he carried over his shoulder. He stopped for a moment and examined me.

"What are you looking at?"

"Just the view."

"Very good." And he tottered off along the track, his curiosity satisfied.

✳ ✳ ✳

Not far from the Thing a small cemetery spread down the hill. The gate was locked, but I hopped over a low wall to examine what appeared to be war graves. Two rows of identical marble slabs paraded in front of a small obelisk as if being reviewed by it. From each grave a uniformed man or woman peered out, their photographs now brownly blotchy with age. Some wore their caps at jaunty angles but all wore the same stern expression. Almost without exception they had died in 1943. An old lady came puffing up the hill towards me.

"How did you get in? I thought that gate was locked," she said.

"It is."

"Yes, it usually is." She ran her hands over a polished granite headstone, and began to weep, sobbing softly to herself with her eyes turned heavenwards. "My husband."

I turned away, not wishing to intrude on her grief, but she called after me, "Young man! Why are you looking at the Partizan's graves? You should see the grave of Pitu Guli, over by that tree. He was a real *voivoda*, a great man."

I looked, and sure enough there was a granite slab adorned with a carved rifle and the legend '*Voivoda* Pitu Guli, 1865–1903' There is a Vlah cultural association named after him.

"Was he in VMRO?" I asked.

"No, he was a *proper voivoda*," the old woman replied, "he and his men fought in the mountains. They never came down. Have some *lokum*." She scrabbled in her capacious bag for a moment then withdrew a box of Turkish delight, proffering it to me. I took one out of courtesy and ate it slowly, savouring the crisp coconut that frosted the revoltingly sweet delicacy. My companion lit a candle and placed it in the ground.

"Are you married?" she asked.

"Yes."

"Then don't go to war. Married people should not go to war."

Pitu Guli was in fact the leader of the Kruπevo battalion of the VMRO at the time of Ilinden, one of very few Vlahs to be directly involved in what was essentially a Slav movement. His name is not present on the memorial to the rising, but someone had recently placed flowers on his tomb.

✳ ✳ ✳

I drifted slowly along the cobbled streets back towards the bus station, breathing in the clear mountain air and scattering squawking chickens out of my path. In the marketplace was a bar with the single word "paradise" above its door in tomato-red paint. What other colour could it be—*paradejs* means "tomato" in Macedonian and Serbian although the same word means "garden" in Persian. I suppose it makes sense— what would you grow in a garden if not tomatoes?

I entered a curious triangular room. The hypotenuse formed the street frontage, pierced by windows. Along the base of the triangle was the bar, while the apex was infested by policemen drinking beer and raki. The room was furnished simply with tables at which people sat on wooden benches. Brightly coloured textiles hung from the walls. At most perhaps 30 people could have sat there. I asked the landlord for a beer.

"You want one of those?" he asked, pointing to the glasses from which the policemen were drinking. Each could have held a quart.

"No, I'd like a small one."

"We do not have small ones."

My tankard, when it came, was half-full of beer. The other half was occupied by froth. A youth was pouring beer from the tap into more tankards and storing them in the fridge. I was soon to find out why. I asked when the bus left for Prilep.

"The last one's at five." I made a mental note, took out some paper and began to write. "Where are you from?" the landlord demanded.

"From London." Someone leaned over from another table.

"From London? Please, sit here. You speak French?" Before I had a chance to reply the speaker had grabbed my glass and placed it next to his own. He was tanned, unshaven and possessed of a large hooked nose and lugubrious hooded eyes. He was smartly dressed in a jacket and a silk tie.

"I am a Vlah." he announced as if this status bestowed access to the secrets of an esoteric religion. Then he pointed to the man seated opposite him. "He also is Vlah."

"It's a shame my father isn't here," I observed, "because he speaks Romanian."

"Really? Is he Romanian? I never heard of anyone who spoke Romanian. That language is very close to Vlah. In fact the Romanians say that we Vlahs are Romanians. That is a pack of lies of course. Never believe anything anyone who is not from Macedonia tells you about this country. Have another beer." It was not an offer. The young man by the bar removed a glass from the fridge.

"How do the Vlahs and the Macedonians get along?"

"Very well. My wife is Macedonian. There are no difficulties because we are all Christians. No Muslim nonsense here." In the nineteenth century an attempt was made to establish a Vlah Orthodox Church. It failed miserably. The Vlahs, of whom there have never been many, have always tended to support whichever group, Greek or Bulgarian, controlled the local church. As Brailsford remarked, "the so-called 'Greeks' of Manastir are Vlahs to a man." Brailsford was very nearly as hostile to Greeks as he was to Turks and Albanians: he firmly believed in the essential Slavness of Macedonia. The Greeks, he thought, lived in Thessaloniki, the Halkidiki and along the Aegean— but then they lived all along the Aegean, not just in Macedonia but in Asia Minor as well. There were just a few pockets of Greekness in the interior, such as the towns of Kastoria and Melnik. These existed in a largely Slav sea; not only were they in the minority, but they were always ready to denounce Slav nationalists to the authorities. Any Slav success would have been a Greek failure, so it was better to fight with the Turks against the Slavs and defend the hegemony of the Patriarch of Constantinoople. My interlocutor was called Šuli. He handed me a business card: "Prota Import–Export".

"Macedonia's OK at the moment," Šuli remarked, "but there's no work for most people. I'm all right with my import–export agency, but I don't know how long it can last. There'll probably be war. Too many people have not enough to do. Gligorov's all right though."

A policeman came in and joined us. "This man is a policeman," I was told.

"I think the fact that he has *Politsija* written on his coat gives it away," I said. The man turned his bulbous nose and twinkling black eyes towards me and issued a bellowing laugh. He had taken the wire out of the crown his cap, and it sagged floppily over the peak.

"*Makedonija* very good!" he proclaimed. A beer was put in front of him.

"No you don't," said Šuli's friend, "You're on duty!" He grabbed the glass and poured its contents down his own throat for safekeeping. He belched. "Have a cola." Somehow another beer had materialized before me.

"Where are you staying?" Šuli asked me.

"Prilep."

"Hotel Lipa? You don't want to stay in Prilep, it's a dump. Stay here."

"Is there a hotel here?"

"Of course. Hey, Zlatko!" Zlatko, in his 20s with curly brown hair falling around his puffy face, came and sat down.

"Yes?"

"This Englishman thinks there is no hotel here." Zlatko took a swig of beer and screwed up his eyes at me.

"Do you speak German?" he asked in that language. "I work in the hotel here. Come on Friday and I will be at the desk, so I will make you a special price of 50 Deutschmarks. I am very pleased to meet an Englishman. No-one ever comes to my hotel anymore because they think there will be war, but there won't. Not if *we* have anything to do with it. The economy's not good, but give it a few years and everything'll be fine, at least if those mad Greeks behave. The embargo's killing us. You should drink rakija."

"I don't like rakija."

"Nonsense! Everybody likes rakija. Just a little one, to try." A glass the size of an egg-cup containing a slightly yellow viscous liquid was placed before me. Screwing up my courage I downed it in one. It burned its way down my throat and proceeded to gnaw a hole in my stomach.

"Drink beer, quickly!" someone shouted and we banged our glasses together. I paused momentarily before taking a draught. It was a fatal error.

"No, you must drink *immediately*," insisted Šuli. This was the cue for everyone individually to give me a lesson in drinking etiquette. I was getting very drunk. Another glass appeared by my elbow.

"I have to get the bus ..." I protested feebly.

"Bugger the bus. It's the First of May! Our friend will drive you later. Anyway you don't really want to go to Prilep. No-one does. What use is Prilep?"

A great bear of a man, ruddy faced and grey haired, plonked himself on the bench opposite and threw a bag of macaroni on the table.

"Macaroni," he observed sagely. "My wife says that I must buy macaroni, so I have bought macaroni, but all that walking makes a man thirsty. I need some wine." The youth behind the bar took a bottle of white off the shelf behind him and emptied the entire contents into a tankard which he set before the newcomer. He drained half of it in a single gulp.

"You speak French? I learnt French at school, but that was 30 years ago. Now everyone learns English. Do you like our country? Do you like our women?"

"I'm married."

"A pity. I have a daughter ..." he leered at me. "Now in Macedonia things are not so good. It is a pretend democracy. The economy is bad, the Muslims are bad, everything is bad. There will be war." He leant back and smiled genially, expelling an enormous cloud of cigarette smoke.

I found myself speaking in French to a neat little man who reminded me of a sparrow. "There are 6,000 people in Kruševo," he was saying, "and half of them are Vlah."

"Yes, there are many different peoples in Macedonia," I said. In my alcoholic fuddlement it seemed like a profound comment. "There is no trouble between them."

"Except the Albanians," said the Sparrow. "They always make trouble, with their university and everything. They should behave like *Macedonian* Albanians. *Albanian* Albanians live in Albania."

"I saw a Muslim village on the road up here. Are they Pomaks?" To my surprise he had never before heard the word. I explained that I meant Macedonian Muslims.

"No!" shouted the Bear aghast, "There can be no such thing!"

"I think he's right," the Sparrow told him, "there *are* Macedonian Muslims, or Muslims who speak Macedonian. Probably Turks really. Everything in Macedonia is very confusing. Turks who think they are Macedonians, Gypsies who think they are Turks ...

"You will find," he continued to me, "that many people here speak French, because it is taught in our schools. Especially women. I don't know why, but women speak French. Why have you come to Kruševo anyway?" I told him I was interested in VMRO.

"VMRO here is very big, very popular. Everyone votes for them. They fight for Macedonia, unlike VMRO in Bulgaria, which is just waiting to conquer us. But that is Bulgaria. This is here."

At a nearby table sat a party of people in their early 20s, Zlatko was now with them. Presiding was a man who sported a sandy goatee and dark glasses. He wanted to speak to me and I went over. He spoke good English, and we chatted about Macedonia's past, its present, its future and the perfidy of the Greeks. More beer. Everyone had the word "embargo" on their lips.

"Macedonia is a good country," I was told. "There will be no war *if* the Greeks lift the embargo and we can trade. We must trade to survive, but the Greeks are making all this fuss about our flag and Aleksandr Makedonski …"

A long-haired youth clad in denim butted in: "All these lies about Aleksandr Makedonski! How can he be Greek with a name like that? *My* name is Aleksandr—Sasha—a Macedonian name. The Greeks say *Alexandros*, which is different. Do you like heavy metal music?"

Šuli and the gang wanted me back. The Bear was on his second bottle of wine and was nursing a glass of raki. He was speaking a polyglot gibberish comprised of French, Turkish, German, Italian, Macedonian and Greek. I was hopelessly drunk and I had missed my bus by several hours.

It was agreed that we should leave. The fresh night air sobered me slightly but the cobbles were heaving like a rough swell in the Solent as we hauled ourselves up hill. I remember that we stopped off in some kind of night-club, all neon lights and blaring music, where we drank more beer and I spoke in English to a girl who understood me perfectly and probably said a number of interesting things. I only remember a pair of legs and pearly teeth ringed with bright red lips. Then Šuli, another man and myself crashed through the gate into Šuli's *kuca*, where we drank raki and a bottle of wine and dined off sheep's intestines in a greasy stew, and watched Serbian singers cavort on the television while children scampered around. Šuli's wife, a poker-faced black-haired woman, was not amused.

The next morning, when I awoke on the sofa, a herd of elephants was dancing a tango inside my skull. I drank glass after glass of water and found a haggard-looking Šuli chain smoking and staring at two cups of Turkish coffee. I drank mine thankfully while his ten-year-old daughter grabbed him playfully around the neck. He spoke to her mollifyingly in Macedonian and she fed him stale chocolates.

Blinking in the bright sunlight we rolled back down the hill to Šuli's shop, a dusty cubby-hole cluttered with imported furniture and kitchen knives.

"I have a friend who lives in Padua and sells *boletus* mushrooms," Šuli said. He showed me a card with a Macedonian name and an Italian address printed on it. "You can make much money that way. It is my new business."

He wanted to go back to the Paradise, but it was shut so we went to the government-run café by the church and sucked up Turkish coffees. The Bear joined us and ordered a glass of *mastika*.

"Isn't it a bit early to be drinking that?" I asked.

"Not at all. I will give you a regime. Before 9a.m. you must drink *mastika*. Then beer until twelve, two glasses of raki and then wine. It is good for your health and will make you strong. But there was a problem with the macaroni last night. My wife told me to get it and I did, but I didn't get home until eleven, and then we fought. She won. That is the history of the Macaroni War."

I left Šuli gazing blankly at the photograph of Marshal Tito that hung in a butcher's shop and fled back down the hill.

✻ ✻ ✻

Prilep will be forever associated with the name of Kralje Marko, the warlord and contemporary of Melnik's Alexei Slav and Kyustendil's Constantine, who carved out a statelet from the ruins of Byzantium. Marko lived to the age of 300, but he is now asleep in Prilep awaiting the time to restore his realm. During his life he slew innumerable Turks and drank their blood whilst running a sideline in combating witches and demons. Edith Durham said of him that "his fabulous and heroic deeds have been sung far and wide, and every kind of savagery justified 'because Marko did it'. It was the excuse offered to me when I denounced the cutting off of Turkish noses and lips in the war of 1912–1913." During that same war a Serbian force took refuge in the citadel of Prilep in the belief that no Turk would dare risk the wrath of Marko in assaulting it.

Marko's horse, Sarach, was no less remarkable. Not only was he blessed with the ability to speak but he could run faster than the wind and liked nothing better than to join his master in a skullfull of wine. The exact whereabouts of Sarach is now unknown. Some have suggested that the animal is dead, but it seems likely that he too is merely asleep. Marko is a national hero in Macedonia. His songs are sung in Bulgaria, Serbia, even as far away as Bosnia. Why Marko in particular should have been singled out for the status of demi-god is uncertain. Durham and others have suggested that in the Marko myth is to be found a folk memory of the mounted Thracian god sometimes identified as Rhesus or Medaurus, but more commonly known simply as the Thracian Rider. Stone tablets carrying the god's image are to be found all over the Balkans, but nothing is known about him save that his cult was favoured by soldiers.

What we *can* say about Marko is that he was the nephew of the Despot Uglješa of Serres, a town now in Greece. Uglješa and his brother Vukašin were killed in battle against the Turks in 1371 and Marko became a vassal of Sultan Murad I, thereby preserving some form of autonomy for his principality. Marko was one of the Serbian nobles who fought against the Serbs at Kosovo, a fact conveniently ignored by the Serbian oral tradition. He died in battle in 1395, fighting Micea the Elder of Wallachia on behalf of Murad's successor Bejazid. Yet, although he fought for the Turks, Marko has been adopted as the symbol of resistance to them. A spot check of a hundred Serbian soldiers in 1909 revealed that all had heard of Marko. Ninety-eight recognized the name of Miloš Obrenovich, who went from supporting the Turks to leading the Serbian uprising of 1814. Just 47 knew that their own king was a man named Peter.

✳ ✳ ✳

Marko's Fortress, which probably actually dates from the time of Tsar Samuel, who alternated his court between here and Ohrid, is a ruin now, frequented only by pink-bellied lizards and young lovers who spread out their coats on the grass and light fires to grill meat. Below, clinging to the rock face like a limpet, is the Monastery of the Archangel. On a sheer cliff above it the name of Tito stands out in white paint. Someone has climbed up there and added VMRO in red.

A path led up the hill to the outer wall of the monastery. Beyond the gate was a courtyard where chickens were scratching in a vegetable garden and brightly coloured rugs hung on a wire. Hard up against the hill are a couple of white *konaks* with carved wooden balconies leaping out over the plain below. Between them stands the church. Originally it was a basilica, but in Marko's time a domed extension was added, its walls a decorative chess-board of white stone and red brick. At one time the exterior had been plastered and decorated with frescos, but now there are just two regally-dressed figures guarding the door beside a sign that reads "Christians! Please leave money to restore our ancient *konak*." Inside, a new concrete floor spans crumbling vaults and fresh plaster reaches down from the dome towards tattered, frescos of statuesque figures. The remaining saints have had their eyes poked out, doubtless by the Turks who held that to remove the eyes was to remove the magic. The saints are named in Greek, but they hold Slavonic texts, a curious compromise. Near the door, where the Dormition of the Virgin should be, Pilate is washing his hands. He still has eyes.

A toothless old man came up to me and asked where I was from. "We have a problem," he said, "I would like to talk to you but I only know Macedonian, no English-French-German-Russian. But please come." We entered the *konak* and climbed creaking wooden stairs to the first floor, past stern icons that frowned at us from the walls. Indicating a door, the man hitched up his trousers and said "You will go in here, but first, this." He swung another door open to reveal a dark refectory. "People eat here," he explained. "Here is fire to cook and here is the oven to make bread and stew." Satisfied that he had done his duty as a guide he pushed me through the first door into a room laced with icons. A couple of wooden tables, one at the back and the other in the window, and some chairs provided the only furniture. A group of people looked up expectantly from their game of poker. The debris of a meal littered the table in front of them. I was introduced, and a haggard man who looked twice his 22 years motioned me to sit, offering a cigarette and pouring me a glass of lemonade. Bright sunlight poured through the windows.

"I'm very pleased to meet you," said the man. His name was Nikola. The others at the table were his wife, his brother with *his* wife, and "a friend". The "friend" was a ragged-looking boy with long jet-black hair whom I guessed to be a Gypsy. He looked about fourteen. He smoked incessantly as he expertly flicked the grimy playing cards through his fingers.

"This is my grandmother's house," said Nikola. "We've come for the holiday, and also because yesterday was my brother's birthday." His brother had a round face which was probably jovial most of the time. Now he looked under the weather.

"Much rakija," he groaned, his cigarette adhering to his lower lip.

"You like rakija?" the friend asked me.

"Of course not. He is English. He likes whisky."

I was aware that a shadow had detached itself from the wall and was noiselessly moving towards me. It solidified into the form of Granny. She stood at my elbow and allowed a smile to play across her moon-like face. She spoke in an insistent voice, her beady eyes twinkling.

"She says welcome to her house. You are her guest. You must eat." She glided to a corner where for the first time I noticed a cupboard from which she removed a plate and cutlery. By my side another plate bore cold fried chicken and some nameless bits of sheep covered in a thick layer of congealed fat. I was offered some terribly salty cheese and a few spring onions.

"Eat!" Granny commanded. Nikola demonstrated by taking one of the pieces of mutton in his fingers and tearing the flesh from the bone with his teeth.

"Where are you staying?"

"The Hotel Lipa."

"How much?"

"Fifty Deutschmarks."

"That is terrible!" exclaimed Granny, throwing up her hands, "Robbery! He must stay here. *I* will not ask for money." She retreated, muttering to herself.

"What do you think of independent Macedonia?" I asked Nikola.

"It is a good country, but there are many problems. Greece makes things difficult and many people are without work, even educated people. Without work you can get no money, and without money you can't eat. In my village—it's only a little one, you won't have heard of it—many people are out of work. Please, you live in London, yes? I would like very much to go to London. Isn't Tower Bridge in London? And Big Ben. Is John Major still president? Margaret Thatcher I liked better."

"I've heard there's a king in England," remarked Nikola's brother.

"We have a queen."

"What's her name?"

"Elizabeth."

"But England is a modern country. How can it still have a king?

Macedonia is a very backwards country, but even we have no king."

"It's our tradition. She's not really important."

"No big part in politics? Then it is just your history. I understand."

"How easy is it to get work in Britain?" asked Nikola. "For us it is very difficult to travel. I still have a Yugoslav passport because the government has not made new ones yet, and it is useless. You can go nowhere with a Yugoslav passport. Perhaps we can exchange addresses and I can be pen-pals with you. Next time you come to Macedonia you will stay in my village. Then you will help me go to your country?"

"Do you think I'll be able to come back? Will there be war?"

"Not unless somebody makes it. It will not come from inside, but we are a small country surrounded by big ones, and when the big ones want a fight they come here for it. This is our fate. Even if there is trouble with the Albanians it will be because Albania has made it. Now that Greece has made our economy bad it would be easy to make trouble with the Albanians. But America will help us."

A bearded, black-robed priest with a curious fire in his eyes strode into the room. Granny rushed to set plates and glasses on the second table. Then a small party of nuns filed in in silence. They were tiny, more elfin than human, and seemingly possessed of immense and profound knowledge. They appeared to have sprung from the pages of a Tolkien novel, moving soundlessly and with intense deliberation across wooden floorboards and down the corridor under the icons. They lived in another wing of the *konak*. They sat at the table and burst into a hymn that sounded like a magical incantation, their voices all but drowned by the priest's booming baritone, while Granny fussed around serving food. The women at our table stood, crossing themselves three times. The Gypsy dealt another hand of cards. Nikola's brother lit a cigarette and coughed, displacing the cards.

The dealer was just about to start again when the bench under him suddenly heaved and a kind of human troll, pendulously breasted and with a tangled mane of strawberry-blonde hair projecting in all directions, emerged from beneath a pile of blankets as if summoned by the priest's chanting. I began to feel that I had stumbled into a work of fantasy, a Balkan Gormenghast ruled by arcane rituals and possessed of bizarre inhabitants clinging to that improbable rock and terrorizing the simple villagers of the plain below by their mere presence.

The apparition shook itself awake, opened its mouth to reveal black teeth, stared at me and said "Liver!"

"Amen," intoned the priest.

I noticed a slimy grey substance lurking under a mound of crushed paprika. The troll broke open some bread and began greedily to push cubes of the stuff into it with her pudgy fingers.

"This is from sheep," Nikola told me. I was relieved.

✳ ✳ ✳

Prilep has moved a couple of miles since Marko's time, but below the monastery a few medieval churches, ruinous now, sit in a maze of dirt roads that weave between houses of burnt mud brick in the Varoš. Bushily moustached and shaggily eyebrowed old men sit on chairs outside their houses, disturbed only by the clopping of horses' hooves as they pass by with their carts.

I retreated back down the tree-lined Marko Street, past Heidi's Milk Bar and its picture of a buxom blonde wench, past the cigarette plant, until I came across a bust. "Lazar Zamenhof 1859–1917. Creator of Esperanto: La mondo estas unu lando; La homaro estas unu popolo." I have never met anyone who could speak this apparently Latin-based language but it is fitting that its deviser, a Pole, should be commemorated in this obscure little town. Where else but Macedonia could a language which is nobody's mother-tongue and is connected to no state have greater claim to validity? Perhaps a Macedonia that used Esperanto as a medium of public communication could have avoided partition, expulsion, genocide. A person who speaks a country's second language is in a sense always a secondary citizen, forced to conduct business in an alien tongue. This is the argument of Macedonia's Albanians when they demand parity with Slavonic for their language as valid for all situations rather than being condemned to the personal realm. But, according to the constitution, Macedonia is "A national state of the Macedonian people". Naturally, their language takes precedence—and why stop at Albanian? Why should Turkish, Romany or Vlah not also be "official"? The country in which *nobody* spoke the official language would be blessed indeed. Language rights are always among the first demands of separatist minorities.

Night was falling as I entered the grid of streets which constitute the old bazaar. Collared doves settled in trees, cooing at one another coyly. All the shops were shuttered. The people who had been madly painting and fitting their new ice-cream parlour in time for the holiday had missed their deadline and brown paper still covered the windows. Even the *korso* had been cancelled in honour of the First of May, even though it was now the Second. If you celebrate Easter a day early, why not celebrate Mayday a day late?

In what had been the town's main square, in the heart of the market, a clock tower which had been built by the Turks but now sported a large cross stood sentinel over a derelict mosque. Great chunks of plaster had fallen away from its walls to reveal the lath underneath and the minaret was crumbling, yet still it retained an air of dignity despite the hard times. Its doors remained proudly green, and a brass padlock secured them as if the imam had unexpectedly been called away to business in Turkey from which he never returned. A group of teenagers sat on the tomb of the mosque's founder, smoking. The sound of music drew me to a lace- curtained restaurant, the only business that was open. Perhaps a coffee and the chance to do some writing.

✳ ✳ ✳

Around a long table sat perhaps twenty people. Before them was arrayed a mound of empty beer bottles and mostly empty rakija bottles. They were singing lustily to the music and a girl with a chiselled Grecian nose and shoulder-length black hair was shaking a tambourine. Within seconds a man in a shabby blue tracksuit had parked himself at my table.

"This is my restaurant," he declared. "You will not drink coffee, you will drink beer, from Prilep! You are from England? Then I will call my brother. He speaks good English. *Hopa!*"

The brother bore a balding head, a leather jacket, squinting blue eyes and a world-weary look. He sucked hard on a cigarette.

"I hear you're from London," he said taking my hand limply. "I lived there for four years, but mostly with other Yugoslavs so I didn't learn very much English. What part are you from?"

"Hammersmith."

"Really? I lived in Fulham for a while, washing dishes in a restaurant. It's a good area, better than Southall where I lived when I was a builder. There are too many Indians in Southall and their food stinks."

"My wife's Indian."

"Then I am sorry. I think maybe you are used to it, but not me. Soon I will go back to London to work. It is a fine city. Everyone in Macedonia wants a nice house and a Mercedes but how can we get such things here? We have to work in other countries. When I was in London I knew many English people who said they wanted to go to Australia. There are many Macedonians in Australia. I could get a good job there, but it is too far, too expensive. So look at me! I have a degree and I wash dishes!" He drained a glass of rakija before resuming his monologue.

"The problem is Greece. They're killing our country with the embargo, and what for? For a name. I'm a Macedonian. I can't think of myself as anything else, I can't be a Serb or a Bulgarian or whatever it is they want me to be. All this stuff about Alexander the Great. He lived on the very edge of the Greek world. He never trusted the Athenians. *His* people belonged to many nations besides Greeks. The Slavs came in the sixth century. Nobody knows where they came from, but they came and they filled this land. They are the Macedonians of today."

"So do you think there might be war?"

"I don't think so but it's impossible to tell." He shrugged. "It all depends on outside powers. Kiro Gligorov is a strong man, a good man, but the war is not up to us. It's out of our hands."

"A lot of people in the West think the Serbs might invade."

"No. Why should they? I have many Serbian friends, and they are good people. If Milosevic wanted Macedonia he could take it, just like that, but why would he want to?" He offered me a cigarette, saying, "I smoke too much. Three packets a day."

All those cigarettes did not seem to have helped his nerves. Like Nikola, he looked far older than his actual years, and he had a haunted air as he edgily surveyed the empty corners of the room, lighting a new cigarette with trembling hands almost as soon as he stubbed out the previous one.

A burly man who was greying at the temples came in and sat down heavily. He ordered *mastika*.

"Hey!" said the tambourine woman, "you speak English. Go and talk to the Englishman!" He lumbered over to my table and collapsed into a chair.

"Hello gentleman," he said. "Beer? How do you like Prilep?"

"Very nice."

"No! Just an overgrown village! There is no culture here. For culture you must go to Skopje, where the university is. I went to university in Skopje. I studied medicine."

"You're a doctor?"

"Alas, no. I studied for four years and then I had to leave. For fifteen years I was very depressed, and then I found God." He put his hands on his heart and rolled his eyes to the ceiling.

One of the party at the other table took out a guitar and began to sing haunting folk songs. He was dressed in a black polo-neck and black jeans and had hair so black it could have been dyed that colour. His eyes smiled and his cheeks twitched with laughter as he threw back his head and sang, joined by the rest of the group. I turned to the owner's brother, who had been silent for some time, and observed that I had been told that singing and dancing were the essence of being Macedonian.

"Dancing, yes. Not singing or playing music. We do not usually do that. Gypsies make music. That is what they are for."

"Tell me," demanded the failed doctor, placing a bottle of beer before me and downing a second *mastika*, "what are these Americans for if they can't protect us? Why have an army if it can do nothing? What is Europe for if it can't help us? This is Macedonia's history, to be the victim of other people's needs. Life is life, and we can do nothing about it. That is all. Life is life. By the Grace of Our Lord there will not be war, but it may come in six years or whenever Greece and Serbia decide. If I was younger I would go to London, but now I am 42 and I am too old. Life is life. We just have to live it."

The guitarist changed his tune: "Hey Jude, don't make it bad / Take a sad song and make it better." Then he handed me a leaflet which extolled the virtues of something called "Herbalife". Written on the back was an address in America.

"Have you heard of this?" he asked. "It's vitamin supplements. I will sell them and get rich."

"Herbalife!" came a chorus of voices from around the table, faces smiling at me drunkenly. They were all going to make their fortunes out of peddling nostrums across the Balkans. Or not.

"You like the Beatles?" the one-time medical student wanted to know. "I like them very much. Also David Bowie. You know he's the same age as me? It's hard to believe. Old music is the best though." He stared down into his *mastika*. "I used to be very lonely. I'm not when I come here, but now I must go. Goodbye gentleman."

I proffered some money to the restaurant owner. "Nonsense! How often do we see an Englishman? Anyway, we are not staying here, we are going somewhere else." I climbed into the guitarist's Lada with his girlfriend and the restauranteur. As we swung into Marshal Tito Street the girlfriend's door swung open and she shrieked, half in fear and half in merriment. Car maintenance is not a highly refined art form in Macedonia, and it is fortunate that they usually drive slowly. The driver put on a tape. "You're simply the best / Better than all the rest" blared forth. He turned around and smiled at me. "Simply the best! Herbalife!"

We rammed into the pavement and then climbed the stairs of an unprepossessing towerblock to emerge into a brightly lit hall where people sat at tables in grim silence facing bottles of wine. The men were staring at a singer who wore a bra, hot pants and very little else and who was singing Serbian pop songs while a bearded man behind her tortured a saxophone, knitting mad rhythms in the smoky atmosphere.

My chauffeur was rattling the tambourine in time to the music as we sat down. From his demeanour and the way the others took their lead from him (as well as the fact that he had the prettiest girlfriend) I guessed that he was the leader of the gang. In a moment the table was piled high with bottles of beer which the men fell upon as if dying of thirst. The women of the party were withdrawn, subdued. They sipped their beer or ordered fruit juice and clearly signalled that they were only there because they had to be, because *someone* had to keep an eye on the men. I remembered Kruševo. The women of Macedonia are a long-suffering lot. Why they bother and don't just emigrate *en masse* to Lesbos defeats me. All day they run the household and raise the children, and all night they have to look after those other children, their husbands.

Someone was attempting, unsuccessfully, to dance on the table, so a *hora* was formed, the women being dragged reluctantly out of their seats. As they circled, encouraged by the singer who paraded before them, I found myself speaking in German to an earnest young man who wore stone-washed denim and had his blond hair in a pony-tail.

"There is no work," he said. "I hope things will become good again, but it is only a hope. Everyone who can is leaving the country. These are not the times of Kralje Marko, however much people may talk of him. We can hope for the future, but we do not control it."

Bitola

The train continues from Prilep across the rolling grasslands of Pelagonia to Bitola. At one time it went further, over the border to Florina. No more. From 1959 to 1967, there had been complete freedom of movement within a strip of land ten kilometres deep on either side of the border. Slavs from Greece used to cross the border to gamble in Bitola's hotel. Nobody knows how many Slavs live in Greece, nor how many have fled to Yugoslavia or further afield, but the bishop of Florina, Augostinos Kandiotis, a noted xenophobe has announced that "even the stones proclaim their Greekness" . He is not a racist—foreigners such as the Slavophones in his diocese are fine, so long as they are Greeks.

Bitola itself has a part to play in Albania's nineteenth-century history. It was here that the Committee for the Liberation of Albania was established in 1905. The Committee formally adopted Latin script for the Albanian language yet to be unified as such from the three alphabets on offer (Muslims, who formed 70 per cent of Albanians, used Arabic, Catholics Latin and Orthodox—about 10 per cent—Cyrillic). The Albanians thus became the first Muslims to abandon the sacred Arabic characters and to look towards Europe for salvation. In addition to this the Committee established yet more armed groups, this time to defend Albanians from the Ottomans on the one hand and from Christian terrorists, such as VMRO, on the other. The crowing achievement of this particular band of brigands came in 1906 when they killed the (Greek) bishop of Korçe, now an Albanian town, who had succeeded in annoying Albanian nationalists, as Greek bishops are wont to do. Bitola has been an important town since Rome moved east, taking advantage of its position astride the Via Egnatia. As Heraclea Lynkestis it was the capital of one of the four provinces into which Macedonia was divided and it was an early Christian centre, the seat of a bishop until the Slavs came and put everyone to the sword—or worse. In 560 Procopios noted that "the Slavs do not kill men with sword or lance ... but thrust them by force onto sharpened stakes."

Under the Turks Bitola, or Manastir as they called it, once again became the administrative centre of a province, one of the *vilayets* which was, according to the Committee for the Liberation of Albania, to have been part of Liberated Albania. It was here that the Military Academy—that were to train a new generation of Turkish officers who would lead a European-style army—were themselves trained. One of the students was a young man from Thessaloniki. His name was Mustafa Kemal.

Edward Lear liked Manastir. He was "agreeably surprised ... at the width and good pavement of the streets, the cleanliness and neatness of the houses". He found the town mostly inhabited by Greeks and Slavs, whom he referred to as Bulgarians, though there were "of Jews a vast number". Rebecca West, who consistently referred to the town by its Serbian name, Bitolj, called it "one of the fairest of all cities ... one of those cities which prove to our amazement that we Westerners have never even begun to understand what town-planning means".

Bitola today is described as "Macedonia's second city" but it remains a small half-forgotten market town, famed chiefly for the production of beer and for its university. A small river tumbles through the centre between two now-defunct mosques and past the covered market, a facsimile in miniature of the Great Bazaar in Istanbul, now occupied by drab state-run restaurants, shops selling spare parts for tractors, and drunks. Downstream, the bazaar weaves a tangled web of narrow streets between low, wooden shuttered shops and past another decrepit mosque to the new market, where people were hawking handfuls of chillies, a few jars of honey or little bundles of carrots and radishes. A few people proudly displayed two or three bottles of Skënderbeü Konjak—Albanian brandy that doubles as paint stripper—or offered Western cigarettes out of cartons at knock-down prices. It was a sorry effort. Of Lear's "long strings of laden mules, four or five hundred together" there was no trace. A black-clad old woman gestured to a bag of crushed paprika and looked at me beseechingly, but I passed on to heaps of plump, blackly glistening olives. They came out of tins marked "Finest Greek Olives". It seemed the embargo was not total.

It was Friday, and time for midday prayers, so I went in search of a mosque, down avenues lined with garishly green lime trees and cobbled back alleys where children played football, shouting "Diego Maradona!" whenever they scored. Minarets showed themselves here and there but the mosques they were attached to proved to be crumbling ruins. One had became a garage called "Dynamo Service". On the ruinous wall of what had once been a *hamam* Goše, Marat, Arap and Naum had written their names in green paint and Latin script. There *were* still Muslims in Bitola—Marat was certainly one, though his friend Naum could only be Christian—but they had effectively become invisible, making Bitola that curious thing one sometimes comes across in Greece, a Turkish town bereft of Turks. There were no fly-bills extolling the virtues of the Turkish Democratic Party of the Republic of Macedonia, no women in pantaloons or men wearing skull-caps. I had expected to see shop signs written in Turkish as I had in Tetovo, but they remained stubbornly Cyrillic. Latin script was reserved for Serbo-Croat, which can be written with equal facility in either script, or the now fashionable English. The only obviously Muslim-owned business I came across was that of M. Nexhipi, dentist and Albanian, but even his sign was written in Latin-script Serbo-Croat. The Jews whom Rebecca West remembered seeing "go softly, murmuring Spanish, into a home refined almost to decadence in its contempt for the exuberant" did not survive the war.

A clue as to what had happened to Bitola's Muslims could be found in the signs over many shops and restaurants: "Solun". Thessaloniki. After the war, when Greece expelled thousands of Slavs over the border, Tito made room for them by granting special leave for the Turks to emigrate to Turkey, and many Slav Muslims proclaimed themselves to be Turks in order to take advantage of the opportunity. So Turkish Manastir died. Unusually for the Balkans it did so peacefully, but were there shops in Istanbul called "Manastir"? Quite possibly. There are shops called "Travnik". For all I know there are shops in Thessaloniki called "Philippopolis"—Plovdiv. Exiles dream of home. They are where they are not by choice but by political necessity, and politics are not made by people, they are made by politicians who, for all their democratic rhetoric, seldom truly care for the people the supposedly represent. What is an abstract "freedom" if it means you must leave your home?

What tension there is in modern Bitola is not inter-religious or inter-ethnic but between the old and the new Macedonia, between the dour, run-down shops which merely proclaim their business ("Barber", "Bookshop") and the neon-lit establishments whose plate glass windows betray imported consumer goods and whose names sound—and in Latin script look—exotic: "Capri" and "Sharon's Boutique".

❋ ❋ ❋

Many of the shops of the bazaar have now become fashionable watering holes, but *the* places to be are the ice-cream parlours of Marshal Tito Street, the pedestrianized main drag that runs away from the river and the old Turkish centre past the Catholic church and elegant town houses dating from the turn of the century, past the ugly bulk of the Hotel Epinal with its casino, the VMRO office and the house of the ARM to a small park by the railway tracks. In the early evening people gather here to drink beer and eat hamburgers and something called a *chizburger* from little kiosks and to chat before moving off to the main *korso* up and down Marshal Tito Street. Two besuited old men wandered past, locked deep in conversation. One was absent-mindedly playing with some lilac blossom which he twirled under his nose. On his head rested a battered grey homburg hat, but we were as far as could be from the German spa town where I drank mulled wine in the snow on Christmas Eve with a girl who played the tenor saxophone. I can't even remember her name now. Yet there was a desperate clutch at the bourgeois European sensibility in that hat—though a touch of the East in the flower.

Studded throughout the undergrowth of the park were busts of Partizans, some designated as "National Heroes"—heroes of a nation that had already died. Some had had flowers of lilac and acacia left on their plinths, presumably on Mayday, for the flowers were sadly wilted now. They were eerie, those dead heroes of a dead ideology, as they peered out of their shrubbery at the fast-food kiosks and money-changers. Nobody had defaced or broken them as in Bulgaria. They had just been left to become overgrown. Left, yes, but somebody still came with flowers. Where was the anger which had erupted in the rest of Eastern Europe and overturned the old idols? Where was the hand of the government, sweeping away all traces of the old Yugoslavia as it had in Slovenia, banning Serbian songs from the radio, renaming streets, removing statues? The Macedonians seemed indifferent to it all. They had sidled out of the federation at the last moment, largely, I was beginning to suspect, because it seemed to be the thing one did. There had been no triumphant change of government. Kiro Gligorov, the last president of the Socialist Republic of Macedonia, had steered the country to independence, quietly dropping the "Socialist" and transformed himself from regional Party boss into a statesman whom the UN deployed to protect, but most people seemed not to care greatly one way or the other. Profiteers profited, the rest went on living life as best they could in the way they always had done. They had been a part of Yugoslavia, now they were not. "Life is life", best get on with it. The people I had spoken to carried with them a deadening fatalism born of their history, a belief that things just happen and the individual is powerless to alter the course of events. They went through life for the most part in a state of utter indifference.

They were not a depressed people though. They had none of the hopelessness of Soviet citizens or of the Romanians under Ceausescu. Far from it. They lived life to the full, and for themselves, for who knows what tomorrow may bring? Firmly believing that the big things in life were out of their hands—and that this was the natural order of things—they busied themselves with the little things, with having a drink or playing football, lighting candles in church and having family meals at which any stranger could be a guest.

However, I liked to imagine that something more than mere apathy had preserved those busts and others at wayside railway stations in the hills where the train paused momentarily to admit some schoolchildren of deposit a party of hikers. Fifty years after the Second World War it is right that we should honour those who fought Nazism. Without them, without the armies that took to the field and these brave young men and women who took to the hills and who died before they were 25, Europe would have been in an era of evil so great the very word seems inadequate to describe it, an evil made all the more horrible by the fact that the vast majority of its perpetrators were not themselves evil. The Partizans were Communists, true, and Communism is out of fashion, but that cannot be reason to tear down their memorials and execrate their memory. To do so is to give victory, if not to Hitler's armies, then to the ideology of Nazism. Yet it is happening throughout Eastern Europe, in Croatia, in Serbia, in Romania, in Slovakia, even in Hungary. The ghost of Nazism has reawoken. The presence of these busts gave me hope for Macedonia, hope that intolerance, of the past as much as in the present, has no place here. History was not being re-written. Heroes remained heroes. I remembered the words of the Croatian journalist in Skopje.

"These people think this is still Yugoslavia," he had said disparagingly, "You still see Tito's portrait everywhere. You don't see that anywhere else." It's true. Tito is everywhere, in portraits in many businesses and in names. Every settlement has its Tito Street. Veles is still *Titov* Veles, when Serbia's Titovo Uzitse has dropped its prefix, and Titograd in Montenegro has become Podgoritsa again. For that I am glad. Yugoslavia was far from perfect (and what country is perfect?), but its people did not slaughter one another in the names of kings centuries dead, they did not seek forcibly to convert their neighbours to another religion. Alija Izetbegovic knew that, and tried to hold the country together in a looser federation. Tito's Yugoslavia was a country worth trying to preserve, but an unthinking West rushed to dismember it. Macedonians in particular have much to thank Tito for. He gave them their language, their state, their church and a peace which continues to this day but which had not been known for 200 years before he came to power.

I never found the old Turkish Military Academy, but on a street shaded by limes and cleft in two by the river a fine turn-of-the-century mansion contained the university and the town's historical archive. Next to it stood an even grander building, its decorative stucco picked out in cream against its grey walls. It was the Josip Broz Tito High School.

✳ ✳ ✳

The next morning dark storm-clouds were rolling threateningly around the mountains as I took the lift to the ground floor of the Epinal and then climbed the stairs to the first-floor restaurant. It is a peculiarity of Yugoslav hotels that the restaurant is usually on the first floor, and there is often no physical connexion between it and the second, which is called the first, where the bedrooms are.

The restaurant of the Hotel Epinal is a hang-over from the days of Communism. Musty crimson velvet curtains fell to the floor over grimy window panes. Brown formica panels covered the walls. The tables were covered with the debris of other people's meals, though their chairs stood empty. At the end of one long table two old men were smoking and talking about politics and the possibility of doing business in Italy or Germany. They poked their fingers and bristled their moustaches at one another as they spoke. I sat at the other end of their table, where mercifully there was some clean cutlery and waited. I lit a cigarette. I stubbed it out. Finally I got up and went to look for the kitchen, where I disturbed the waiter's interesting conversation with a scullion. When I returned to my seat I found that the place opposite me was occupied by a tall middle-aged man who wore a leather jacket and leaned back casually in his chair. He said something to me. I told him I didn't speak Macedonian.

"Neither do I," he said. "You English? I speak a little English. I am from Croatia. Do you know how are things in Croatia at the moment?"

The waiter brought me a plate of ham and eggs, some stale buns and the world's smallest coffee pot, from which I extracted half a cup of a luke-warm infusion of roasted acorns.

"I'll have what he's having," my companion told the waiter before returning to me. "What are you doing in Macedonia? Business?"

"Sort of. I'm a writer. I'm trying to find out why there's no war here." He smiled mirthlessly.

"By a miracle!" He flashed that humourless smile again, then lapsed into silence.

"Are you a businessman?" I asked to keep the conversation going.

"Not really. I'm in business, but I'm not what you would call a businessman." I pondered what he meant. Either he was an extortionist—an "insurance broker" rather—or he had a part in spiriting all those olives over the border from Greece. Or both. A millionaire from Petrich possibly. He said nothing more until his ham and eggs were brought.

"English breakfast," he remarked. I left.

Lurking half underground just a stone's throw away from the two central former mosques the Church of St Demitrios is huge, delicately painted in cream and beige and dated 1830. In the sunken nave, for the benefit of a feeble audience and accompanied by a feeble choir, a priest was warbling feebly before a vast gilt iconostasis sporting the intricate high relief detail that marked it as the work of Debar craftsmen. Old ladies shuffled about in the gloom, but the church was built for grander things than this. Massive stern icons gazed down disapprovingly on the small group huddled in its belly. Almost without exception their inscriptions were written in Greek. Just a few near the back, including those of Clement and Naum, which marked this as a Macedonian place of worship, bore Slavonic texts. Forests of candles burned brightly before the iconostasis, but almost as soon as each supplicant turned away from their devotions his or her offering was greedily snatched up by a blue-coated janitor and thrust into a bucket for re-cycling.

The iconostasis was so massive it had five doors rather than the usual three. When the service ended a second priest, an imposing man whose eyes betrayed great depths, emerged from behind the fifth door and intoned a blessing for a private party in a strong baritone voice. I wished he had presided over the main ritual. The church needed a presence like that. He could have filled it on his own. A dimpled girl touched my arm and offered me some roasted chickpeas which had been blessed, a kind of *prasad*, as Hindus call food which has been offered to the gods. More people were arriving now, circulating, lighting candles, leaving offerings of money or flowers. I went outside to an arcade which ran the length of the church, where I was grabbed by a widow whose voice came out in a garbled screech.

"Buy this!" she demanded, thrusting a picture of a saint into my hand. "You can keep him close to your heart and he will protect you."

"No thanks." She squinted at me, bobbing up and down agitatedly.

"Where are you from? England? Are you Catholic?"

"Protestant."

"Does that mean you don't believe in the Holy Virgin?"

Before I could explain that the Blessed Virgin Mary is, like most things, optional in Anglicanism, she was leading me off indignantly towards a priest. Unlike policemen, you can always find an Orthodox priest when you need one. He was rather a ramshackle affair, his cassock stained, his hands callused with labour and an untidy scrub of grey stubble on his chin. When he spoke you could see that his yellow teeth were mostly broken. He had an idiot grin.

"This man is English," declared the crone, "and he is Protestant!" She huffed with indignation at the idea.

"So what?" he replied. "All Christians are the same. It's a level table."

"But he doesn't believe ..."

"I don't care what he does or doesn't believe. I have told you. Stop talking and listen to me. All Christians are the same." He took my hand, smiling innocently. "Welcome friend." I took an immediate liking to him. He understood my Bulgarized Russian perfectly, though I was less sure of his Macedonian.

"Most Macedonians are Orthodox. It's very important to our people. I'm not sure about other Christians, but there's a Catholic church on Marshal Tito Street and I think some Protestant ones. There *are* some Muslims here I think, but if you really want Muslims you must go to Ohrid. They have many there, but be sure to go and see St Naum as well. He lives there. Here we're Christians. You must see our new churches, this way," he gestured, "and that." I promised him that I would.

As I left the church, along a cobbled alleyway with the words *Hristos Voskrese, Vistima Voskrese* strung across it, I pondered the its dedication. Demitrios is patron and protector of Thessaloniki. More than once he has personally intervened to save that city from barbarian hordes. A warrior, his icons depict him mounted on a horse with an infidel impaled on his lance. He and St George feature in most Balkan churches. As with Marko, some have sought to connect his cult with that of the Thracian Rider. It's an attractive theory, and one that perpetuates the idea of the Balkans as being essentially mysterious, a place where dark currents run deep, but it is at once too clever and too simple. What could be more natural than for a subjugated Christian people to dedicate their church to a warrior saint, especially so soon after the Greek revolt? After all, the congregation, even if it had been Slav, was loyal to the Greek Church.

I followed a road uphill towards one of the new churches, clearly visible on a hill outside the town. Asphalt gave way to cobbles, cobbles to dirt. Finally a path plagued by chickens and miniature dogs whose bark would probably have been worse than their bite had I stayed to find out, wound up through damp, intoxicatingly scented pine trees. Goat-herds sat looking over the plain, smoking and keeping an eye on their flocks of five or so animals. I reached the church just as the downpour began and sheltered inside. Only the brick walls and a cluster of pre-cast concrete domes had been completed and there was no sign that work was ongoing save for a stack of red roof tiles. A Gypsy trudged by leading a horse and followed by a boy who carried a scythe three times his size over his shoulder. One man, his horse and his little brother went to mow a meadow.

✳ ✳ ✳

I was overtaken by the rain again as I made my way back into town, so I took refuge in a nearby *türbe*, an open-sided brick pavilion in the midst of a chaotically overgrown Muslim cemetery. It took me a while to realize that not all of the graves were old. Once it had stopped raining I emerged from my tomb and looked at the last resting places of Ahmad Karo and Turka Pochiva Osmanova and family, whose dedication was written in Macedonian using the Latin alphabet, since Cyrillic is sacred to the Orthodox. All the other memorials were broken, their headstones, even modern reinforced concrete ones, flung hither and thither. I began to feel uneasy, a feeling which increased when I saw VMRO graffiti on a couple of memorials. It seemed the cemetery had been desecrated. I only hoped it had happened a long time ago and not recently. The only purely intact grave was marked with Communist insignia.

Desecrating a grave must be one of the lowest, most cowardly acts. The dead harm nobody and they have no means of redress. They should be left in peace. Only the most pathetic of people could vent his frustration on a grave, like those feeble specimens who daub swastikas on Jewish graves. What is it meant to prove? It makes its perpetrators feel big, true, and they will never be brought to justice since it is a quick, easy operation that takes place by dead of night, but how can anybody regard it as an act of heroism? How can anyone feel proud about taking on someone who is not merely defenceless but already dead? The dead are the softest of all soft targets, ideal for people who for all their bravado, their marches and banners, are themselves soft. Assaults on graves has been a feature of the Bosnian War. In some ways it is the ultimate act of genocide, an attempt to deny not only a people's present and future but its past as well, to eradicate all trace of its ever having been. Yet it is a crime that is usually carried out by people who have lived with the victims for so long that without the latter the former would not be, in any sense that a Nazi would understand. I left that hill in the blackest of moods.

* * *

I cheered up a bit as I walked upstream through quiet streets of patriotic name and mud dwelling, punctuated at frequent intervals by little public gardens. The clouds parted and the sun came out, and then at last I found my Muslims. A dainty mosque with a neat octagonal dome sat in a delightfully overgrown garden studded with graves of the purest white. None had been overturned. Adorned with fez or turban according to the occupant's rank, they were being slowly smothered in purple-flowering convolvulus as if the bindweed was unwilling to let the deceased leave this earthly paradise for the heavenly one on the Day of Judgement. Nearby a shack, which I took to be the imam's house, rested under a crescent moon which projected from the apex of its pyramidal roof. It was nearly time for prayer so I sat under the newly added porch and waited. A terrier came and yapped at me till it grew bored and wandered off. A line of ants crossed the path by my feet, each intently busy on some nameless task. I felt like a sluggard (Isaiah) and was duly chastened. The appointed time came and went. No *ezan*. A middle-aged man drifted past in slow motion, a bottle of *mastika* in either hand. Whatever else the Muslims of Bitola were, they were not fanatically devout.

I moved, fixing another minaret as a landmark and arrived at a small house-mosque distinguishable from a dwelling only by that tower. From inside came the sound of prayer and I sat on a bench to await its end. An attractive young woman in a headscarf, with a brood of young children clutching the hem of her regulation raincoat, peeped around the corner of the building to look at me. The group conversed rapidly in a mixture of Macedonian and Turkish.

At length the worshippers came forth, all five of them. You don't, of course, have to pray publicly, except at noon on Friday, but this was ridiculous. Four old men extracted my personal details while the fifth, a young man with curly raven hair, locked the building. Then they looked at each other, said "Lunchtime," and vanished.

Some mad impulse took me towards the mountain on the other side of town, where I thought I could see a monastery. The walk became hot and dusty as I passed between blocks of flats through streets across which teenagers had strung red ribbons to symbolize volleyball nets. I took a chance turning across a stream and there ahead of me was my "monastery", now looking like a range of farm buildings. Down a dirt track just to my left another unfinished church nestled in a grove of willows. When complete it would be beautiful, a neat domed cross-in-square tucked in beside the stream. An off-duty soldier lazed outside a café cradling a bottle of beer in his hand, staring at me. From the unfinished church two middle-aged women emerged backwards, crossing themselves thrice after the Orthodox fashion, and picked up their bags of shopping.

I entered the building and was surprised by the gentle gurgle of running water. It was not long before I found the source. Three steps down from the concrete floor of the nave was a spring gushing from a lead pipe. To one side hung an oil lamp, the kind that hangs before icons. A cross dangled from the church's floor over a well into which people had cast one- and two-denar coins. Someone had lit a candle and laid out a sprig of lilac. The explanation was to be found in an icon with a Greek text. St Panteleimon. He was a doctor by trade, and is thus charged with healing. Here *was* something ancient. Holy wells are found all over Europe and as often as not they are associated with miraculous curative powers. Here in this unprepossessing suburb I had stumbled across just such a well, held holy long before the church which housed it became sacred.

In the nave a table had been placed where the iconostasis should be. It was adorned with icons, St Panteleimon taking pride of place. Candles had been placed on it along with flowers, red and yellow tulips, blue irises, wallflowers and wisteria, together with a couple of Easter eggs dyed red. This place was sacred without the church's blessing, but the reverence with which it was held was expressed via Orthodoxy.

Nearby was a barracks, the very one from which the Secret Macedonian-Revolutionary Organization (Officers) had organized to expel the JNA. It is a part of Macedonian tradition: any organization must be both revolutionary and secret. An open, democratic organization would be a welcome relief. I was never able to discover whether there had been a Secret Macedonian-Revolutionary Organization (Other Ranks). A departing member of the JNA had carved the dreaded Serbian cross into a plaster wall. It had been hastily scratched out. Within the perimeter fence, the ARM had its shirt off and sat in the shade drinking coffee. When the JNA left, they took all of their weapons with them, leaving the ARM with coffee cups. I had a feeling the latter liked it that way. According to Hugh Poulton, the JNA's peaceful withdrawal was "a triumph for Gligorov's diplomacy". I only hope the proximity of the healing spring to the barracks was not a reflection of the esteem in which the Army Medical Corps is held.

* * *

I ambled on through the town at random. Bitola was more of a Christian town than I had given it credit for being. I had been deluded by the Atatürk connexion, forgetting Lear's comment that in his time most of the Turks had been soldiers or government officials. Just past a wall on which a graffito read "Punk is not death" (*sic*) in English, I came across a tiny monastery. Around an open courtyard, which was the area of the average house, was a group of buildings painted a murky cream. The church was forced to stand on stilts projecting over the yard. It was hard to imagine more than two people inhabiting the complex at the best of times. A sheep bleated from behind a wooden door, and as if on cue a layman appeared. We exchanged pleasantries.

"Would you like to see inside the church?" he asked before leading me up a flight of rickety wooden stairs. A portly red-haired woman, whose face was deeply lined, was sweeping the corridor. She joined us, leaving her broom.

The church was peculiar. We are used to churches being long and thin with the altar at the end, but this was long and thin with the altar at the side, the result both of the constraint of space and the need to face east when praying. The man began to light lamps before the icons. It would take him a long time, for the entire room was a seething mass of icons. They covered every inch of the walls, nineteenth-century paintings, cuttings from cheap Greek magazines, even a photograph of the as yet uncanonized Russian mystic Father John of Kronstadt, darkly mysterious behind his black beard.

"Monastery of St Naum!" announced the woman. "Brother of St Clement. See, here is the icon of Naum." She waved her arm towards a heap of images of the monk. "And here Clement," another pile, this time of bishops. "The monastery is very old, 70 or 80 years."

"The iconostasis is much older, perhaps 1,000," put in the man in his tobacco-rasping voice. He exaggerated. "When this place was rebuilt the iconostasis was moved here to the new church."

"How many monks are there here now?" I asked.

"None, alas. There are two who live in the mountains. They come sometimes. It is not much but it keeps us going. There may be a resident in the future." I toyed with the idea of a horde of two descending from the hills, but it didn't really work. What did they *do* up there anyway besides pray and live off roots and berries? Nothing probably, but then St Anthony, the founder of Orthodox monasticism, found the Egyptian desert too crowded and retreated further to a completely inaccessible place. People would keep bothering him so, which is tiresome for a recluse.

The woman left. I mentioned that the icons in St Demitrios' had had Greek inscriptions. The man spilled the oil he had been carefully pouring into the lamps and exploded.

"What do you expect? When that church was built there was no real Macedonian Church, although there had been one in Ohrid in the old days. The Greeks got it closed down. Just like now, they refuse to accept that Slavs exist. So you see all this embargo mumbo-jumbo that is killing our country is not new. There has always been Greek propaganda against Macedonians. The people I feel sorry for are the Slavs in Greece, 500,000 of them who don't officially exist. What can they do? To us it doesn't matter who you are so long as there is still peace, but with them always war." He was standing on a stool to light a lamp as he spoke these words, and he nearly fell off. I thought it wise to withdraw. According to the Greek census of 1951 there were 47,000 "Slavophones" in the country. The government of Macedonia claims that there are 1 million Slavs in Greece. Most independent observers put the number at no more than 200,000.

In the street, the woman was taking the sheep for a walk. It was nibbling dandelions, which would make it sick. Not far away another church raised itself above the square two-storeyed houses, a hideous 1970s pile of concrete, spikily uncomfortable but beautifully cool inside. The icons were mostly new and mostly Greek. There was St Paraskevi (Parskeva in Macedonian or Petka to the Bulgarians), the woman who carries her eyes on a dish and gave a special gift of inner sight to Vanga—the sight perhaps to see that an icon is an icon regardless of language, and that God is God whether *Allah, Bog* or *Theos.* A Macedonian folk song runs "God damn the Christians from Legen who do not respect St Petka or Sunday".

✳ ✳ ✳

I found yet another church next to the Cyril and Methodios Ordinary School. Built in 1870, the Church of the Virgin had later had an onion dome added *à la Russe.* Coupled with a modern and as yet unfinished belfry the effect was not a happy one. Descending into the sunken nave that I had come to expect I found a four-man choir and a couple of priests officiating at a service. A score or a score-and-a-half of women aged between 30 and 90 lined the walls in box-like pews with high rests where you could put your arms during the long hours of standing during the service. Under a black marble slab in one corner lay Metropolitan Kliment, Archbishop of Ohrid 1912–17: the first archbishop since the Turkish occupation, during whose brief reign two wars had been fought and another started, each of the warring parties seeking control of his see. To my surprise the icons were written in Slavonic. That meant either that they were younger than the church or that they had been retouched by some Serb or Bulgarian hand.

One of the choir had an exceptionally strong singing voice. He carried the rest with him and offered fierce competition to the priests, both of whom were quite young and like most of the priests in Macedonia sported neatly trimmed goatees. An old woman at the back added her thin voice to the music, going through the more than hour-long service from memory. She must have been doing the same for 60 years.

After the service the population of the church exactly halved. One priest, two choristers and half of the women left. The others gathered around two tables on which were set funerary cakes and candles draped in black crêpe. Memorial services were to be held. Neither widow was aged more than 40. The priest swung his censer and chanted while the two men behind him sang ominously dark hymns. Then they stopped and the priest was reminded of the names of the departed in a whisper. He didn't catch them and they were repeated, but just to make sure an old lady shouted them into his ear. He understood and, still chanting

217

solemnly took a spoon and made the sign of the cross in each cake and poured what looked like brandy over them.

A blaring of horns warned me. It was wedding time. Smartly dressed people began to gather by the door. Then the bride appeared. Her beauty was marred by the fact that she seemed to have been bodily crammed into an outsized meringue. Layer upon layer of white cloth billowed around her. Fearful of being smothered by this apparition, I left. Outside another wedding party was gathering.

I hung around under a cedar tree watching kids play football in the schoolyard. Two men came up to me. One was deeply tanned, balding, with grey hair. His blue eyes squinted terribly. The other was an entire head shorter than me and stocky. Black hair spread around his face in a soft beard and his eyes twinkled merrily. He was the chorister who had sung beautifully.

"My name is Zoran," he said, stretching out his hand. "Where are you from? This is no good! I do not speak English. Do you know Greek?"

"Try Russian." He smiled pleasantly.

"So you like churches and things like that?"

"Anything to do with religion or politics."

"I don't want to talk about politics. Have you seen our new churches? These are very important times for us because now after Communism the Macedonian people can return to their true selves as Orthodox."

"But there's a Catholic church here, and many Muslims."

"Not so many Muslims. There are many mosques, but they do not work. Besides, the Muslims are not Macedonians, they are Turks. As for the Catholics they are very few. Have you seen our other church, St Demitrios?"

"I have, and I was surprised to see all the icons written in Greek." I wasn't, but Zoran might throw a new light on the matter. He did.

"You should not think of it as Greek. It is *Byzantine*. All this area was Byzantium, East Rome, and because they spoke Greek you will see Greek in our churches. It is because we are Byzantines, not because we are Greeks. What is your religion, Catholic?"

"No, Protestant."

"Of course, you are English. That's all right. You're a friend of the Orthodox. The head of your church went to the Holy Mountain. Have you been there?"

"Athos? No."

"You should. It will be good for your soul." He shook my hand and left.

Athos, *Sveta Gora* or the 'Holy Mountain' in Slavonic, is in many ways the nerve centre of Orthodoxy. It is a religious republic at the very end of one of the fingers of the Halkidiki near Thessaloniki, a part of Greece yet independent of it. No female may set foot there. When the writer Alexander Kinglake visited in the 1830s, the Turkish pasha governing it had begged him not to let on that the pasha's cat, his only friend, was a queen. What they do about female birds or insects I don't know, but it is said that cruise-ships lie off its shores filled with wailing mothers lamenting the loss of their sons to its grim, fortified monasteries.

That Saturday night the young people of Bitola were taking the air along Marshal Tito Street, hanging around the ice-cream parlours and coffee shops or lingering for hours over a small beer in bars that were so badly lit as to be almost pitchy. Some surveyed the trips offered by travel agents to Paris, Zurich or Düsseldorf, though "Palasturist" still offered weekend breaks in Sarajevo for anyone mad enough to take one. A group of shabby off-duty soldiers pondered the posters outside the Macedonian Cinema. *Ljubavni Marathon* was playing and the posters graphically illustrated what kind of marathon a *ljubavni* one might be. *Hamlet* at the National Theatre had no takers. Perhaps it was too close to the bone. In the park people were eating *sendvichi* and *tost* under the statues of the Partizans. I went to my usual haunt, a kebab shop by the river on the edge of the bazaar and ate succulent cubes of grilled pork.

The only other people in the place were the landlord and a young man with a single gold stud in his ear and a flushed face. The landlord was possessed of a prominent nose and tightly curled grey hair. I had hoped to do some writing, but the young man, Kiro, wanted to talk. He bribed me with some pistachios and a few cigarettes. He was more than slightly drunk, and very angry.

"Everything is wrong with this country! Chiefly, there is no money here. The Greeks see to that with their idea that there is no such thing as a Macedonian. *I* am a Macedonian. Have you been to Heraclea? The ruins of a great Macedonian city are there."

"Heraclea was built centuries before the Slavs came."

"True, and it was on the very edge of Macedonia, but I live in modern Heraclea, and *I am Macedonian!* In some ways Yugoslavia was better than this. There was work, there was trade. Now there is nothing, no money you see. Only the Mafia and the politicians have money, and there's no real difference between them. No-one cares, and you in Europe least of all!"

"Do you think there'll be war then?"

"No, that never. Why? Because the war will come from outside not inside and we all do 20 months' National Service. We'll fight the bastards to the last man. If only we had more money, a lot more money. Now people emigrate to Canada or Australia and they forget the people they leave behind. They are traitors, giving us nothing. They listen to Serbian songs and say 'this is good Macedonian music'. Bastards. We can do nothing without money and there is none now."

"I agree Macedonia's biggest problem is economic but what about religious tensions? I have seen many new churches being built here. Why?"

"Because Orthodoxy is very close to the Macedonian soul. The Communists would not let us express our religion freely, but now we can, so we're building the churches we need. Of course our church is not recognized. We are not recognized! It is a plot against Macedonians. But when you talk about religious problems I suppose you mean Christian–Muslim problems. There are none. This is not Bulgaria! The problems are ethnic, not religious. With Turks and Gypsies there are no problems, but the Albanians want rights which the Macedonian people in Albania do not have—rights to religion and language. In no country, Albania, Bulgaria or Greece are we recognized, yet they all make claims on us. In all these countries there is only one language, in ours many ... Albanian, even Romany. Why? Why should *we* always give and no-one else?" I had no answer to that. Kiro continued: "I will stay loyal to my country whatever, but now there are no laws. Bigger than the problem of Albanians is the problem of no laws. Anybody with money or a gun can do whatever he likes. And the politicians are the biggest criminals. They have money and guns."

Kiro left and the landlord came to my table, drawing deeply on a cigarette and looking down his long nose at me.

"It's all down to money," he said. "That is our real problem. Look at me. I have a business that nobody uses because they do not have the money to pay for what I have to offer. I can't afford credit at 20 per cent interest. I even have a family room upstairs. Always empty. Where the money will come from I don't know but it must come."

Ohrid

I walked back through the forest of Partizans and the graffito which read "Macedonia for the Macedonians—VMRO" to the bus station. That writing had been there for at least five years. When I first saw it back in 1990 it had seemed radical, even threatening. Now it was perfectly normal. A notice in the bus station advertised services to Istanbul, Sofia, Gothenburg, and Lerin. Lerin is the Slav name for Florina, just across the border. Would people ever be able to cross that border again, to go shopping or to visit relatives or even just for the hell of it? I hoped so as I boarded a bus going in the opposite direction, to a place that is at once the heart and the very edge of Macedonia. To Ohrid.

In a way, Ohrid *is* Macedonia. Situated on a rock by the lake that bears its name, a lake which is bisected by the Albanian border, it has been an important town for centuries. Like Bitola, it was a staging post on the Via Egnatia and a centre of Christianity before the arrival of the Slavs, who named the town for its citadel: *Vo Hrid*, "On the Cliff". Centuries later, after the mission to Bohemia had failed and Cyril had gone to Rome to die, two of his followers, Clement and Naum, made their way via Belgrade to the Bulgarian court at Pliska. Clement was immediately sent to Ohrid as bishop and Naum joined him there in 893 after establishing a school for the new Slavonic letters in Pliska. Clement and Naum made Ohrid the pre-eminent centre of Slav learning before Naum retreated to a monastery at the other end of the lake, which is now regarded as proof against mental illness and is revered by Christian and Muslim alike. Clement's school was famed throughout the East Mediterranean long before the universities of Oxford or Paris emerged from the West's Dark Ages.

For the next 100 years Ohrid grew as a centre for propagating the Byzantine political idea of a Christian federation with a single Emperor and became embellished with many fine churches. It was from here that Tsar Samuel, having risen in revolt against Byzantium and himself imbued with that ideal, mounted his campaign for world domination, after re-establishing the lapsed Bulgarian patriarchate. It was to this place that those 14,000 blind men stumbled across miles of mountain and rocky plain after their encounter with the imperial army of Basil II in 1014. Samuel died in a fit of apoplexy at the horrible sight, but his son Radomir continued the struggle until he was murdered by his cousin the following year, along with his wife and his brother-in-law. In 1018 Basil "The Bulgar-Slayer" entered Ohrid in triumph. Bulgaria was at an end for the time being.

Ruthless though he was in war, Basil was fair in peace. Though the patriarchate was demoted to an archbishopric it retained a measure of autonomy, with a Slav archbishop who was appointed by the emperor rather than by the patriarch of Constantinople, although this was a temporary measure. After 1037 all the archbishops were Greeks, but Ohrid remained a centre of Slavonic learning despite the complaint of Archbishop Theophylact that he was forced to live in a "filthy marsh" among "unclean barbarian slaves who smell of sheepskin."

Two hundred years later the tables were turned. A new Bulgarian Empire had been founded and one of its leaders, Kaloyan, had gone so far as to style himself "The Killer of Romans". In the chaos that followed the sacking of Constantinople by the Crusaders in 1204 Kaloyan's nephew Ivan Asen vastly extended his realm, picking off Crusader states one by one and eventually coming to govern most of the Balkans, including Ohrid, subsequently proclaiming himself "Tsar of the Bulgarians and the Greeks". Despite that, his contemporary, the Byzantine historian George Acropolites noted approvingly that Ivan did not "strain himself with the murder of Byzantines ... Among the Barbarians he was the best of men." After his death the empire broke up, attacked both by Byzantium (then temporarily removed to Nicaea) and the Mongols, but the Byzantine Emperor Michael VIII reaffirmed Ohrid's ecclesiastical pre-eminence in the northern Balkans. The city experienced a final flowering of church-building before the arrival of the Serbs in the form of the army of Stefan Dušan in 1334. Dušan's death and the collapse of his empire into petty principalities made it an easy matter for the Ottomans to conquer Ohrid, which they did in 1371.

Eventually the town's ecclesiastical power was broken by the Turks in 1767, when, under Greek pressure, both the Bulgarian Church of Ohrid and the Serbian one of Peæ were merged and placed under the direct control of Constantinople, but the town was and in some ways still is regarded as the home of Bulgarian Christianity, an essential part of Bulgaria, and it was the subject of impassioned debate in the late nineteenth and early twentieth centuries. Was it Bulgaria, Serbia or Greece? None of these, apparently, though up until the First Balkan War Bulgarian priests had been active in Ohrid, and during the Second World War members of the Bulgarian General Synod made a point of travelling there. The Macedonian Orthodox Church claims itself to be the true spiritual heir of the earlier Ohrid patriarchate. But then so does the Bulgarian. It is another of those interminable, irresolvable disputes. Why the two modern Churches cannot *both* be heirs to the medieval one is beyond me.

Lear found "Akhridha" "full of exquisite scenes" to draw, but he had problems with the Muslim inhabitants: "seeing me unescorted, a crowd of the faithful took aim from behind walls and rocks, discharging unceasing showers of stones, sticks and mud." It was the third time he had been pelted, and he was obliged to secure an armed guard from the pasha before he could continue sketching. The Albanians of the time— and Lear makes much of Ohrid being an Albanian town—took strong exception to the making of images, which they associated with Satanic practice. Albanians are more sophisticated now.

I rented a room above a restaurant beside the lake in the old town. Every morning I awoke to the sound of frying and delicate fishy smells wafted up the stairs to me. My landlord, as well as being a restaurateur, was a master wood-carver and the building was filled with his work— impossibly contorted friezes showing writhing masses of vegetation with strange goblin-like figures peering through the leaves and peacocks pecking pomegranates. He was a long-haired man who always dressed in denim and reminded me of a St Bernard dog. His forehead would wrinkle as he stared at me with sad brown eyes and ask "And what will you do today?"

✻ ✻ ✻

Ohrid is a UNESCO listed World Heritage site. On a hot Sunday afternoon I wandered along the narrow stone-flagged streets of the old town past graceful overhanging *konaks*. People sat listlessly under coloured umbrellas outside cafés listening to the gentle splashing of the azure-blue lake at their feet. The road twisted uphill and from behind shuttered windows came the sound of a wedding reception. The *konaks* crowded in on one another, tumbling towards me and from time to time I passed tiny ruined churches sheltering under the embrace of wisteria. Sleek cats rolled in the dust. My object was the Church of St Clement, a neat late thirteenth-century structure at the top of the hill, sitting in a small courtyard under cypresses, commanding a view of the town, the lake and Tsar Samuel's fortress on the hill opposite. The inevitable wedding party was just leaving as I sneaked through the door. A woman in a bottle-green dress, long permed brown hair and sunglasses challenged me in the *narthex*, or porch.

"Where are you from?"

"London."

"Well then I'll let you in for free, but this *is* a museum you know." A priest was clearing away the wedding crowns.

"A museum *and* a church?"

"Well, OK, sometimes one, sometimes the other. We're not quite sure yet."

Inside, St Clement's houses some of the finest frescos in the Balkans, but they have deteriorated slightly and the saints' puffy faces all had a slightly green tinge to them as if they had died some time ago—which in truth they had. A stone iconostasis that had not been there on the occasion of my last visit was hung with icons which seemed to have been looted from the museum next door. Some of the stones in it were recently quarried, but there were curious recycled early-Byzantine pieces, pre-dating the arrival of the Slavs and adorned with dolphins and pomegranates.

In one corner stood a small shrine to St Clement, who appeared in the company of Cyril and Methodios on an icon dated 1863. The inscription, in Greek, was crudely scratched into its gold covering, and several pairs of socks had been draped over it. The saint's image on the iconostasis, dating from 1779, very shortly after the Bulgarian church

had been merged with the Greek, was smothered in finely worked silver. No wonder the church was watched closely.

The Green Woman appeared at my side again.

"You see," she said, "in the *narthex* the Old Testament." The Virgin squatted in the Burning Bush, holding an infant Jesus who was blessing Moses. "In the church, first people who believe in Jesus, above that the life of the Virgin and then the life of Christ. You know Orthodox iconography." The warrior saints who stood around the walls with their swords drawn had a vague air of discomfort, as if they had been persuaded against their better judgement to take part in a fancy-dress parade. I looked in vain for the prophet Elijah, Ilja, the Macedonians' favourite but I was rather taken by a stylite who had hung his beard outside the bucket he was sitting in and let it dangle down his pillar.

"The porch was added in the nineteenth century, to protect the outside frescos." Under the lean-to extension, which Rebecca West compared to a byre, traces of fresco were to be seen. A river of blood flowed into the gaping maw of a dragon in the vision of hell, and—yes, there was the mysterious woman riding on a pair of fish and carrying a ship, whom I had first seen in Transylvania. I have no idea who she is or what she is doing. My guide didn't either.

"When I was last here this was a museum not a church," I remarked.

"It is not *really* a church now! People have been using it as one since 1991, although strictly speaking they shouldn't."

At the end of a slight promontory, on a cliff above the lake, stands the little church of St John the Theologian, just a few years older than St Clement's and also dating from that curious period between the collapse of the Second Bulgarian Empire of Tsar Ivan Asen and the rise of the Serbian Empire of Milutin when Byzantium briefly regained a form of control over the Balkans. I walked to it along a path flanked by white irises and blossoming hawthorns above a tiny beach where blue-painted fishing boats were drawn up. One had pictures of saints painted in the bows. "Clement" it said on one side and "Naum" on the other. The calm waters of the lake shimmered silver, and all around the great walls of the mountains fell to the shore in a blue haze. On the Albanian side white peaks glinted sharply. A few people with a priest were coming slowly towards me, laughing and smoking as a bee buzzed drunkenly by.

The monastery buildings that had once encircled the church have been torn down now. I rather wished they had been left in place—they must have been white *konaks* with those graceful arcades of wooden balconies which are so typical of Macedonian monasteries. The little church seemed naked, exposed, without its protecting huddle of buildings. The siting was perfect, magically beautiful, and completely still. A light breeze rose off the lake, and a dinghy chugged around the promontory. There was a cough behind me and an old man emerged from the church and struggled to light a cigarette. Inside the building were a few battered medieval frescos and a modern oil-painting depicting Elijah having his vision of the Flaming Chariot against a backdrop of Lake Ohrid. A typed notice in French lamented the theft of nine icons in the 1980s.

I climbed on up the hill behind the church. The air was heavy with the scent of pines and the light wind roared through their needles like some far-off ocean. Birds twittered irritatingly near at hand. I was beginning to feel thirsty, but before long I came across a ruined mosque. Where there is a mosque there is always water and, sure enough, a spring of pure sweet liquid bubbled up from which I drank long and hard.

This was one of the first mosques in the Macedonia, built above the tomb of St Clement after his bones had been removed to the church that now bears his name. Excavations around the ruin had revealed the foundations of an early basilica and below the mosque's floor the truncated legs of Christian saints could be seen in frescos. But the name of the mosque, "Imaret", the hostel, testified that it had remained a place of pilgrimage throughout the Turkish years. Old habits die hard, and it was not long before I found an open pavilion that contained the tombs of two prominent Muslims. Who they were I do not know, but people still made pilgrimages to this place. A pile of boiled sweets had been left on one of the graves. Nobody had dared touch them. Instead families sat on the grass eating picnics and enjoying the view.

Not far from the mosque lay the foundations of another basilica. Its floor was covered with sand, but when I scraped it away fragments of mosaic of the fourth or fifth century were revealed. I uncovered a drunken-looking bird, perhaps a partridge, then another came cautiously into view, followed by a creature that may have been a horse but looked more like an okapi. It became compulsive work. I squatted in the hot sun, rubbing my hands raw, scraping away at the remains of the city that was here before the Slavs the Turks or the Albanians, at the very beginning of Christian civilization, while the pines gloomily closed around me with their stifling deadness, soundless spectres watching my desecration of the holy place. A cuckoo called as if commenting on my labour and in the shadow a family of Gypsies materialized clutching guitars. They watched me suspiciously.

At the top of the hill the shattered ruin of Samuel's castle stands sentinel, impassively looking down on the jumble of churches and white houses flowing below it to the edge of the lake which spread broad and blue between its enclosing mountains. To the landward a plain three miles across, just large enough to feed the medieval city, spreads out until it is closed off by the purple hills. Minarets sprout from the town below like the fresh tendrils of newly germinated seeds. Butterflies staggered from flower to flower and lizards flashed their vermilion bellies at me or paused to poke out their forked tongues in disgust. By the gate leading into the citadel a poster had been stuck. "Peace and health without tobacco, alcohol or drugs" , it read. "Tobacco, alcohol and drugs or health. It is your choice. Society Against Alcoholism, Nicotinism and Narcolepsy of Macedonia."

As I lay on the grass breathing in the scent of wild thyme I tried to conjure Samuel's court, a provincial version of the one in Constantinople, but I couldn't. I thought of his tragic army fumbling its way over the hills and gradually spilling into the plain, but again it eluded me. The events were too remote, the sun too warm, the grass too soft. Sleep crept over me gradually. When I awoke a brown-eyed puppy was staring at me quizzically. It let out a startled yelp and ran off when I moved.

✳ ✳ ✳

Well away from Samuel's castle, outside the city walls, a plain whitewashed mosque like a thousand others in the Balkans sits near the market on the edge of a square. It looks like just another mosque, but down a side street is a grand gateway decorated with terracotta panels depicting fruit and loaves of bread, and visible from that street is an enormous octagonal *türbe* which thrusts its roof high above the eaves of the neighbouring shops. A crescent-shaped finial holds between its horns a mass of detailed calligraphy.

I walked under the gateway and peered through one of the windows of the *türbe*. Inside lay three vaulted tombs sumptuously clad in green cloths with Arabic writing embroidered on them in gold thread. At the head of each the occupant's turban had been preserved, draped in black; and two strips of starched white cloth ran the length of the apex of each vault. Two bearded men, one in his 30s the other ten years older, with greying temples, fiddled with a crystal chandelier that dangled from the roof of the structure. A porch adorned the courtyard side of the *türbe* and a 60-year-old woman stood under it, looking through the building's door. She wore black and had a light shawl draped over her head. As I approached she turned kindly blue eyes to me and smiled.

"Welcome, stranger," she said in a softly musical voice filled with warmth. "From where have you journeyed?" Her gentle words seemed to be reaching deep into me. "From London."

"What a pity," she murmured, "I have no English. How can we talk?"

"Russian perhaps?" I suggested. "Is a Sufi sheikh buried here?"

"Oh yes! Our *Pir*, the founder of our *tariqa* here in Ohrid. His name is Pir Muhammed. This is his *türbe*."

"In Persian they say *mazar*," I commented pointlessly.

"Really? That is interesting. Pir Muhammed came 300, perhaps 400 years ago and now he lives here with us." She spoke as if he was still alive. Then as an afterthought she added, "He came from Khorasan."

Khorasan again! The wellspring from which flowed so many Sufis, with at its heart the great shrine-city of Mazar-i Sharif, The Noble Tomb which is said to house the remains of Ali, son-in-law and cousin to the Prophet and focus of the Shi'i faith.

"What is the *tariqa*?" I asked.

"Helveti. In England you have Naqshibandi, with your Sheikh Nazim of Cyprus, but here we are Helveti. There are many dervishes here, all Helveti. In Struga you will find Bektashis and in Skopje Rifa'is."

"I know about Skopje. I have seen the *tekke*."

"I can see you are interested in dervishism. Would you like to see the inside of our *tekke*?"

She led me to the door of the mosque and we removed our shoes. My hostess—whom I shall call Ayesha, since Ayesha was known as "the beloved of the Prophet" and I never learnt her real name—led me through a door into a room furnished with green sofas around the walls and a central table on which rested two ashtrays. Everything was spotlessly clean.

"This is the guest room, where our sheikh greets his visitors," I was told. She led me on into a larger room. A wood-burning stove stood in the middle of the floor, while against one wall was a fireplace with traces of a charcoal fire in it. A low divan covered in lovely kilims ran around the remaining walls, which were themselves adorned with calliagrams and a Turkish calendar.

"This is ... I can't think of the word ... where they make *zikr*."

"The *semahane*."

"That's it. Thank you. Sheikh-dede sits here on this sheepskin, his guests here to his right and all the dervishes around the walls. On this sheepskin near the fire sits the man who makes coffee. They must have coffee you see, and only coffee. No sugar." She lifted a cloth to reveal neat rows of ceramic thimbles on a tray.

"Do women join in the *zikr*?"

"Oh no! That only happens in America, where there are many women dervishes. Here we are traditional."

A mosque opened off the *semahane*. A neat wooden *minbar* stood in one corner beside an extravagantly decorated grandfather clock made in Paris. Like everything else about the *tekke* it was scrupulously tidy, a far cry from the chaos of Skopje. As if reading my thoughts, Ayesha said

"We restored the whole complex a couple of years ago."

"Where did the money come from?"

"Our own work. Who would not work for the *tekke*? To be a dervish is to have a second family, and you do anything for your family. Many young people are dervishes. You grow up with it, and you do not leave."

Outside in the glazed porch, Ayesha said "This is where they pray in the summer," then she lightly sprang up some stairs to another room like the *semahane* but brighter and painted a pale blue.

"Also in the summer they make *zikr* here, in this room."

"I notice you say *oda* for 'room,'" I ventured. "*Oda* is a Turkish word."

"Naturally it is Turkish. I am Turkish. Most of us here in Ohrid are. The Albanians live in Struga, which is why there are Bektashis there—Albanians like Bektashis."

Someone downstairs was calling for Ayesha so we descended. I went and looked at the line of ten tombs which filled the porch of the *türbe*. Each was a copy of the main tombs, with a turban, an green cloth, and a towel at the feet. Little plastic labels on the towels gave the name of each resident. One was described as *Sheikhzade*. *Zade* is a Persian suffix meaning "son of". Ayesha materialized by my elbow.

"Soon it will be Bayram [holiday], so the *türbe* is being cleaned. There is *zikr* tomorrow. I will see if you can attend. Come at six minutes past five."

I returned at the appointed time to find the *tekke* deserted. Perhaps I had misunderstood Ayesha. Was it "six minutes past five" or "between five and six"? A church bell rang and I climbed the hill to the building. In its smoke-blackened interior a priest was chanting for no-one's benefit but his own and grim saints stared at me disapprovingly as if they knew I was an impostor. Back at the *tekke* a lugubrious man eyed me suspiciously. He twitched his moustache and drawled "Where are you from?" I told him, and explained my interest in dervishism. Asif spoke Schwytzerdeutsch, the peculiar German dialect of Switzerland, and I found him hard to understand, but it seemed that now would not be a good time, what with Bayram and everything.

"Friday would be good. There will be a Frenchman who wants to take photographs." A group of mostly elderly Albanians gathered around us.

"Why not tomorrow?" one of them suggested.

"Not tomorrow—Bayram."

"Then today."

"The sheikh has said no."

The sheikh himself appeared, a dignified man of about 60 wearing a pressed blue suit and the white fez and black turban denoting his rank. He was a stark contrast to the Rifa'i sheikh in Skopje, slim, erect and with a deeply lined face surmounted by bushy white eyebrows. It was agreed. I was to come on Friday. I took it as some kind of test, to see how serious I was.

✳ ✳ ✳

If Bitola's market was a sorry affair, Ohrid's was the exact opposite. Spreading over a large area just around the corner from the *tekke* and overlooked by a low stone church which clung to the hillside was a jumble of stalls among which people of all kinds milled. Trestles were piled high with mounds of gleamingly white rice, sacks of spinach and baby carrots which would fetch a fortune in London. Bags of herbs and pulses rubbed shoulders with plumply glistening Kalamata olives from Greece and Arabian dates. Women ran their hands lovingly through mountains of curd cheese, savouring its oozy squelchiness between their fingers. One alley was lined with stalls selling eggs in pallets of two dozen. Some of the eggs seemed to have been kept too long, as fluffy yellow chicks, cheeping anxiously, struggled to escape from cardboard boxes. Old women held the adult birds up by their feet and prodded them critically. Stallholders doused their vegetables with water from time to time to keep them fresh and green. Country women offered dripping honeycombs and home-distilled raki. Bundles of notes were changing hands. Nor was it food alone that was being offered for sale. One man gingerly ran his thumb along the blade of a vicious-looking axe. Another had coils of rope and some scythe blades spread on a low table before him.

"I am a Gypsy-man," he told me. "Rope is for horse, cow, anything. Everybody comes on market day. The market is where all peoples mix."

Behind him a group of young children was staring in fascination at a tank of tropical fish for sale, along with budgies in cages. A man in a smart grey suit and a floppy black cap examined some horseshoes, banging them together and listening intently to the ring they produced to determine whether they had been forged true. Above it all floated a joyous hubbub of voices speaking a medley of languages as stallholders extolled the virtues of their cabbages and would-be purchasers berated them for trying to pass off such poor produce.

I sat outside a coffee shop sipping thick sweet Turkish coffee and watching the crowds roll by. Fine-faced Albanian men with hooked noses and leathery skin drifted by under their white felt caps, absent-mindedly playing with their rosaries. Macedonian matrons clad in black pushed through the crowd, a single thick plait of grey hair tumbling down their back to the waist from beneath scarves with flowers embroidered on the borders. Muslim women from the villages spread their wares on the ground and sat on camp stools, their brightly coloured scarves wound tightly round their head and their floral dresses swirling to the ground around them. When they smiled they revealed mouths full of gold. They contrasted sharply with the respectably bourgeois Turkish women in their plain scarves and dress-cum-raincoats, who kept their gold strictly on their wrists. A toothless old man, his face a gnarled mass of wrinkles, staggered by, bent double by the weight of two huge bags of shopping which he hung from the walking stick slung over his shoulder. Groups of policemen stood around idly as a young man in dark glasses, black leather jacket and blue jeans carefully carried an enormous earthenware pot in the wake of his girlfriend, who teetered on perilously high heels, her legs constricted by skin-tight black jeans. A tall, straight-backed Macedonian woman of about 60 strode past, gloriously attired in the traditional costume few people still wore: a long white dress under an embroidered white waistcoat and a dark apron richly adorned in red and gold. Everybody was in good humour. Everybody took time to exchange a few words. Above all, nobody seemed to be in any hurry. There was no rush. Every type of Macedonian seemed to be here, jostling shoulders in perfect harmony. I hoped it would continue like this, that there would not come the fateful Monday when any one of these people was absent, or even that the market failed to open at all.

Clement of Ohrid Street runs from the market to the lakeshore, where there is a miniature harbour and a square flanked with smart cafés where the young people congregate in the evening. In a square at the other end of the street's polished stone flags stands an ancient oak tree, cleft in two by lightning but still alive, which is shown to the tourists. Along the street are travel agents, banks and little shops which sell the usual tat you expect to find in a popular resort—painted shells with "A Souvenir of Ohrid" written on them and the like. At one time this was the main street of the commercial district, just outside the town walls where the land became flat enough to build the bazaar. Now it is the centre of Ohrid's battered tourist industry, a loving recreation of the Old East with more than a touch of Disney about it—preserved to death.

A rusty iron gate leads off this street into a tiny courtyard dominated by the octagonal bulk of mosque. Its minaret is gone now, and the entrance front is crudely patched with bricks and breeze-blocks, but it is a living thing. Ohrid's true past survives hidden from the gaze of the tourists who pass unknowingly by within feet of it, making for the tree.

Men were washing themselves at the *sadirvan*, the hands first, then inside the mouth and nostrils, the arms up to the elbows, a splash on the head and a good scrub inside and behind the ears. Finally they doused their feet as a warbling *ezan* struggled through the open door. They were a motley crew of all ages. Two were dressed, bizarrely, in the tracksuit of the England football team. One elderly man wore a smart light blue three-piece suit with a gold watch chain strung across his tracksuit. His nicotine-stained moustache exactly matched the colour of his blotched white fez and bushy eyebrows adorned sad blue eyes. His tap wasn't working properly and he struggled to turn it off, looking at me half-beseechingly and half-despairingly. Then he hurried after the rest, leaving the tap dripping.

At the end of prayers a tall man was the first to emerge from the building. His bald pate, deep set eyes and bushy white beard reminded me of Alexander Solzhenitsyn. We salaamed and I introduced myself.

"What do you want to know about Islam?" he demanded. I took him to be the imam. He spoke slowly and almost monosyllabically in answer to my questions.

"The Muslims here are mostly Albanians, though there are a few Turks and Gypsies. We have a *mekhteb*, but if you want to go to *madrasa* you have to go to Skopje or to Kosovo, to Pristina. There isn't really any difficulty with the Christians. Our relations are good. What problems there are are low-key. They keep themselves to themselves and so do we."

A young man of about 25 appeared at my elbow. His jet-black hair was swept back from his forehead and he wore the sleeves of his T-shirt rolled up. A gold chain hung around his neck.

"Do you speak German?" he asked in a strong Swiss accent. "I lived in Switzerland for three years, working."

"What was your work?"

"Oh, many things. I worked as a baker, I washed cars, that kind of thing. Now it is too difficult for us to travel. It costs a lot of money, but there is none. Without money you cannot travel, without travelling you cannot get money. It is hopeless.

"Most of the Muslims here are Albanians. There are some Turks, but they now have many Macedonian words in their speech. Also there are some Muslims who genuinely speak Macedonian."

"And they are called Pomaks?"

"No, they are just known as Muslims. That is what they call themselves too. But Islam is a religion, not a nationality. *Within* Islam there are no nationalities, only Muslims, but it is wrong to say 'Muslim' when someone asks you your nationality. My father is right to say there are no problems with the Christians, but that is because the problems that we have are political not religious. They are problems with the state, not with Christians as such."

The imam, or *hoxha* to use the Albanian title, was getting anxious to leave. As we walked over the flags of the street outside, made smooth by the passage of countless feet, I mentioned the *tekke*. How did they feel about dervishism?

"I should not say this," said the youth, whose name was Fadil, "because they are Muslims and you shouldn't say bad things about your fellow Muslims, but I do not think they are healthy. They make good *namaz* but then they add things which are not in the Qur'an, and so they are changing Islam. Sometimes I think that they worship their sheikh. They are very hierarchical, and that is against Islam. Whether you are a king or a worker it doesn't matter, we are all equal. My father is an imam but that is purely by chance, there is nothing special about him. Also the dervishes encourage the villagers, uneducated people, to do things like visit tombs and even monasteries to pray. It is a foolish thing and it is not in Islam, but now it is a tradition and you can't stop it. If they made their pilgrimage to Mecca they would be cured, but who can afford to go to Mecca?" Islam may be one, but it is vary varied.

We stopped outside a shop and the imam pulled a hefty key from his pocket and unlocked the door. The interior was beautifully cool and glittered with cheap jewellery. We sat on low stools and ate bananas that the imam took out of the drawer of a desk. I absent-mindedly used my left hand and was jokingly told off for it.

"I know it's *haram*," I admitted shamefacedly, "but I can't help it."

"They call this a democracy," complained Fadil now that we were in private, "but sometimes I wonder. It won't be a proper democracy until we get our university. They won't give it to us because you can only work in what you've been trained for and they don't want us to train for good jobs. You go to the town hall and see. All the people working there are Macedonians. An Albanian *can* get a good job, but it is very difficult and you must be able to pay much *baksheesh*. This is a police state, run by and for the police, all 13,000 of them. Can you imagine in such a small country? Germany does not have so many police. They are all Macedonian."

In a state without laws and with high unemployment government jobs are always desirable. They are secure and lucrative—you can sell favours. You are in a position both to give and to receive patronage, but a desk job depends on political favour. A policeman can be far more of an independent operative, which is precisely why they are all Macedonian—the police are armed, and the government doesn't trust Albanians with guns.

"Is there not one Albanian policeman?"

"Maybe a few, but not many. Albanian areas should be policed by Albanians. Ohrid is only 30 per cent Muslim, but Struga is 90 per cent Muslim, and from there right the way up the west side of the country, Kichevo, Debar, Tetovo, is solidly Albanian. But we are not treated as equals. It is forbidden to fly the Albanian flag, we cannot learn Albanian history, and we must add *-ski* or *-ov* to our names to make them look Macedonian." I had seen no evidence of that last claim, which mirrored Bulgarian policy and its reverse operated in Hoxha's Albania, where "religious" names—which in practice meant Slav and Greek names—were outlawed (it is hard to think of a more religious name than Hoxha).

"Before the Slavs there were the Greeks, and before them were the Illyrians. We are descended from the Illyrians. This is our land," declared Fadil. "We should have more freedom."

"We were here first"—it's an almost childish cry but, like anything which appeals to the childish in man, it carries great force. It is the very essence of the Greeks' claim to copyright on the name "Macedonia". Its strength comes from its simplicity and from the way it appeals to a child's sense of justice: "I had it first, so it is mine, all mine and I don't have to share with anybody". But like all childish ideas it is not only simple but simplistic, and we live in a complicated world, a world where simplicity can be a dangerous thing.

"The politicians are fools anyway," Fadil continued. "Take the flag. That is the thing which does the most damage to this country. It, far more than the name, is the cause of the Greek embargo. Greece doesn't make a fuss about Thrace being divided into three because there is no "Thracian" flag. And they're right. The flag of Macedonia is a Greek flag, not a Slav one. It has a Greek symbol on it. How can the Slavs claim it when it's much older than any Slav presence in the Balkans? The Slavs still lived in the Carpathians when that symbol was used. The flag should be changed, because it is meaningless here. It would not be a hard thing to do."

The imam changed the subject: "Do you know Cat Stevens?"

"Not personally." I told him a little about Islam in Britain and Yusuf Islam's struggle to establish a government funded Muslim school in North London. In turn I asked him about the grand mufti in Skopje.

"We call him the reis."

"From *Reis-al-'Ulema* [Chief among the Learned]" I put in.

"Exactly. He draws up a programme for what Muslims in Macedonia should do, religiously, but it is up to each imam to decide whether to follow his programme. Mostly we can do what we like." Fadil interrupted.

"At the moment my brother is in Mecca studying *hadith* so he will become an 'alim. We need more people like that, but because he is doing it, I don't have to bother with religious questions." He smiled, but I was less easy at the news. I feared that the brother would return from his studies in Saudi Arabia infused with that country's austere and humourless interpretation of Islam, Wahhabism. Founded in the eighteenth century, it is particularly opposed to dervishes, saints, Shi'ites and anything smacking of the Western intellectual tradition, although after some struggle the Saudi monarchs managed to get Western technology accepted; a famous and possibly apocryphal story is that of the introduction of radio into the country. The *'ulema* was strongly opposed on the grounds that it was diabolical, but the king, in a stroke of genius, caused the Qur'an to be broadcast. Nothing diabolical could ever say the Word of God, so radio passed. Unfortunately, where Wahhabis all too often excel is in intolerance and bigotry—contrary to Islamic law, the practice of Christianity is forbidden in Saudi Arabia. I feared that when the brother returned, with all the kudos of having studied at the heart of Islam, he might see the government's policies on Albanians as an attack on the faith, an attack which must be met with *jihad*. I mentioned Bosnia.

"That war is political not religious. Bosnians are Muslim in name only. They do not practise their religion. They drink and all that. It is becoming religious though, because people are coming from outside to wage *jihad*, people who do not know Bosnians, people who think they are fighting for Islam."

A friend of mine who studied British Islam once told me that he had overheard a British Muslim who was not yet in his teens ask his imam whether it was his religious duty to wage *jihad* in Bosnia. The imam told him that *jihad* could take the form of helping refugees from the war, but not all imams have that authority, or would take that line. From the Muslim point of view, with no necessary knowledge of Bosnia or the events leading to the war, the events in the central Balkans look very much like another case of Christians killing

Muslims. It does not help that the news media, especially in the West, continually refers to "The *Muslim* government" and "The *Muslim* army", when both are multi-confessional. It is misleading, dangerous and born purely out of journalistic laziness. It seems that whenever Muslims are in the news a point is made of their being Muslims, as if that fact alone was the key to understanding events. So we have "Muslim Chechens", "Muslim Azerbaijanis", "Muslim Albanians" even when religion is irrelevant to the news item. It doesn't happen to anyone else. Nobody talks about "Christian Americans" or "Buddhist Thais".

So the Bosnian conflict is reduced. The Serbs, who are Christian, are fighting the Muslims (they are also fighting the Croats, who happen to be Christian as well, but we don't want to confuse the issue). All this is due to "age-old rivalries and deep-seated ethnic hatreds" which no rational person can hope to understand. Therefore we should just let them fight it out, since they are all as bad as each other. The Muslim world can see "Muslims" in Europe being slaughtered by Christians on television every night, and they can see Europe doing nothing about it. Inevitably the widely held belief that Europeans are fundamentally hostile to Muslims becomes more deeply rooted and results in a reciprocal hostility to Europe and to all things European. Militant Islam then becomes more attractive, and militancy must be active. Sooner or later, the largely secular Bosnians, seeing their only help coming not from secular Europe but from militant Islam, themselves become militant. This helps no-one, least of all the many entirely peaceful Muslims living in the West who find themselves branded as irrational fanatics. A war which started as a purely local political affair becomes an international religious one with no obvious solution. I hoped Macedonia's Albanians—and her Slavs for that matter—would have the common sense not to see their disputes as being founded in religion.

A young woman who wore a bright headscarf with tassels that fell in a line across her forehead poked her head around the door. It was time for lunch. I returned to the coffee shop in the market and listened to the clattering of a dozen games of backgammon. The Gypsy rope-seller sat by me.

"It is very hot," he observed.

Struga

Struga, the home of the Bektashis, lies just over ten miles west of Ohrid across the fertile plain on the northern edge of the lake. It is here that those crystal waters flow out to form the river Black Drin, which runs north to Debar where it merges with the White Drin and as the Drin pure and simple turns west to become Albania's main river. The lake water rushes out in a foaming torrent only to be calmed by a dam downstream, creating a pool between straight embankments through the centre of town. Every year millions of elvers swim up the river to their secret lairs in Lake Ohrid—or they did until a dam was built near Debar. For a while it seemed that the delicacy of eel would vanish from the tables of Ohrid's best fish restaurants, but now the elvers are transported around the dam in tanks on the back of trucks. An Ohrid without eels is as unthinkable as an Ohrid without its famous trout.

On the pedestrianized main street people were sitting outside cafés sipping cappuccinos in a scene of almost Italian grace. Indeed, Struga was a part of Italian-occupied Albania during the war, the Bulgarian zone ending a short way outside Ohrid. Behind was a maze of narrow streets that gave way to villas swathed in vines reaching to the lakeside and streets lined with poplars, which ran down to a sandy beach where the townsfolk were painting their boats in readiness for the summer season. Struga is the scene of an annual international poetry festival, and it would be hard to find a pleasanter location, "an enchanting little place, white and clean like a peeled almond ... pretty enough to eat", as Rebecca West put it with her characteristic effusiveness.

An attractive little mosque sat coyly nestling under a lead dome in the shade of some spruce trees to one side of a square filled with sports cars and BMWs with Tirana plates. From its minaret a green flag bearing a star and crescent hung limply. A canopied *sadirvan* hung around with clean towels sheltered under wisteria in the small garden. Worshippers began to arrive on ramshackle bicycles and sat around smoking and chatting. Presently the imam arrived in his dark blue suit and his red fez, and the *ezan* gurgled sleepily from the minaret. One by one the men filed inside.

I had been going to wait for the end of *namaz* but somehow the idea of another struggled multi-lingual conversation seemed too wearing so I left and wandered through dirt backstreets on the landward side of town. In each courtyard a sheep with a tether around its waist was grazing, blissfully unaware that tomorrow was Bayram, the Feast of Sacrifice when Muslims remember Abraham's willingness to sacrifice his son Ishmael. By tomorrow these docile animals would be kebabs and the poor of Struga would feast on meat given to them by the pious. It would by a joyous day—except for sheep.

I sat for a while in the shade of some spruce trees near a small modern church by the river, listening to the soothing whoosh of water as it flowed through a sluice. Aromatic blue smoke floated over me as a man wrapped in muslin tended his beehives, the insects buzzing soporifically. People were fishing and they occasionally hauled out tiny silver fish with yellow tails which they cast glistening into buckets.

Later I came across a mobile still which was puffing quietly to itself, filling the street with a heady mixture of woodsmoke and alcohol fumes. It squatted like a giant copper toad on an iron frame, its maw open to receive the wood that was proffered it. A thick pipe extended from its domed roof for a yard or so before entering a cooling vat which was replenished by a green plastic hose. Water splashed playfully down the outside and from the bottom a clear liquid dribbled into a basin covered with a muslin filter which was held in place with clothes-pegs.

An old woman who can't have stood more than five feet in her rope sandals emerged from a nearby house. Around her waist was tied a heavily embroidered red woollen apron.

"Young man, what are you doing?" she asked me, smiling.

"Just walking. Are they making rakija there?"

"Oh *yes!* Would you like some? Come. Where are you from?"

Sitting in the shade on upturned logs was a middle-aged couple, staring intently at the thin trickle that emerged from the still. He was tall and lugubrious, she short, mostly spherical, and possessed of a black and grey fizz of hair. Nearby sat a younger woman whom I took to be their daughter or daughter-in-law.

"This young man has come all the way from England!" announced the old lady. "He speaks some Russian but no Macedonian, which is a pity. Give him rakija." She let fall a light, mellifluous laugh which seemed to come from the girl she had once been. I was proffered a log to sit on, and a glass the size of an egg-cup was filled for me from a demijohn. I sipped the liquid gingerly. It was still slightly warm from distillation, almost pure alcohol, and it burned my tongue and throat before settling in my stomach and gradually inching its way towards my fingertips.

"Second distillation," the man said. The old lady peered into my face.

"Are you all alone?" she chuckled.

"Yes. I left my wife in London."

"Ah, you are married. And children?"

"Not yet."

"He is young," said the distiller's wife, "there is plenty of time."

"Yes, time," agreed the other.

Two young boys came out of the house behind, singing patriotic songs. They carried sticks on strings strung over their shoulders, and saluted me smartly as they went by. In 1903 youngsters in Skopje also went around singing nationalist songs in the streets: they sung in Slavonic and neither the Turkish police nor their Greek informers could understand the words.

"Would you like coffee?" asked the old lady. "I will make some." She retired to her house. I sat on my log becoming slowly intoxicated by the rakija and the heady red-wine scent of the crushed remains of grapes which lay around in heaps.

"Are they your own grapes?" I asked.

"No, they belong to our neighbour, the older woman you spoke Russian to."

She returned carrying the only known antidote to rakija, strong Turkish coffee.

"Tell me," I asked, emboldened by the drink, "most of the people in Struga are Albanians, yes? How do you get on with them?"

"Not so bad," the old woman said, "but," she lowered her voice conspiratorially, "they can't be trusted. *Not Orthodox* you know. You *are* Christian I presume?"

"Of course."

"Well then." She pointed to a villa which had beautiful Isfahan carpets hanging from its balconies. "In that house there are *Albanians!*" She tutted, scandalized. A ten-year-old cycled by over a crossroads. A blue Lada, travelling much too fast, shot out of the side street and screeched to a halt, missing the child by no more than a yard. The driver was wearing a white skull-cap. "Muslims!" exclaimed the old woman.

Somehow another egg-cup of rakija had materialized in my hand. I sipped it slowly and felt a relaxing comfort creep over me. I dozed, with my eyes open. Life was good. Everything was peaceful. A dustcart which seemed to have been 'liberated' from Germany drove down the street. A sign on its side admonished "Fifty per cent of household waste can be recycled!" in German. The Macedonians recycled more than that, I knew. I had seen them in the bazaar in Ohrid hammering out old Greek olive tins and re-soldering them into pots for brewing Turkish coffee.

"Would you like some rakija?" the dustman was asked.

"No, thanks all the same," he replied.

✳ ✳ ✳

In the concrete shed of the market posters in Albanian urged me to cast my vote for the Party of Democratic Progress, as opposed, I guessed, to those of Democratic Regression and Totalitarian Progress. A church loomed above the outdoor section, and I stopped to take a photograph.

"What are you photographing?" asked a short, greying man who stood near a barrow piled with jeans.

"Only the church."

"You'll get a better view from over here." He indicated his barrow. He was wrong.

"Where did you learn English?" I asked.

"I learnt in school for a year, but also from songs. I have a big collection of songs. I like heavy metal the best, Iron Maiden, Deep Purple—the first Deep Purple that is. They are no good now. I went to see them in Belgrade, but Ritchie Blackmore was singing not Ian Gillan. Ritchie Blackmore is good, but not in Deep Purple." His voice came in a quick, rasping staccato.

"This is the Church of St Nicholas," he added. "That's my name too, Nikola. We have four other churches in town but this is the best. It has sixteenth-century wall paintings inside. You're a Christian aren't you? What branch?"

"Protestant."

"European Protestant or Church of England? There are so many new churches here now, Pentecostal, Baptist, Hare Krishna … All mad. Fuck them."

"I saw a new church out by the river …" I ventured

"That? That is the Church of St Petka. It is a *parekklesion* really, only a little church with no priest. What do you say in English?"

"A chapel."

"That's it, a chapel where people go to pray. Only the building is new—there was another one before. Underneath it is water, not a river, just water. It is good for people who are sick in the head. Many people go there, even Muslims. This is only a small town, but there are many Muslims; Albanians, Turks, Gypsies. Macedonians also, but most of the Macedonians are Orthodox. The only other Orthodox are the Romanians. I don't mean Romanians from Romania. *Old* Romanians."

"Aromani" is a term sometimes used for Vlahs. Nikola paused for a moment.

"There is a Catholic church in Ohrid. Well, it's actually just a house which they use as a church. It was for the families of soldiers from Slovenia and Croatia who were posted down here. Now I think there are just a couple of missionaries there. They are good people though."

"How do the communities relate? There's that trouble with the university."

"All that is bullshit. Politics. What do the Albanians want with a university? It is just the politicians making trouble. Real people have better things to do. We have to work hard just to live. Look at me. I run this stall. I make perhaps 1,000 Deutschmarks a month after I have given money to my boss, and it is hard to live." I thought 1,000 Deutschmarks was a very high figure. The "boss" I took to be a local Mafioso. Nikola continued.

"It is terrible. You see women—even Muslim women—on the streets selling themselves. Sometimes I have seen as many as 25 in a single night, here in the market, and remember this is only a small town. You will put that in your book please, so that everyone in the West will know the shocking things that are happening here, the terrible things we must do to live. And now people come back from Switzerland with their money and their expensive cars. And AIDS. This is a very big problem, but our biggest problem is that there is no work. We Macedonians are happy to work hard for a little money—we don't want much—but there is no work. It is all the fault of the politicians. Take Milosevic. Bastard. Serbs are good people, really they are. My wife is Serbian, but the politicians just like to mess things up. An old Communist. I hate Communists. My family, clan I think I should say, has lived here for 400 years. My grandfather was in the textile business like me. He had three houses here in Struga, seven children and a daughter, and $4\frac{1}{2}$ million Deutschmarks. Not paper money either. Gold Napoleons and Austrian crowns. Then the Partizans took everything and my family lived as beggars for 20 years.

"Never trust anyone who calls himself a leader. I am a devout Christian and I go to church every day, but never when the priest is there. Priests lie. They just want money. Now Christianity is split, because Rome wanted all the money. What is the difference between Catholics and Orthodox? They say *Filioque*, that the Spirit comes from the Father *and the Son*, and they show Jesus on the cross with a single nail through both his feet. We say the Spirit comes from the Father *through* the Son and our Jesus has a nail through each foot. Also we cross ourselves from right to left not left to right like the Catholics. And out of that the lying priests and politicians make wars. Even now the Croats are killing Serbs because they hate the Orthodox, but it is all one religion. Jews worship only the Father, not the Son, and Muslims follow Muhammed, but it is all the same. Lies, lies, lies to make people hate each other! I went to Jerusalem with a group to celebrate our Christmas [6th January] and I saw all the priests just taking money like everyone else. Then I realized that Christmas is not a place, it is in our hearts. Politicians, priests, the Mafia, they are all the same. They just want money and more money." It is true that visiting a major pilgrimage site can be enough to put you off religion for life.

Three young men began inspecting the wares laid out. "Excuse me," said Nikola and he went on the commercial offensive, expertly slipping a tape-measure around the waist of one of them before the man had even noticed. They spoke in Albanian. No sale.

"There are so many Albanians here now I had to learn their language," Nikola said when he returned. "There used to be just 2,000, but when the Turks left after the war they came from Albania because it was better here than there. You will see if you go to Albania. They live like animals, perhaps fifteen in a two-room flat with no water. No-one should have to live like that. Not everybody does of course. The Mafia have nice houses like here in Struga. They go to the *dzamija* five times a day and what do they do? When I go to church I go to pray, but they get the *hoxha* and they talk politics. The *hoxha* says 'do this' or 'do that', and they do it. That is no way to behave in a place of prayer. Mafia, priests and politicians!" This seemed to be his bugbear. A young couple strolled by arm in arm.

"Now that's something you didn't see five years ago," remarked Nikola, "Muslim women being so free like that." How he knew they were Muslims I could not tell. "Even now if you go to the villages around here, as I do to sell my textiles, the Muslim women look away when they see me coming. I don't mind—they are not so beautiful—but it is not civilized.

"Bosnia was civilized. Sarajevo was the most beautiful city in the Balkans. After Dubrovnik, but that had the sea. Everyone could live there, Croats, Macedonians, Muslims, Jews. Everyone. I lived there for four years and I had a Muslim girlfriend. Her name is Lejla. They were civilized Muslims there. I could speak to Lejla's mother quite openly. But her parents were devout and they didn't want her to marry a Christian, so we moved to Subotica. You know where that is?"

"In the Voivodina."

"Yes, where the Hungarians live." Before the First World War, the Vojvodina, the part of Serbia north of the Danube, had been a part of Hungary. The Habsburgs allowed Serbian refugees to settle there in the seventeenth century, and they established a patriarchate in exile. In exchange for not having to convert to Catholicism, the Serbs were expected to defend the frontier from the Turks as a kind of warrior-peasant class like the Cossacks. They were led, of course, by a *voivoda*, from whom the province gets its name. It the most ethnically diverse part of Yugoslavia, with Germans, Romanians, Slovaks and many others in its population. The tennis player Monika Seles is a Hungarian from the Voivodina.

"We had a good business in Subotica selling textiles. People would come from Italy and sell us jeans and then the Magyars [Hungarians] and the Romanians would come and buy them. Lejla still has that business. I don't know where the jeans come from now. I had to come back to Macedonia but her parents wouldn't let her move south, so she stayed with our son. Although I'm married here now I still love her, and I visit every week—not Subotica but Belgrade, there's a bus from Struga. I give her 25 Deutschmarks and I buy clothes for her. Things are very hard in Yugoslavia, harder even than here." The average monthly wage in Yugoslavia was 30 Deutschmarks. It was a sad story, but how many other Yugoslavs could tell tales like it?

Somehow we got back onto the subject of religion—or of para-religious activity, which seemed as close to Nikola's heart as it is to mine. Nikola's wife (the one in Macedonia) had had a back problem and they had gone to visit a woman in the Soviet Union whose name was Dzuma. Her family name, which I have forgotten, was a Georgian one. Nikola claimed that even Margaret Thatcher had consulted Dzuma once. The back problem had been cured, and as a party trick Dzuma had laid her hands on a bald man's head. Within an hour he had sprouted thick black hair and complained that he felt hot.

"Dzuma's house is full of icons. She prays all the time. They say that if she stops praying all her power will leave her." I mentioned Vanga and her church in Rupite.

"That is not good. The Witch of Petrich. She claims to tell the future, but Jesus tells us not to follow prophets—like Muhammed." I remembered Him telling us not to follow *false* prophets. The whole point of Islam is that not only was Muhammed not a false prophet, but he was the last of the *true* ones. The word originally meant "one who reveals the true nature of the present", not "one who foretells the future". Nikola expanded his theory: "You have to sleep with sugar under your pillow and Vanga 'reads' that. She has no eyes you know. It's like people who 'read' the coffee in the bottom of your cup."

"Gypsies do that in England."

"Gypsies will do anything for money. I went to see Vanga once. Nothing!" That was the source of his scepticism. If it works, like Dzuma's magic, it is true. If it doesn't, it's false. It is as simple as that. The attitude of the supplicant, which is often crucial, did not feature in the scheme of things. Vanga was just another person lying for money.

A bulbous Suzuki rolled past. It was registered in Tirana, the double-headed eagle standing proud on its number-plates. "Some rich Albanian," I remarked.

"Probably an Albanian Mafioso from Macedonia," riposted Nikola. Anyone with an expensive car is Mafia. We're happy with a Zastava, a Fiat really. Honest people don't want much. Look at me. I have a house, a Zastava, two children and a daughter, and another child in Subotica, and I sleep well next to my wife. They have lots of money, a big house, and they die young."

✳ ✳ ✳

I never did find the Bektashi *tekke*, much to my disappointment. Of all the strange religious movements in the Balkans, the Bektashis must rank second only to the Bogomils—in fact many believe that the Bogomils *became* Bektashis, however implausible that might be. They were dervishes, and their creed caught on like wildfire, becoming the favoured sect of the janissaries. During the 1930s the glorious King Zog of the Albanians even tried to make Bektashism the state religion of his country. From what is said of them, they are not orthodox Muslims. Women have an equal role in their faith and their *zikr* involves drinking rakija. Most remarkable of all, they believed in the transmigration of souls, in reincarnation, and Bektashis are said to wear bells around their ankles to warn stray insects of their approach, lest the hapless beast be trod upon. I wanted to meet some to see if any of these claims was true.

✳ ✳ ✳

Walking down to the bus station I passed a Muslim graveyard. It might seem morbid but I couldn't help going in. The story it told was very different to that of Bitola's vandalized necropolis. Smart white headstones stood erect, each facing Mecca to ensure that on the Day of Resurrection the faithful arose facing the holy Ka'aba. As Fadil had intimated, some of the names ended with the suffix -*ski*, but the fact that the memorials were inscribed in Macedonian intimated that the grave was occupied by a Slav. There was no shortage of purely Albanian names.

Near the back was a grave sporting a turban recently painted green. To judge by his mildewed photograph Hysni Qemal had been a fine old man, possessed of a huge white beard and piercing eyes. He had been a sheikh, and the green indicated that he was also a *sayyid*, a descendant of the Prophet. An earthenware ewer had been left by the side of the grave, while on it a pool of solidified wax marked the remains of a candle.

Behind Hysni's grave a whitewashed enclosure stood open to the sky. Inside was the grave of a much older holy man. with a tree growing from it as is usual. A niche in the wall was black with soot and a river of once molten wax flowed from it. Clearly the zeal of the "fundamentalists" had not reached the shores of Lake Ohrid. Hassan al-Banna of Egypt, whose followers killed Sadat for making peace with Israel, was revolted by the "accretions" of dervishism. Abdul A'la Mawdudi, the leading light of South Asian "fundamentalism", is buried in a plain unmarked grave. No doubt all this would change when Fadil's brother returned from his studies and mounted the *minbar* on his first Friday home. I feared that gradually Macedonian Islam would become humourlessly intolerant. The last thing Macedonia needs is an Islam—or any religion—with no flexibility, with no room to accommodate a disparity of views within its mantle. For Macedonia to survive her people must be flexible, boundaries between groups must to a certain extent be blurred, because hard boundaries grate against each other and produce sparks. There is more than enough dry tinder lying about.

Bayram in Ohrid

If you spend any length of time in a place you quickly develop a kind of routine, going to the same places at the same time for the same things, and after a while you begin to be recognized and to feel at home. It was not long before the staff of the coffee shop in Ohrid market learned that I liked my Turkish coffee sweet, with a glass of water on the side. "My" table was always free at the *gostilnitsa* where I ate in the evening and where the sheikh and his cronies gathered for coffees after *zikr*. The freedom of travel, of going where you will without ties, carries with it the penalty of always being on the outside, of not belonging. Having roots, having a place, seems to be a vital human need, and besides if you stick around you gradually pass from the barely human category of "tourist" to become a fully-fledged person. Settled people have never liked nomads precisely because they have no place. The *gostilnitsa* (in Macedonian the word means "restaurant" but in Russian it is a hotel) was run by a Turkish family and the regulars spoke Turkish among themselves. This was their place, where they could shelter secure among their own people.

The morning of Bayram dawned in bright sunlight. From my room by the lake in the old town I could hear the dull wet slap of an old woman washing clothes in the sparkling water and beating them on a rock to shift the dirt.

At the turn of the century, Brailsford remarked that "one seems in such a place as Ochrida to move in a long pageant of strange and beautiful things which has no more reality than some symbolical procession." As I walked by the water on my way to breakfast two pale, cadaverous men in linen suits emerged from a side street that ran up to the churches of The Virgin of the Hospital and St Nicholas of the Hospital. They carried notebooks under their arms, and one was considerably older than the other. They seemed to be refugees from the 1920s, when male British aesthetes with slight literary pretensions and a rather greater interest in brown boys haunted the Mediterranean in couples, being languid and cursing the natives.

"Was it just a dream?" the elder murmured in English.

✳ ✳ ✳

On down the cobbled alley, past the cobbler's shop with its heaps of soft, pointy-toed sandals heaped in the window, its bridals and its unlikely sign saying "Dutch spoken" on cracked yellow paper was my usual breakfast haunt: "Slava Paskali's Pastry Parlour". It was a tiny box of a room furnished with low stools and metal tables where people went to eat the Turkish pastry known as *börek*. You could have it with meat, cheese or spinach stuffing, but you could only have *börek*. That and *ayran*, the Turkish yoghurt-based drink which is so refreshing on a hot day. As had been pointed out to me in Skopje, everything in Macedonia is backwards. *Ayran*, which is essentially the same as Indian lassi, is called *yogurt*. What the English call yoghurt is *kiselo mleko*—literally "sour milk".

"I'm sorry," said Slava, "I have no spinach for your *börek* today."

The tea shop in the market was shut for the holiday but not far from Slava's was another where I sat under a faded portrait of Marshal Tito and a tri-lingual calendar with a picture of a mosque in Gostivar. I took out my cigarettes and lighter, laying them on the table. Before I knew it the lighter had been grabbed by an excited five-year-old boy whom everyone addressed as Gigi. I tried to retrieve it, but the kid ran off. It was a good lighter too, a Clipper which had travelled the world with me.

I finished my coffee and went up the broken and overgrown steps to the rough wooden gate through which the urchin had gone. It swung open to reveal a garden and a group of women from a Flemish painting. One, in her 30s, sat at a rickety table peeling and slicing onions. Behind her stood a slightly younger woman wearing a garish scarf on her head and washing clothes at a tap. Between them an immensely old crone swaddled in black dandled an infant on her knee. By her side stood a vase of lilacs from the tree that only partly shaded them. The perpetrator of the theft eyed me from the doorway of the ramshackle hut that was their home.

"Excuse me," I said hesitantly, "your son's got my lighter." The youngest of the three stopped her washing. She would have been pretty if she had had better teeth.

"It's yours is it?" She turned to the crone. "Give him the lighter."

"What?" she croaked. "What is this man doing?"

"The lighter is his. GIVE IT TO HIM!" The others yelled, one into each ear.

"All right, all right, don't shout at me. I may be old but I'm not deaf," she grumbled, fishing the desired object from the folds of her clothes.

"Where are you from? England?" the youngest said to me. "Please sit down. Would you like coffee? England is a very good country."

"Where did you learn English?"

She giggled. "You understand me? I learnt in the school."

I sat at the alarmingly wobbly table and answered the usual questions. The little boy, who seemed to be hyperactive, was called Muhammed.

The gate swung open and a burly, round-faced man lumbered into the yard and sat down heavily. I guessed he was about 40. He was 30, son of the crone, husband of the woman who had learned English and father of Muhammed. His name was Adnan: "A pity my other name is not Kashoggi.

"Macedonia is a good country," he proclaimed. "Many different people live here, and they all get along. I speak five languages. Macedonian of course, Romany, Turkish, Albanian and Serbian—but that is no good."

"Why not?"

"I must speak an international language, English or German. You are the first man I have met who spoke Russian."

Granny hobbled into the house and returned with a large cauldron which she placed ceremoniously before Adnan. It contained a large, fatty lump of lamb onto which a note had been pinned. Adnan took it and read. The meat was a Bayram gift from a Turkish family to the poor Gypsies on the hill. "Would you like to eat?" he asked me. I declined.

"Today is Bayram, a special day for Muslims, so today I have work. I am a musician. I play a very old national instrument. Later there will be dancing—Muslim dancing—and I will play."

"Not the *zurna*?" I asked in some trepidation. The *zurna* is a type of oboe found throughout the Middle East. It has an exceptionally unpleasant sound.

"No, not that." He hunched himself as if at a drum kit.

"Have you heard of Ivo Papasov?" I asked.

"Ivo Papasov! He is the Maestro! A genius, almost a god. Our *zurna* player tries to copy him, but Papasov is this high and our man is only *this* high." He indicated the difference. "Some people do not like us to play Bulgarian music, but it is all the same really. Do you know Ivo Papasov? Have you spoken to him?"

"I don't know him personally. My brother's a musician by the way."

"That is too good! What does he play? Not heavy metal I hope. I like Rod Stewart very much. English music—Eric Clapton, Mick Jagger, Bob Dylan ..."

"Bob Dylan's American."

"I did not know that. He is not so good then."

A number of ten-year-old boys pushed through the gate. Adnan pointed to one of them. "This is my son. He will get my instrument." It was brought, a goblet-shaped drum on which Adnan beat a sharp tattoo. He looked up at me.

"Do you have a car?" he proffered me his driving licence. I reciprocated, showing mine. Daniel, his son, looked at it in fascination.

"It has 'UK' on it. Is that Ukraine?"

"United Kingdom," his father corrected him, "but," turning back to me, "it has no photograph. What kind of identification is this? I could take it and say I am you. Perhaps you have one of these?" He produced his identity card.

"We have no such thing in my country."

"No? We need them to go *anywhere*. They're not passports, no good for international travel to Switzerland or Bulgaria. We need them to travel in Macedonia."

A tracksuited man who was even burlier than Adnan came into the garden. He was Adnan's brother. I went through a by now well-practised routine.

"I don't have children either," he said, "but my brother has three."

"That is because I am strong!" proclaimed Adnan, flexing his arm playfully. "I am Samson. My wife is Delilah!"

His brother turned my name over a few times, trying it. Then he gave his judgement: "A beautiful name. William Tell."

"William Shakespeare," I retaliated.

"I am Romeo, my wife is Juliet!" Adnan's wife threw a spring onion at him and he chased her screaming into the house, emerging after a while with a satisfied look. "Everything is normal. Now I will get beer."

When he returned, carrying a couple of bottles of Bitola-brewed Pelbier, he said "You must come at half-past three. Then we will make music for the Muslims." He pointed to a battered minaret which soared over his house. "Sky-rocket. Space shuttle!" He laughed.

"Aren't you Muslim?"

"I make my own religion," he laughed. "There are many good things in the Bible, also in the Qur'an, so I am half-way." I remembered the despairing words of a Transylvanian German: "as for the Gypsies, no-one knows *what* religion they are!" I was presented with a Bible and a Qur'an, the former printed in Serbian in Belgrade, the latter in Zagreb with parallel Arabic and Croatian texts.

"I do not go to church or to mosque because priests and imams only want money. God is in your heart. I suppose you believe in evolution? I do not. God made us, we did not come from monkeys. In the Bible it says we came from mud, but of course that isn't literally true. What it means is that, as the earth contains all the elements, so do we.

"In England there are many people from the colonies, yes? Like Hong Kong?"

"Yes. My wife is Indian."

"That is too good! Does she worship Buddha or Shiva?"

"Shiva."

"And does she eat cows? In India cows are holy."

"Not in England, they're not."

We paused. A puppy came out of the house and began chewing my bootlaces. Daniel showed me his English school-books. They featured the Brown family who lived in London and went to see the Changing of the Guard, and the Greens who lived in America and didn't. Out of the blue Adnan said:

"It's 50 years since the end of the Second World War. We should be glad about the end of Fascism. As long as there are pictures of Tito in the shops here we are safe from war, but in Serbia they took the pictures down. Milosevic is an evil man. I hate him."

"What about Ratko Mladic or Radovan Karadzic? There are too many *voivodas* in Bosnia now. They are all mad."

"Mad all right, but they are not real *voivodas*. In the old days VMRO were real *voivodas*, but now they just pretend to be. Gligorov thinks he is a *voivoda* but the true *voivodas* were the Partizans. To be a *voivoda* you must fight Fascism, not support it." He grew gloomy.

"I think there will be war with the Albanians," he said. "No-one wants it except their mad leaders This nonsense about a university. What do they want with a university? *I* don't need a special university, and anyway there are plenty in Albania. There will be war with Albania. It will be a catastrophe. War with everyone. The Third Balkan War. War with Albania, Greece, Serbia, Bulgaria, Russia ... we have no friends. We will all die."

He sat staring into his by now warm beer as the sun turned and the lilac threw its shadow over the pestilential plastic bags of rubbish people threw over the walls of Samuel's castle through the nettles into his backyard.

"Albanians are only part of the problem. We have no economy. The denar is nothing, worthless. Without money young people turn to prostitution, become drug addicts or worse. We *must* have work. The only people with money are people who have worked in Switzerland. If I worked in Switzerland or Germany for a year I could be a big man here, a big man. The minimum wage in Germany is more than most people here earn. But you must have money to go, and you see I have none. People here are happy to have little, but most have less than that. If my band gets work we make maybe 500 Deutschmarks, but there are five in the band, so that makes just 100 each. Mostly we play at weekends, at weddings, so I get about 400 Deutschmarks a month. It is not enough. Always we have problems, but we only want to live our lives in peace. But the Greeks hate us, and the Serbs. As for Bulgarians, they are bad people."

"I've always found them very hospitable."

"Hospitable to English people, yes, but they look down on people from Macedonia. They always have their noses in the air. They say there is a Macedonian state but no Macedonian people. Of course there is a Macedonian people—people who live in Macedonia. I am not a Slav. My people live everywhere from Delhi to Dublin, but *I am a Macedonian!*"

✳ ✳ ✳

I left that run-down house, saying that I had to telephone Shaoni. On the wall of the town hall some departing Serb had scratched the Serbian cross—'Serbia Alone is its Own Saviour'. Over the four Cyrillic letters, "*CCCC*", in the quadrants of the cross someone had written his reply: "*BMPO*". Internal Macedonian Revolutionary Organization. In the post office I found a line of shabby booths where bright red telephones were screwed down to wooden shelves. I dialled London, leaning against the broken glass of the booth. Nothing happened. In a kind of glass cage outside a young woman with curly black hair was taking payment for calls.

"Is it possible to telephone England?" I asked her.

She jumped and stared at me, quivering, her brown eyes growing wider and wider. She looked like some wild animal which had had a nasty fright. At length she regained control of the situation.

"You want to call England?" It wasn't such a strange desire. "Write down the number. Now ... the code ..." She scrabbled through a sheaf of papers on her desk until she came up with a list of international dialling codes. England was not on it.

"Try Great Britain," I suggested. It was there. She wrestled with her own red telephone to no avail before lifting the receiver on a direct line to Skopje.

"Hello. This is Ohrid. Can you get me a line to England?"

She went back to the red instrument. The connection was made, but the line was terrible.

"Thank God you're safe!" said Shaoni through the jumbled fuzz of 100 languages and 1,000 people all speaking at once.

In Bulgaria making an international call involves nothing more complicated than going to a public telephone box. Macedonia's lines are routed via Belgrade. I was the victim of one of the side-effects of the sanctions on Yugoslavia. Suddenly this brave new country seemed terribly isolated and I began to understand the sense of hopelessness that had pervaded so many of the conversations that I had had. Just a stone's throw from Ohrid was Greece, a member of the EU, of NATO, of the OSCE, an equal player at the card table of European diplomacy. In Greece you buy a piece of plastic, insert it into a machine, and speak to anyone in the world. For all its geographical proximity this tiny country of 2 million might as well have been Mongolia. The forces of politics, both internal to Yugoslavia and international, had shut it out of the "Common European Home" announced by Mikhail Gorbachev and seized on by the West as meaning hamburgers for all. Macedonia doesn't need hamburgers—they have their own speciality of the same name with the chips *inside* the bun and the meat liberally sprinkled with paprika and oregano. What Macedonia *does* need is to be taken seriously, as seriously as Slovenia or Estonia. It cannot be written off with a shrug as 'Former Yugoslavia'.

✳ ✳ ✳

In the afternoon I returned to Adnan's house. Daniel led me across the market and through a maze of streets to where the band was playing. They could be heard several blocks away. They had set up on a patch of grass surrounded by housing estates and were playing away furiously. The music was amplified to such an extent that it was virtually inaudible. A solid wall of sound washed across the grass towards a group of people standing at a safe distance, but I had to brave the aural assault to be introduced to the musicians. Adnan pointed to the clarinettist. "He plays Ivo Papasov!" he yelled above the din. "This is what we call Wedding Music. It is good, yes?" Retreating, I found that I could, just, make out a tune that I recognized, but it was a struggle.

A cart was drawn up and crates of beer and soft drinks were unloaded for the benefit of an anticipated audience. That audience never appeared. Groups of young people dressed in their best clothes, red chiffon dresses and tight dinner jackets with white bow ties, idly drifted by and stopped for a while to listen before moving on. A fat man on a bicycle rested for ten minutes before peddling off again. Some children hung around but they were hardly enthusiastic. The performance was a flop. The beer sellers began to pack up again and the band called it a day. Adnan, Daniel and I crammed ourselves into the tiny Zastava—a 1950s Fiat Cinquecento—belonging to the bassist whilst Kemal the synthesizer player shot off in his own model in a cloud of dust. I know his name was Kemal because it was written on the back windscreen. On the front was written "Maπallah [By the Grace of God] Rally Sport". Adnan was not in a good mood.

"No people, no money," he moaned as we puttered past mosques gaily adorned with green flags.

✳ ✳ ✳

Down by the water in the old town are two basilicas. St Nicholas' still functions as a church, with a charmingly naïve iconostasis, brightly painted in bold primaries. Stacked in glass cases around the walls lie icon upon icon, cracked and blackened by age and devotion. The saints emerge gradually through the layers of the ages, and I felt that they wished they hadn't. They frown and grouch and huddle together for comfort. From a tape-recorder placed behind the bishop's throne came the sound of plainsong. A young woman switched it off and came up to me.

"Do you want to light a candle? Only I must close the church now."

By complete contrast, across a square where grass pokes up through the flagstones, is the Church of Holy Wisdom, St Sophia. In parts it dates from Clement's time, an almost derelict barn of a building which seems in imminent danger of collapse. It had once had a dome but the Turks demolished it when they turned the building into a mosque and erected a minaret which has itself now vanished. It served as a mosque until 1912 and was then left to collapse, although it had been gradually falling apart for many years before the Muslims vacated it. Then in 1951 the experts moved in, stripping away years of plaster to reveal superbly flowing frescos, executed by craftsmen from Constantinople shortly after the defeat of Samuel, as a means of reasserting Byzantine hegemony. Here Jacob dreams of his ladder, there Abraham prepares to sacrifice his son—Isaac or Ishmael, according to taste. In the semi-dome of the apse the Virgin holds the Infant Jesus aloft on a plaque and the grown man can be seen preparing crowns for the Forty Martyrs, Roman soldiers who refused to renounce Christ and return to the old gods. They huddle naked, blue and shivering, as they slowly freeze to death on an ice-bound lake.

In one corner a *minbar* still stood, confected out of pieces of the old iconostasis, marble slabs with stylized fishes and intricate abstract swirls. The piano which had once stood in the apse had vanished and in its place were a couple of icons with sadly wilted flowers laid before them. Dead churches always seem peculiar, and this was even odder, neither living nor dead, a place both sacred and secular. Outside, I sat on an overturned column and lit a cigarette. The custodian of the monument came and parked himself beside me.

"Did I tell you this place dates from Clement's time?" he enquired. "Clement was a great man: he founded the first university in the Balkans 1,000 years ago. In those days there were no schools, only monasteries, but in Clement's school you could learn more than just religion. He introduced many new things: science, mathematics, new forms of agriculture. Ohrid was the centre of learning for all of the Balkans."

"The church you see today dates from the ninth to the thirteenth centuries," he added, "but its foundations are much older. The archaeologists found the foundations of a fourth-century church, from before the Slavs, when Christianity was new. And there may be the remains of an even older pre-Christian basilica here. They think it's pre-Christian because it doesn't face east as a church should. Will you excuse me? There is a tree I must plant." True, he loved his church, but he loved his patch of public garden more, and he dug frantically with a long-handled spade until he was satisfied, and then tenderly patted the earth around the roots of his new tree.

The Monastery of St Naum

Clement was an intellectual. Naum was a mystic. He retreated to the southern shore of the lake to where a pool fed by fifteen springs (and later found to contain another 30 springs underwater) replenishes Ohrid's pure waters. Here he wrought miracles, a craft which seems to have declined since the middle ages. The most famous of the miracles concerns a peasant who was returning home in his cart when his mule was mauled by a bear. Naum ordered the bear to replace what it had taken and the animal obediently took its place between the traces and pulled the cart to the peasant's home. Icons of Naum frequently depict this miracle.

Today the monastery is on the very edge of Macedonia. Just 100 yards from its lakeside setting can be seen a red flag with a yellow smudge on it. Facing that is another with a black blur fluttering in the light wind. The border with Albania. The grim concrete blocks of Pogradeci on the Albanian side can be seen plainly just a few miles further on and a swathe had been cut through the dwarf oaks that cover the hill a stone's throw away. In the old days, the days of Enver Hoxha, that border could not be crossed. The guards were reputedly bored and trigger-happy. Now the border is open and a trickle of cars, mostly with Albanian numbers, dribbles through.

The complex rises steeply from the lake as the monasteries of Athos do from the Aegean, looking more like a fortress with its parapeted outer walls and solid whitewashed buildings. In the courtyard a youthful monk chatted to a family which seemed to be resident. None showed any inclination to include me in their conversation. A gnarled old man sat on the parapet dangling legs clad in pink wellingtons over the lake and perused the opposite bank through binoculars. I don't know what he was looking for, but he sat there an hour and more without speaking, just turning his glasses first to Ohrid and then to Pogradeci.

In the centre of the courtyard was a tiny church, or rather a group of churches. At the heart the usual cross-in-square thrusts an elongated dome skywards. Its *narthex* links it to another domed structure which itself sprouts an extravagantly arcaded *narthex*. To the south a third dome pokes between the two. Yet this mess seemed oddly harmonious, an arrangement of things in such a way as to suggest that there *was* a reason for the apparent disorder of the universe and that that reason is a divine one, that despite all its overt jumble, to the person of God the world is not only ordered but perfectly so. And the buildings at Naum's monastery are perfectly ordered. They are not romantic. They do not hint at tumultuous forces beyond humanity's control. Byron would doubtless have found them trite, domestic. But the whole point of religion is precisely that the universe is not out of control, however that might appear to ignorant humanity to be the case, for "He divided the waters from the firmament and He saw that it was good."

I ducked through the portal of the church to be met with the usual pudgy-faced saints who glowered at me, though the Virgin looked down encouragingly from the dome. On their frozen lake the Forty Martyrs shivered to dissuade the Slavs from backsliding whilst Christ made crowns ready for them. St Steven turned his eyes towards the Trinity while the mob of Jerusalem stoned him. A female saint was tearing a devil from a man's mouth.

The main part of the church was homelier, despite the ascetic whose beard reached to his toes and the stylite on his pillar who was looking down his nose at me. From a delicate iconostasis St Clement and St Naum gazed at me from a Greek icon, bearing between them a scroll inscribed with the Cyrillic alphabet. As usual John the Baptist, "John of the Stream" or Jovan Bigorski, as he is called by the Macedonians, carried a spare head under his arm. The head looked rather apologetic, as if disclaiming any responsibility for its predicament. To my right Daniel was surrounded by complacent, almost cuddly lions, and on my left Meshach, Shadrach and Abednego warmed their toes in the furnace. A smattering of candles guttered before the iconostasis and the church reeked of incense. The smell seemed to revolt St John the Evangelist, since he looked away in disgust, but St Luke was quietly adoring an icon he had just completed.

Matthew was being bothered by his attendant angel but Mark's lion looked more like an overfed neutered tom. You could almost hear it purr. The iconostasis was dated 1711. The frescos were, I think, later but it was hard to tell. The whole effect was comforting; there was no mystery in this faith.

The next room contained Naum's tomb. A velvet cloth of a rich crimson covered the slab under which he lay: unlike those of his brother, his bones had not been disturbed by the Turks. The dark little room was decorated with scenes from Naum's life and death. There was the episode of the bear, and elsewhere he baptized some cautious Bulgarians. Around the grave itself bishops and monks gathered in Holy Awe. Each figure was named in Greek, yet they had all come to pay homage to one of the founders of Slav Christianity. Outside a peacock screeched like some soul in torment, making me jump: "*oo-á-gh, oo-á-gh*". Peacocks are not allowed in churches except in effigy on the iconostasis. Like the pomegranates that adorn early Christian art, they represent Paradise, the Persian garden whence came the idea of Eden.

I sat on the parapet looking 20 feet down into the limpid waters of the lake. The man with the binoculars continued to stare at whatever it was he was staring at and four soldiers clumped past in heavy boots. A solitary monk appeared briefly and the peacocks scrabbled on the roof of the church. An electric green beetle settled on my arm momentarily before flying off and I could hear the endless jabbering of a rookery coming to me from a grove of poplars. Below a dinghy put-putted by in a wide arc past the monastery. It contained a couple of Arab men and a single woman swathed in voluminous black and white drapes. At the end of a short mole someone was fishing, and 20 miles away in Struga I could see that it was raining. Dark clouds swirled around the mountains, but the calming hand of Naum protected the monastery.

I walked back to the pool where the springs combined their output before feeding the lake, past a battered notice reading, in Macedonian and English, "Attention! Border Zone! Only people with permission are allowed!" A Muslim family sat on the grass under a weeping willow and one of the men lit a fire. Before long kebabs were sizzling merrily and the air was filled with the mixed scent of grilled lamb and wood-smoke. Standing beside the pond was a small square white building. Inside was a small pool from which water overflowed downhill. On the outside

wall was written "*Sveta Petka, Sveta Voda*"—St Petka, Holy Water. More than Cyril or Clement, Petka seemed to be Macedonia's saint. If ever the people of the Balkans needed foresight and sanity it was now. People had lit candles inside, further blackening damp renditions of the Virgin and Child, the Baptism, Clement, Naum and the Archangel Michael. Two-denar coins, the ones with the picture of the Ohrid trout on, had been cast into the well in supplication.

It's a remarkable beast, that fish. There ought to be a miracle associated with it. It is found only in Lake Ohrid and the neighbouring Lake Prespa, to which the former is linked by tunnels under the mountains. By some utterly inexplicable evolutionary freak, it also occurs in Lake Baikal in Siberia. A single fish will feed two people, though I was once present at a meal where four dined off just one exceptional specimen. Tourists who know no better get offered it grilled or fried, but it is best eaten *Ohridska*, perfectly filleted so that the fish, whilst whole, contains not a single bone, and stuffed with sweet red peppers and fried onions before being baked. The flesh is pink and firm, not oily, and delicately flavoured, somewhere between brown trout and salmon.

✳ ✳ ✳

It was beginning to rain as the final bus of the day back to Ohrid drew up opposite the cafés which line the final few hundred yards up to the monastery. About 20 Japanese got off it carrying hard suitcases and looked around them with bewildered expressions. Their presence was utterly inexplicable.

Clement and Naum knew what they were doing when they established themselves at Ohrid. The basin which the lake almost completely fills abounds with holy wells. I paused for a while at the village of Peštani, a cluster of buildings sheltering under a low cliff beside the lake. Its church is dedicated to Sveti Vrachi, the holy doctors after whom the Bulgarian spa of Sandanski had been named before being accorded a modern revolutionary protector.

On the edge of the village I came across a whitewashed shrine, its interior adorned with icons, Easter eggs and faded purple flowers. It faced a deserted hotel and the "Good Luck Casino", a handy place to pray for success or repent your folly. Three men were excavating the hillside beside the shrine.

"We are building a new one," one of them explained. "It will be bigger and better. You can pray here for anything. Your prayer might not be answered but you can always try."

"There's no *Sveta Voda* here?"

"Not here, no, but there are a couple of places up in the mountains with small churches. They will cure you of any illness."

"And what about at the church? Who were the holy doctors anyway?"

"There's no holy well there, only in the mountains. As for the doctors, they lived a long time ago, perhaps as long as 300 years ... I don't really know. If you come back on Sunday you can ask the priest."

One of his friends slowly uncurled himself from the pile of rubble he had been sitting on and blinked at me twice. "Can you take our photograph with the old shrine behind?" he asked. The three struck heroic poses, grasping their shovels. Then one of them wrote down an address, struggling with an unfamiliar alphabet. "Be sure to send three pictures, one each. Then we can remember." Months later I received a postcard from them, written in a careful Latin hand: "Hello! Greetings from Ohrid. Thank you." The postcard had been printed in Zagreb.

I didn't fancy hunting for springs in the mountains so I retraced my steps along Peštani's only surfaced road to the village's dusty waterfront square. Cars from Pogradeci stumbled over the potholes, making for the border, and a Tirana-bound bus harried a tiny Zastava from Pristina. Considering that, a mere five years earlier, car ownership had been illegal in Albania it was remarkable how many Albanian cars there were. Some would be expensive even in the West, Volvos and Mercedes, the property of the old *nomenklatura* and their offspring, able through their contacts to escape the grinding poverty that afflicts their country. It would not do to enquire too closely into how they came by these cars though.

The fish restaurants around the square were empty, and signs vainly advertised bed and breakfast. Groups of men hung around with no work to do, and grannies clad traditionally in their white dresses and embroidered waistcoats were sitting by the water simply staring over the lake towards Albania. A dinghy crammed with fishermen chugged by as I sat on the pier listening to the gentle slapping of the waves against its stones.

✳ ✳ ✳

I tried the *tekke* one more time. There was no-one about. Four men entered the courtyard and tried the door of the mosque. It was time for *namaz* but the door was locked. An old man came with the key and opened the building and eventually *ezan* drifted out feebly. After the prayers the keyholder came across and looked at me suspiciously.

"What do you want?" he demanded.

"I was told that if I came now I could talk to someone about the *tekke*."

"Come back again at eight. The sheikh will be here then."

I was being stalled again, but I duly returned at the appointed hour. Groups of smartly dressed middle-aged men were coming down the ally clicking their rosaries. A couple of them recognized me and smiled, placing their right hand over their heart in greeting. An old man, not the one I knew as the sheikh, was wearing a sheikh's black and white turban. A sharp-eyed lad of about 20 with a piece of paper stuck to a cut lip approached me as night began to fall. I told him my story.

"Wait a moment," he said, and disappeared around the corner of the building. He returned with a lanky man ten years his senior and a spry young woman in a leather jacket whose auburn hair was carefully styled to frame her face. She spoke English well, with a careful deliberation.

"Perhaps we can help you. You cannot speak to the sheikh because now it is the time for prayer." As she spoke, a neon lights sprang on at the top of the minaret. Looking up, I saw that the *muezzin* had climbed to the balcony and stood outlined against the increasingly inky sky inviting Ohrid to prayer as his predecessors had done for centuries. These days it is more common for the *muezzin* to recite his message into a microphone from the comfort of the mosque's interior.

"Can you ask some specific questions?" asked the woman, whose name was Linda. I started with the obvious one. When was the *tekke* founded?

"Four hundred years ago. Our *pir* came from Khorasan." The tall man removed the cigarette from his mouth and said something in Turkish. His voice was a gravelly growl, the product of too much smoking. "He says that at first there was only a *madrasa* here. All our sheikhs are buried over in the *türbe* with their wives. Here we are Helveti. Have you seen the *tekke* in Struga?"

"I looked but I couldn't find it." They laughed.

"It's near the police station! You should have asked. Everyone knows where it is. Actually it's not in very good condition. They're talking of restoring it."

"Where did the money come from to restore this one?"

"Many people gave, but mostly it was the sheikh's family."

"The *tekke* in Struga, what *tariqa* is it—Bektashi? And can you move between *tariqat*? How do they differ?"

"The Struga *tekke* is Helveti also. I think there are Bektashis in Kichevo, but I'm not sure, also in Debar and some other places. The *tekke* in Skopje used to be Helveti, but it's Rifa'i now. I don't know why." The tall man spoke again.

"There are twelve *tariqat*, Helveti, Mevlevi, Chishti and so on. There can be neither more nor less. Although they are all the same on the inside the *zikr* varies so it is not usual to move from one to another. You wouldn't know what to do."

"That man is the sheikh," smiled Linda, "or at least he will be. He is the present sheikh's son. It's hereditary. You can't just set yourself up as a sheikh—you're born with it. Like your king."

"What about relations with the *'ulema*? I spoke with the imam of the mosque on Ulitsa Sveti Kliment Ohridski and his son, who speaks German, and they did not like dervishism."

"The man with the big beard? He doesn't have a son here. His family is in Tetovo. That is where he is from."

"Then not his son but another young man. By the way, his brother's in *madrasa* in Mecca, learning Wahhabism."

"Thanks for warning us!" they laughed. The sheikh's son, who seemed to be called Errol, added, "Seriously though, we should not say bad things about our fellow Muslims but that old man's very strict, almost fanatical. We never say anything against the *'ulema* but they seem to think they can say anything they like about us. In Yugoslavia there was a *reis al-'ulema* and a head dervish. Now there is only the reis in Skopje and he favours the *'ulema*, which is wrong. He should represent *all* the Muslims in the country. Islam should not be divided in this way."

Linda expanded: "The fanatics think I should wear *hijab*, but the Qur'an says that you should adapt to changing times. The point of *hijab* is not to draw attention to yourself. I'm at Skopje University in my final year studying English. All the other students are Macedonians. If I wore *hijab* I would draw attention to myself just as if I was wearing a short skirt. Many people in Ohrid wear *hijab* just because the imam says they should but it doesn't mean anything. I feel strongly that I am a Muslim, but my Islam is in my heart not on a piece of cloth."

The dervishes, about 30 in number, emerged and lined up in the courtyard behind the sheikh facing the *türbe*. They said a brief prayer and the meeting broke up. The sheikh turned his hooked nose and hooded grey eyes to me and clasped my hand, saying something in Turkish.

"He says that he is very sorry but he must go to a memorial to pray for a dead man. But ask a question."

"Why do people become dervishes?" I asked. He answered slowly, picking his words with care. With a shock, I realised that he was speaking in blank verse.

"Anybody *can* become a dervish, nobody *has* to. You can become a dervish by helping the *tekke* or simply by being pure of heart. That is the most important thing. You cannot be a proud man. Now I am sorry but I must go. My son will answer your questions." He took my hand again.

"The sheikh is a very hospitable man," I was told, "but a busy one. Hospitality is very important to us Muslims. So is humility. It took a very long time for you to be able to speak to anyone here, but you must realize that we had to make sure you were genuinely interested. We get a lot of tourists coming to the *tekke*, but we're not here just to give them something to look at."

"Can you tell me something more about the *türbe*? Do people who are not dervishes pray here?"

"Oh yes, all the time. They fill the courtyard."

"To get the *baraka*?"

"Exactly. Our *pir* has much *baraka*. Would you like to see inside the *tekke*?" Errol excused himself.

"I can't go in. I've been drinking beer."

Inside the *semahane* Linda turned to me and said "I suppose you can read all this writing, being the expert."

"Only the words 'Allah' and 'Muhammed'," I admitted.

"Then you're like me." She pointed to one of the divans. "This is where the president of Turkey, Mr Özal, sat when he met our President Gligorov." We went into the mosque.

"I think this is called *minbar*," Linda said uncertainly, pointing to the pulpit. In one corner a furled flag which I hadn't noticed before rested against the wall.

"What's the flag?"

"No idea."

"Are many young people interested in Islam, or, specifically, dervishism?"

"There is some interest, but in general people feel themselves to be Muslim but don't do anything about it. It is very difficult to pray five times a day and do everything else that is required ... We haven't really had a lot of interest from Arabia or Turkey. They're more interested in Albania and Bulgaria. In Albania people will say they are Muslims but they know very little. They will make *namaz* and laugh about it. It seems strange to them. I suppose some day I should read the Qur'an but it takes a lot of time and I don't speak Arabic. I'm a Muslim and I trust what my elders tell me about our religion. I'm no imam."

We went around the corner to where the sheikh's house was and sat outside under a veranda. Night-time insects were twittering somewhere near at hand. Ayesha, the woman I had met on my first visit to the *tekke*, put bowls of fruit before us and placed a fresh packet of cigarettes at my elbow. Then she poured tea into tulip glasses.

"Turkish tea," said Linda. "Not like English. You put milk in yours." She shuddered involuntarily. "I have heard about your weather too. All that rain! I could not live in such a place. Rain makes me depressed."

Errol joined us and Linda asked him about the flag.

"It's the flag of Ali, two hands and a sword with two blades. We keep the flag of our *tariqa* in the *türbe*. In the old days, when the Muslims armies went to war each *tariqa* fought under its own flag."

"Why Ali?"

"It just is. The Rifa'is revere Ali especially and celebrate his birthday. That is when they put metal spikes through their cheeks. We celebrate Muhammed's birthday but of course we respect all great Muslims."

"You have told me that being a sheikh is hereditary. What would happen if a sheikh died with no son?" They exchanged wry glances.

"Then it would go to his nephew, either his brother's or his sister's son." Later I learned that was a sore point. They were engaged. Linda preferred girls. I asked about intermarriage.

"It happens," said Linda. "The sheikh's wife was born Christian but she has converted. My uncle married a Serb. She is still Christian. It can be difficult though because the families put a lot of pressure on the couple. Some people call Christians *giours*, unbelievers, but we should not do that. We all believe in one God. The biggest problem is nothing to do with religion. Just look at Bosnia They're not Muslims there. It's nothing to do with Islam against Christianity, it's all politics. Ask a Bosnian about Islam and he'll say '*What—what is Islam?*'. Islam is a very tolerant religion. We must respect others."

"In England many people say Islam is intolerant."

Linda spluttered with indignation. "There is no such thing as an intolerant religion. There are only intolerant people. Take this thing with the Albanian University. I'm Turkish but I'm happy to study in Macedonian. Why not? One language is much like another, you just use them for different things. Arabic for prayer, Turkish at home, Macedonian for local business and English for international business. What's the point of an Albanian degree? Who speaks Albanian? Politicians are just twisting things for themselves. The people who already have power just get more. There's this programme of privatization. All of a sudden the man who used to be the manager of a factory is its owner and he's a big capitalist."

"And how did he get the money to buy the factory in the first place?"

"Who knows? Mafia I suppose. They become millionaires overnight. Now there's a big gap between rich and poor which there never was before. Most people don't have work—the sheikh's retired now but he used to work because you can't just be a sheikh, you must be something else as well A poor man is a dangerous man, easily led by false promises. You've seen the pictures of Tito? He was a great man. Just one man holding Yugoslavia together. We believed in Yugoslavia. We felt that we were a part of something bigger than ourselves, all the people together. The world knew who we were. Even we Turks felt that we were Yugoslavs, that this was our home. When, say, a Croat won a medal at sport we all felt proud. Yugoslavia was a good idea, but in the end it was only an idea. Now it's all gone, but as long as Tito is there in the shops we will still believe in Yugoslavia. We lived so much better then! We could travel. I have been to Istanbul and also to Greece. I like Greece, but now they hate us for living in Macedonia. They are trying to kill us. Have you been to Istanbul?"

"Are there dervishes in Istanbul?" Errol interrupted.

"I don't know," I confessed. "There's a Mevlevi *tekke* but it's a museum now. Atatürk didn't like dervishes, but if you go to Konya you will see that people still pray at Rumi's tomb."

"It is not true that Atatürk hated dervishes," objected Errol. "It can't be. My grandfather the sheikh always had a picture of Atatürk on the wall. What happened is that many people said they were dervishes to avoid military service. A single *tekke* might have as many as 1,000 members, but they were not real dervishes. If Atatürk hadn't closed the *tekkes* and forced the people into the army there would be no Turkey today."

We got on to the subject of British Islam and somehow I let slip that I am married to an Indian.

"Does she worship cows?" Linda asked. Her knowledge of India was based almost entirely on reading E. M. Forster. In her mind the country was filled with church-going people who sent their children to England to be educated. I had to tell her it was not so.

"But," I added, "the English did educate their children in England. My grandfather was born in Bombay and went to school in England."

"So you were colonialists!"

"Like the Turks in Macedonia."

Linda smiled gently and shrugged: "Yes, just like the Turks in Macedonia."

✳ ✳ ✳

I walked a mile or so away from the town and sat on a bench at the end of the smooth arc of the promenade while the sun gently slid towards the hills. A faint breeze rustled the reeds. A couple of cormorants wheeled past me and a grebe bobbed on the lake's rippled surface. From far away I could hear the shouts of children playing football and the water sploshed and gurgled soothingly by my feet. As the sun sank lower the mountains of Albania hardened their silhouettes from a hazy blue to steel grey and another, higher range emerged behind, glinting

crisply in the last light of the dying day. Standing on its little promontory the Church of St John showed black against the slate-coloured hills beyond and Samuel's ruined castle, perched on its rock above the town and the lake, caught the last rays of sunlight. A fishing boat made its way back to Ohrid chugging gently to itself. A great peace seemed to come over the land, and with it a kind of melancholy. Why should so beautiful a place be heir to so much suffering, suffering which has bequeathed it only bitter unresolved disputes?

"Time," I thought. "There will always be time." It was an idle thought.

A cold wind began to blow out of Albania and the calm lake became jagged, angrily splashing over the promenade. Some teenagers, a boy and a girl, enjoying their first love, and two of the girl's friends, jumped away from the spume, laughing. Behind me a torn poster flapped. "Save the children of Macedonia" it said in English. Did Macedonia have the time it needed to steel itself against that wind blowing from Albania, from all points of the compass? I could not tell. For the first time I felt the ghosts of 14,000 blind men come crowding round me. They said nothing. What was there to be said? For me, time here had run out.

GLOSSARY

Note: Where a word is designated as Slavonic, it is common to Bulgarian, Macedonian, Serbian and Russian. South Slavonic indicates words common to the first three but not to the last.

Alafranga	"In the Frankish (European) style": from Italian, a popular style of decoration in the nineteenth-century Balkans drawing on Western forms, especially Baroque.
'Alim (*pl.* 'Ulema)	Arabic = "Scholar", especially one learned in Islamic law.
ARM	Army of the Republic of Macedonia.
Baksheesh	A gift offered in consideration of services to be rendered. Not to be confused with a bribe, which is illegal.
Baraka	Arabic = "Divine blessing".
Bashibazouk	An irregular, Muslim, soldier of the Ottoman Balkans especially charged with putting down Christian insurrection.
Bayram	Turkish = "Festival". Celebrated by Muslims twice a year to commemorate Muhammed's birthday and the intended sacrifice by Abraham of his son Ishmael. Arabic = *Eid.*
Bey	Turkish = "Lord". An honorific applied to those one respects and especially to the governor of a province or a tribe.
BVM	Blessed Virgin Mary. An Anglican usage.
Camii	Turkish = "Mosque".
cheta	Slavonic. An armed band, often under the leadership of a *Voivoda* (qv).
Chetnik	Member of a *cheta.* In Bulgaria also sometimes called *Komitadzi.*
Çiftlik	Turkish. An estate often owned by an absentee landlord. Balkan lands given by the Sultans in the early years to valiant warriors but later often used as dumping grounds for intractable nobles.
Da	"Yes".
Dervish	Turkish and Persian = "Poor". Member of an esoteric Muslim movement engaged in ecstatic activities aimed at proximity to the Divine. Dervishes are frequently believed to earn their living by begging.
Despot	Byzantine title: rank just below Emperor. By the nineteenth century the term was often used of Orthodox bishops.

Devsirme	A levy extracted by the Ottomans on their Christian Balkan subjects, comprising the forced abduction of boys and their conversion to Islam prior to induction into the Janissary Corps. This was in addition to the legally-sanctioned *jizya* or Poll Tax paid by non-Muslims in lieu of military service.
Divan	Persian. An assembly. The room or seat in or on which people assemble. The topic discussed at an assembly. (Many Persian poems intended for discussion rather than pure entertainment are called *Divan*.)
Dobre	Slavonic = "Well, Good".
Dzuma	Arabic = "Assembly", especially the assembly at noon on Friday for communal prayers. Hence Camii/Dzamiya, the place where such an assembly is held (Arabic *al-Meschit al-Juma*, Assembly Hall). Also connected to *Jama'at* = Society, League.
Dzamiya /Dzamija	Slavonic = "Mosque".
Ezan	Arabic. The call to prayer.
FIS	Islamic Salvation Front. An Algerian political party, winners of the last democratic election in Algeria and demanding Islamic Law.
FYROM	Former Yugoslav Republic of Macedonia.
Ghazi	Turco-persian = "Warrior", specifically one who defends Islam.
Gospodin	Slavonic = "Lord", "Mister".
Gyuvetch	Meat and potato stew.
Hadith	An authenticated saying of or about Muhammed. One of the sources with the Qur'an of Islamic Law.
Haiduk	A brigand.
Hajji/Hadzi	One who has made pilgrimage (*Hajj*) to Mecca. In the Balkans also sometimes used of Christians who have been to Jerusalem.
Halal	Arabic = "Permitted".
Hamam	Turkish. A bath-house.
Haram	Arabic = "Forbidden".
Hijab	The requirement in Islam that women be modestly dressed.
Hiz (*pl.* Hizi)	Slavonic = "Hut".
Hoca/Hoxha	Turkish and Albanian spellings of a word often synonymous with Imam (qv). One learned in Islam. (Arabic: *Hujjat al-Islam* = "Proof of Islam".)
Hora	Slavonic = "Circle". A ring-dance common throughout the Balkans.

Imam	Arabic. In Sunni Islam, the leader of prayers in a mosque.
Imaret	Arabic. A pilgrims' hostel.
Irredenta	Latin = "The Unredeemed", referring to members of a people outside that people's nation-state. The movement to bring them within such a state.
Jihad	Arabic = "Holy War", either literal warfare against the enemies of Islam or metaphorically as the struggle for faith.
JNA	Yugoslav Peoples' Army.
Kaškaval	A kind of sheep's cheese similar to feta.
Kâšta	Bulgarian. A house.
Khan	A Central Asian honorific. "Lord", today often used as a personal name.
Konak	Turkish. A villa.
Korso	Slavonic, the same as Italian *passagiata*. An evening promenade along a street of a town designated by mutual consent of the community at large. The object is to be seen with the right people.
Kuca	Macedonian. A house.
Lev (*pl.* Leva)	Unit of Bulgarian currency, divided into 100 *stotinchki*. At the time of writing Lv.100 = £1. Literally, 'Lion'.
Lokum	Turkish Delight.
MACSAM	Macedonia Sanctions Assistance Mission. An EU/OSCE agency.
Madrasa	Institute of Islamic higher education.
Marhaba	Turkish = "Hello".
Mastika	A spirit flavoured with mastic gum, which is also used in the manufacture of glue. Very nasty.
Mazar	Persian = "Tomb".
Mehana	Slavonic = "Inn".
Mekhteb	An Islamic institute of primary education.
Mihrab	The niche in the wall of a mosque indicating the direction of Mecca.
Millet	Turco-persian = "Nation". Originally specifically a foreign nation such as Christians, now used as in the West to denote any people politically constituted as such.
Minbar	The pulpit in a mosque from which the sermon is delivered on Friday.
MRF	Movement for Rights and Freedoms. Bulgarian political party advocating greater tolerance of Muslims.
Muezzin	The man who gives the *ezan* (qv).
Mufti	Often synonymous with *Imam* (qv). Graduate from a *madrasa*.

Namaz	Turkish = "Prayer" (Arabic *salat*).
Narod	Slavonic = "People, Nation".
Narthex	Greek. The entrance porch of a church.
Nasdraviye	Slavonic = "Cheers!"
Natsionalnost	Slavonic = "Nationality, Ethnic Group". Lower than *narod* in the Communist hierarchy of peoples.
Nekroloz	Slavonic from Greek, literally "words about death". Notice attached to e.g. trees, walls, doors announcing a death or the anniversary of one.
Nema	South Slavonic = "There is not" (literally). Otherwise "Go away and stop bothering me". An annoying word.
Narodnost	See *natsionalnost* (qv). Between this and *narod.*
OSCE	Organisation for Security and Co-operation in Europe.
Osmanli	Turkish = "Ottoman".
Pasha	Turkish = "Lord". Governor of an Ottoman province, but also used of anyone to whom respect is due.
Pazar	Turkish = "Market".
Pir	Persian = "Master". The founder, less commonly the current leader, of a dervish (qv) group.
Planina	South Slavonic. A mountain range.
Pomak	Derogatory term for Slav Muslims = "Half a Muslim".
Rakija	Brandy. Not to be confused with Turkish *raki* which is flavoured with aniseed.
Reis al-'Ulema	Literally "Chief among the learned". The most respected Islamic scholar in a given group of Muslims. Often the titular head of the Muslims in a country.
Sadirvan	Turkish. The fountain for making ablutions at a mosque.
Salaam Aleikum	Arabic = "Peace be with you". The common Muslim greeting to which the reply is *w'aleikum salaam.*
Salvar	Turkish etc. = "Trousers".
Sandzak /Sanjak	Turkish *sancak*. Ottoman administrative district. Roughly, "county".
SDS	Union of Democratic Forces. Bulgarian political party.
Shari'a	Arabic. Literally "the road". Islamic law.
Sheikh	Arabic. Literally "Old Man". An honorific often used of the leader of a dervish (qv) order.
Sljivovista	Slavonic. Plum brandy.
Sv/Sveti/Sveta	Slavonic = "Saint, Holy".
Tariqa	Arabic = "The way". The teaching of the various dervish orders.

Tekke	Range of buildings where dervishes meet.
Theme	A Byzantine administrative unit peopled by a peasant militia.
Türbe	Turkish = "Tomb".
'Ulema	See 'Alim (qv).
UMO-Ilenden	Bulgarian political party-cum-terrorist group advocating unity and independence of all three parts of Macedonia.
UNPREDEP	United Nations Preventative Deployment (Macedonia).
UNPROFOR	United Nations Protection Force (Bosnia).
Utro	Slavonic = "Morning"
Vakif	Turkish (Arabic *waqf*). A pious legacy of e.g. land to provide for the upkeep of mosques, hospitals etc.
Vecher	Slavonic = "Evening".
Vilayet	Ottoman administrative district. Roughly, "province".
VMRO	Internal Macedonian Revolutionary Organisation.
VMRO-DPMNE	Democratic Party of Macedonian National Unity. Chauvinist political party in FYROM.
VMRO-SMD	Union of Macedonian Societies. Bulgarian political party advocating union between FYROM and Bulgaria.
Voda	Slavonic = "Water".
Voivoda /Vojvoda	Slavonic = "Warlord".
West (the)	United States of America.
Zakat	A tax payable by all Muslims to maintain religious institutions. Usually 10% of disposable income.
Zikr	"Rembrence". Religious ritual performed by dervishes to induce a state of ecstasy. May include chanting, singing, dancing or all of these.